Violence

Violence

A New Approach

Michel Wieviorka

Translated by David Macey

SAGE

Los Angeles • London • New Delhi • Singapore • Washington DC

First published 2005
Translation published 2009
Reprinted 2010

SAGE Publications Ltd
1 Oliver's Yard
55 City Road
London EC1Y 1SP

SAGE Publications Inc.
2455 Teller Road
Thousand Oaks, California 91320

SAGE Publications India Pvt Ltd
B 1/I 1 Mohan Cooperative Industrial Area
Mathura Road
New Delhi 110 044

SAGE Publications Asia-Pacific Pte Ltd
33 Pekin Street #02-01
Far East Square
Singapore 048763

Library of Congress Control Number: 2008938815

British Library Cataloguing in Publication data

A catalogue record for this book is available
from the British Library

ISBN 978-1-84787-545-7
ISBN 978-1-84787-546-4 (pbk)

Typeset by C&M Digitals (P) Ltd, Chennai, India
Printed in Great Britain by Ashford Colour Press Ltd, Gosport, Hampshire

CONTENTS

INTRODUCTION

If we define and desire modernity as a progressive stage in humanity's history or as an advance on the part of reason and a retreat on the part of traditions and obscurantism, two main conceptions of violence fall almost naturally into place. The first grants it great legitimacy and expects it to play, if need be, a revolutionary role. As Frederick Engels puts it (1976 [1878]: 235–6), 'In the words of Marx, it is the midwife of every old society pregnant with a new one … the instrument by means of which every social movement forces its way through and shatters the dead, fossilized political forms'. According to the second, violence will inevitably decline as reason comes to the fore. This latter conception has inspired broad socio-historical approaches, as in the major (1994 [1939]) study in which Norbert Elias reconstructed the civilizational process that allowed Europeans to internalize, control and therefore reduce their violence from the Renaissance onwards. It has also provided the theme for more empirical and less ambitious studies, such as Jean-Claude Chesnais's long-term statistically-based (1981) study, which demonstrated that the number of acts of violence has quite simply fallen.

But both the history of the twentieth century – the history of wars, genocides and other mass murders – and the social changes which have for example, seen an almost systematic rise in the statistics for delinquency in Western societies since the end of the Second World War, suggest that we must be wary of images of a general decline in violence in the contemporary world. That suggestion is consistent with the broader picture. The exhaustion of the workers' movement and its 'grand narrative', and the return of God and the rise of ethnicity, urge us by the day to abandon evolutionist modes of thought. We can no longer see contemporary modernity as the ever-more triumphant march of peoples and nations as they automatically advance towards further economic and political progress. Some thinkers even take the view that we are no longer modern but postmodern, whilst others (Eisenstadt and Schluchter, 1998; Göle, 2000) prefer to defend the idea of 'multiple modernities' and reject both the idea that all societies are moving in the same direction and the view that there is 'one best way' to go forward. The vast majority of those who try to reflect upon modernity or contemporary post-modernity have one thing in common, namely an idea that Alain Touraine (1995 [1992]) has definitely formulated more clearly than anyone else. In his view, the characteristic feature of modern times is certainly not the progress of reason but, rather, the dissociation that divorces reason from cultural identities and passions, including religious identities and passions.

From that perspective, there is no particular reason why there should be a decline in violence. On the contrary, violence can appear and spread in countless spaces. It can be encouraged both by reason, which turns it into an instrument to be used by actors for whom it is a resource or a means to an end, and by identities and religion, because it is part and parcel of their demands and aspirations which can sometimes be unlimited. With every passing day it is becoming difficult to articulate the dichotomous registers that constitute modernity, no matter whether we describe them as body and soul, reason and the passions, action and being, instrumentality and identities, or the universal and the particular. The gap between these registers can also lead to increased violence.

The more we look at contemporary modernity, or post-modernity if we prefer to put it that way, in terms of a splitting or dissociation, the greater the danger that we ourselves will be divided in our approach to violence. We must therefore consider, on the one hand, its objectivity, including its empirical objectivity, its factuality (possibly in quantitative terms – the number of people killed in wars or terrorist attacks, the statistics for delinquency, crime, and so on), and we must on the other hand recognize the way subjectivity influences how it is experienced, lived, observed, represented, desired or undergone by individuals, groups and societies. There is no avoiding the need to adopt this double perspective, which makes it remarkably difficult to define violence. An objective definition will, for example, speak of a violent assault on the physical, intellectual or moral integrity of an individual or group of individuals.[1] It will, however, quickly be objected that this definition forgets the subjectivity – individual or collective – of the author, victim or observer. We simply cannot ignore the fact that what we describe as violence is subject to considerable variation in both space and time, depending on which individuals and groups are concerned. The objective, or objectifying, point of view implies a strictly universal perspective, as it claims to be applicable to everyone and at all times. The subjective viewpoint, in contrast, is relativistic as it changes, depending on the position of the individual who is speaking. There is therefore a danger that we will find ourselves in a difficult intellectual dilemma. The specific feature of the contemporary era is that it confronts us with this type of divorce, which constantly threatens to paralyse or subvert the analysis, and to make any action designed to respond to the challenge of violence delicate, or even counter-productive. We will return to this point in our discussion of the media in Chapter 4.

Before we even begin to explore the huge topic of violence, we have to recognize its diversity. The word 'violence' is in fact applied to countless phenomena, and used to describe all sorts of events and behaviours, both individual and collective: delinquency, crime, revolution, mass murder, riots, war, terrorism, harassment, and so on. Its spectrum of application can be extended almost to infinity, depending on whether or not we include its moral, and not simply physical, dimensions, and depending on whether or not we follow Pierre Bourdieu by introducing the notion of symbolic violence – the violence used, in this perspective, by a dominant system such as a state or actors that are so powerful as to prevent the dominated from producing for themselves the categories that would allow them to under-stand their own subordination.[2] This book is not devoted to one or more given forms of violence, and is primarily interested in its physical modalities, and especially those that prove to be most murderous. Although the author has devoted several empirical studies to the phenomenon, the ambitions of the present study are much more theoretical. It seeks to provide a coherent and sophisticated set of analytic tools that will allow us to approach the question of violence, to understand the logics of its appearance and spread – and, perhaps, to resist it.

These analytical instruments are not just described one after the other, as though laying them out side by side was enough to provide us with a toolbox. This book is based upon something that became obvious to its author in the course of his research: in either the 1960s or the 1970s, we entered a new era which both demanded and authorized the use of not only the classic modes of approach, but also of new ways of thinking about and approaching violence, if we wish to understand it. There is something mysterious about violence, which is never reducible to the explanations that the market for ideas offered us in the 1970s and the 1980s. That strangeness, which is what gives literary and sometimes journalistic accounts of violence their power, is the very thing that makes the phe-nomenon still more intolerable. And ultimately, that is what defines it best. That, at least, is what we have to deal with here, as we first (in Part I) demonstrate the need for a new paradigm and then outline an original approach that gives a central role to the subjectivity of the actors and to the processes of the loss of meaning or the over-production of meaning that give rise to violence.

Notes

1 See, for example, Yves Michaud (1978: 20): 'We can speak of violence when, in an interactive situation, one or more actors act, either directly or indirectly, either once or on more than one occasion, in such a way as to attack, to some degree, either the physical or moral integrity of an individual or group, their property, or their involvement in symbolic and cultural activities'.

2 For a critical discussion of this notion, which runs through all Pierre Bourdieu's work, see Addi (2002), and especially Chapter 7, which deals with symbolic violence and the political field.

Part I

TOWARDS A NEW PARADIGM

INTRODUCTION

The concrete forms of violence that give every era its 'repertoire' (see Tilly, 1986) vary from one period to another, as do the representations to which it gives rise. This idea, which has yet to be developed, finds its most complete expression when it is possible to discuss both violence, as defined by a specific era, and the general characteristics of the context in which it operates. It then becomes legitimate, in certain historical conjunctures, to speak of a 'new paradigm' that can deal with everything pertaining to the phenomenon and the preconditions for its expression.[1] In this perspective, the conceptualization of violence must take into account its tangible manifestations, the actors and issues involved, the discourses that refer to it in both public opinion and the media, the policies that attempt to deal with it, the way the law adapts to it, and the ways in which the social sciences approach it.

If we are to discuss violence today, we require a new paradigm, which means that we need to use new theoretical tools. And in order to produce, or at least update our analytic categories, we must first take stock of the profound mutations that make earlier categories unsuitable, inadequate or secondary, so great have been the changes that have taken place, often at a breath-taking rate, in the overall landscape at every level: global, international, social, local and individual.

We will take as our starting point the 1960s, which in many respects signalled our entry into a new era characterized at the international level by the US's war in Vietnam and, in many societies, by the various political, social and counter-cultural movements whose fallout would lead to the temptations of terrorism, by the importance of guerrilla movements and by the continuous increase in delinquency in Western societies, but also by new ways of looking at violence, especially in the USA, where the Johnson Administration appears to have discovered that the phenomenon had historical and social dimensions internal to American society. This era was characterized by significant experiences of political violence, by certain intellectuals' commitment to that violence, and by the importance of revolutionary ideologies. That era is well and truly over: we have entered a different period, some elements of which were already being outlined at the end of the 1960s.

Note

1 For an initial formulation of this idea, see the special issue of *Cultures and Conflicts* edited by the author (Wieviorka, 1997).

1

VIOLENCE AND CONFLICT

When life in industrial societies was structured around the basic conflict between the workers' movement and the masters of labour – the class struggle – and when international relations all over the world were overdetermined by the major confrontation between two blocs known as the Cold War, the arena of violence exhibited characteristics that are not necessarily relevant today. The very notion of 'society' now seems to be coming under attack because there is no longer any central principle to structure conflict. In the case of many countries, the adjective 'post-industrial' is almost as obsolete as 'industrial', and we tend to speak, rather, of networks or a globalized economy. Inter-state relations are no longer determined by the face to face clash between two super-powers – the United States and the Soviet Union – that were able to avoid escalating things to extremes.

But even before we develop this idea, we should, perhaps, emphasize its ambivalence. It in fact combines two registers and, if it is pertinent, must have both a sociological value and an historical import. On the one hand, it requires us to accept that, rather than going hand in hand, violence and conflict are the products of distinct or even contradictory logics. That is a sociological point of view. On the other hand, it offers us an historical balance sheet: as a result of the decline of the workers' movement, which was the main incarnation of protest in industrial societies, and the end of the Cold War, violence now takes on unexpected and broader dimensions and forms. Those dimensions and forms are on a different scale and have new implications.

We do not need to dwell here on the notion of violence, which has already been touched upon in the Introduction (and elsewhere; see Wieviorka 1989, 1999). It is, however, very helpful to specify what we mean by the word 'conflict' which, like so many terms in current usage, quickly becomes confused because it refers to so many different social and political experiences as well as interpersonal or intra-psychic experiences. We will speak here of conflict in the restricted sense of an unequal relationship between two individuals, groups, or ensembles that compete, within the same space, with the aim or purpose not of liquidating an adversary, and the relationship itself, but of modifying the relationship, or at least strengthening their relative positions.

If we accept what is admittedly a narrow definition, a conflict is the opposite of a rupture. Ruptures occur when two individuals, groups, or ensembles separate and, at best, contemplate the gulf that separates them and ignore one another or, at worst, contemplate the destruction of the other camp. From the perspective adopted here, 'conflict' therefore does not mean war, or at least not the type of war which, rather than being the continuation of politics by other means (to use Clausewitz's celebrated formula), is intended to annihilate an enemy. The notion of conflict adopted here is in some respects similar to that outlined by Georg Simmel.[1] It departs from Simmel, however, not because it describes conflict as non-violent but because, according to Simmel, the 'unity' brought about by conflict may involve the destruction of one of the parties concerned. The sociologist does indeed make a distinction between conflict and violence, as I do, and that suggests that we should think about the difference between the two, even though one may merge into the other. Some conflicts, he explains, do seem to rule out everything but violence. One example is the conflict between 'the robber or thug and his victim':

> If such a fight aims at annihilation, it does not approach the marginal case of assassination in which the admixture of unifying elements it almost zero. If, however, there is any consideration, any limit to violence, there already exists a socializing factor, even though only as the qualification of violence. (Simmel, 1955 [1925]: 26)

Some conflicts are stable, structural, or even structuring. Others, which are less long-lasting, can be transformed. They are unstable and or may even be resolved in the shorter or longer term. According to the perspective adopted here, conflict does not involve enemies, as an approach inspired by the thought of Carl Schmidt would have it, but adversaries who can stabilize their relationship by institutionalizing it, by establishing rules that allow them to negotiate, or by finding modalities that allow them to maintain both the links between the actors involved and the differences that divide them. Not every aspect of conflict is negotiable, and there is always the possibility of violence. And yet my general thesis is that, on the whole, conflict is not only not to be confused with violence: it tends basically, to be its opposite. Violence closes down discussions rather than opening them up. It makes debates and exchanges – even unequal exchanges – difficult and encourages ruptures or even pure power relations, unless it breaks out because a rupture has taken place.

The Experience of the Workers' Movement[2]

Throughout the industrial era, the societies that were fully involved were animated by the protests of workers, many of them deriving from the same oppositional principle and from a central conflict that was all the less violent in that the protesting actors were powerful in their own right, could organize in the long term, and could develop militant commitments that allowed them to negotiate their demands or to bring political pressure to bear without necessarily abandoning their long-term plans to construct different social relations. Let us briefly recall, then, the meaning and import of the protests that shaped what certain post-modern thinkers call one of the 'grand narratives' of modernity.

The apotheosis of the workers' movement

The working-class consciousness is a product of the privations or dispossession suffered by workers who find it impossible or difficult to control what they produce. It is also the embodiment of a project, or a call for a different society. It is an assertion of an unhappy subjectivity, and at the same time of an ability to project itself into the future, to invent possibilities other than those offered by the present, or the here or now. It is capable of imagining a radiant future.

This capacity is embodied mainly in skilled workers who, because of the positive principles they derive from their craft, expertise and skills, have a certain pride and are convinced that they have a role or a social utility, that they deserve respect, and that they must not betray their self-esteem; they are therefore inclined to negotiate. In contrast, unskilled workers who are left to their own devices are, more so than other workers, prone to becoming involved in rebellions that lead nowhere, and to explosions of anger. As Alain Touraine demonstrated in the mid-1960s (Touraine, 1966), and as subsequent research carried out under his direction has confirmed (Touraine et al., 1987 [1984]), this working-class consciousness's ability to integrate and its capacity for action were at their greatest in situations in which the proud consciousness of skilled workers and the proletarian consciousness of unskilled workers came together and could be articulated, especially in the big Taylorized factories that dominated industry from the inter-war period until the 1970s.

During this period, when there were strong working-class communities with a dense social life, and when the labour movement and its struggles led to the establishment of forms of political life, a community life, and intellectual and social debates, violence was not a mode of political action, or at least not in the most serious forms that lead deliberately to a loss of life. Strikes could be hard and long, tensions in the factories could be high, and discourses

---

11

could be aggressive, but murderous violence was not a resource that was used by the actors involved, even when they met with brutal repression.

The end of the industrial era

Everything changed when we emerged from industrial society in North America and Western Europe in the early 1970s. Our emergence from industrial society did not come to mean the death of industry or even, as some were rather too quick to prophecy, the complete demise of Taylorism, whose principles still rule the lives of some companies. Its real meaning was that the opposition that existed between the labour movement and the masters of labour was no longer central.

The conflict between these two had once informed all collective life, and had given a meaning to other social, peasant or urban struggles, struggles in the universities, consumers' struggle and so on. It was the basis for the political split between left and right, it animated intellectual life, and was extended at an international level by ideologies that contrasted an East that spoke in the name of the working-class proletariat, and a West that was supposedly the embodiment of capitalist domination. As the workers' power became more powerful, it became more institutionalized, and usually took the form of a social democracy that, in many countries, succeeded in taking power without using violence. In the West, it was not the structural conflict of industrial society that gave rise to violence and its political derivatives in the second half of the twentieth century. That violence was, rather, the result of a destructuring of that conflict. This encouraged forms of hyper-institutionalisation and bureaucratization within the trades unions, and unleashed the anger of those workers they no longer represented. It could also lead to far-left terrorism (we will come back to this) or to the rise of more or less racist populist leaders and movements that filled, without any serious collective violence, the political void it left behind. They ranged from Ross Perot in the United States to the Northern League in Italy, from the *Front National* in France to Vladimir Jirinovsky in Russia. What is more important, the end of the industrial era also resulted in a serious crisis within the trade union movement and created major functional difficulties in systems of industrial relations, even when, as in Germany and Scandinavia, they embodied a great vitality. It had spatial effects, helped to generate the phenomena of urban decay, and destroyed many working-class neighbourhoods, from the black hyper-ghettoes of the great American cities that had been orphaned by large-scale industries which were themselves in decline (see the fine studies of William Julius Wilson (1979; 1987), to the *banlieues* of France which, now that they were no longer 'red suburbs' held and organized by the Communist Party, became the theatre of the hate – a theme that provides the title for

Kassovitz's major film – anger and rage of the young people described by François Dubet from the mid-1980s onwards (Dubet, 1987).

In this context, workers whose very existence was shattered by the shock of deindustrialization, job losses, unemployment, exclusion and insecurity, or who were simply frightened witnesses to these things, also lost the points of reference that had once allowed them to have a positive self-image, exploited and dominated as they may have been. They often found themselves prostrate and turned in on themselves, and were incapable of doing anything. Whilst they too paid a high price, their children did not experience the same feeling that their social existence had been destroyed, and were more likely, or more ready, to turn to social violence. In many Western societies, and especially in the working-class areas that were hardest hit by factory closures and job losses, juvenile delinquency and urban violence are largely the products of the exhaustion of the central social conflict that had characterized the industrial era.

In such cases, violence is a combination of a fairly classic delinquency or criminality, and an expression of a feeling of social injustice. It is sometimes impossible to distinguish one from the other. The urban riots that hit Britain and then France in the 1980s and 1990s, or the virulent violence of the skinheads, whose violence reveals a style that is itself disconnected from any content, or any truly social or working-class overtones, were in many respects also products of that decay.

At this point, we need to be careful and to qualify our remarks. It would be a mistake to conclude from the above remarks that there is a direct or one-way link between social or political violence and the exhaustion of the social relations characteristic of the industrial era. The link between the two is neither automatic nor immediate. When there is an upsurge of violence in such a context, we need to introduce mediations if we are to understand it; it is not a necessary or direct expression of decreased social mobility or of the crisis. The riots that broke out in working-class areas in France and Britain, as well as in the big American cities, in the last two decades of the last century, occurred as a result of police brutality or unfair court decisions and were not really protests about unemployment. This was, for instance, the case in Los Angeles in 1992, when a white jury acquitted the police officers who were filmed beating up Rodney King. Young people's anger and hatred certainly found expression in various urban spaces and against a backdrop of social difficulties, but they had more to do with their powerful feelings of injustice, non-recognition and racial or cultural discrimination. By the same criterion, unemployment and poverty do not, as we know all too well from Lazarsfeld's (1972 [1932]) study of the unemployed of Marienthal, immediately or directly lead to social violence, even when they are an expression of a sudden social collapse, as in the countries of the former Soviet empire. They are much more likely to give rise to a passive frustration which, over time, may make individuals susceptible to hate-filled racist or anti-Semitic ideologies or radical political projects (such as Nazism in Germany), to calls for a return to the most Stalinist forms of communism in the countries of the former Soviet bloc, or even to national-populism or nationalism in many Western countries.

Once the conflict between workers and bosses has completely lost its structuring capacity, we see the emergence of a culture that is very different to that of actors who are involved in a relationship of domination, especially amongst young people. The dominant values cease to be those of individuals who see the fruits of their activity or of what they regard as socially-valuable work being appropriated by others. There is no longer the same feeling of being of great social utility, or even of being dispossessed of all control over one's labour and what it produces. The dominant feeling is much more likely to be one of being useless, or at least of being outside society and being denied access to its values. The new culture comes to be defined by the winner/loser couple. What matters is being a winner and avoiding the scorn that is reserved for losers. Some of the 'disposable', to use an expression current in Latin America, or the rejected, develop an acute fear of losing their social status. They are overwhelmed by a feeling of absence or loss: 'I serve no social purpose; I'm on the scrapheap, or as good as.' When the structural conflict is over, individuals are left to their own devices, and there is a danger that they will blame themselves for their failures or existential difficulties. There are no adversaries to fight in order to defend what is now a non-existent contribution to collective life. Violence is much more likely to occur in such a context than in a working-class culture where the lived experience of domination or exploitation, or even the feeling of being oppressed and exploited, was inseparable from an awareness of being socially useful.

The dissolution of the conflict detaches individuals from society and plunges them into one ordeal after another, and they experience them as so many personal challenges. This encourages them to expose themselves to personal danger, so as to avoid being despised by others, and to worry about what Erving Goffmann calls 'face'. The problems of social domination are replaced by personal problems and personal fragility. Individuals are encouraged to respond with violence to any expression of disrespect, real or merely perceived. One of the great lessons to be learned from contemporary studies of the young people in working-class areas who have, in France, becomes involved in riots and various other forms of violence, especially at school, is that their behaviour is an expression of their resentment, of their feeling of non-recognition and, perhaps at a deeper level, of their inability to give a meaning to their lives, now that there is no social relationship that might allow them to define themselves in relation to an adversary, or to an oppressor, or to an exploiter (Wieviorka, 1999; Lepoutre, 1997; Dubet, 1987). As

Lord Scarman demonstrated in his (1982) report on the Brixton riots in England, they are, rather, faced with an enemy, or with someone who is perceived to be an enemy or adversary, namely the police and its racism. We therefore have to conclude that conflict and violence are very different things, and that we cannot be satisfied with arguments that are too elementary, direct, or determinist, because there are so many intermediary dimensions and mediators.

When a conflict as massive and central as that between the workers' movement and the bosses structured collective life and public space, upsurges of violence on the part of, for example, gangs of more or less delinquent adolescents, provided a spectacle that was relatively easily to tolerate. Such spectacles were less tolerable when the conflict in question was imperceptible because it was new and under-developed, and the same is true when it loses its centrality and importance. As Louis Chevallier (1973 [1958]) has clearly demonstrated, when the labour movement was coming into existence in Paris, the bourgeoisie's perception of working-class actors confused the labouring classes with dangerous classes. Similarly, Régis Pierret (1996) and Michelle Perrot helpfully point out that the *Apaches*, who were the young Parisian hooligans of the early twentieth century, belonged to a working-class youth whose existence as a group was denied. They were therefore seen as threat. Neither the parties nor the unions showed any real interest in them. The *Apaches* were a product of a new industrialization which was 'tearing apart the urban fabric, breaking up ethnic groups and neighbourhood and separating the sexes'. In so-called traditional society, in contrast, young men had had 'specific forms of existence and intervention'. At the turn of the century, 'autonomous forms of industrial organization, which had persisted for so long and which had in fact always emerged again, were being undermined by the discipline of the factory' (Perrot, 2001: 359–61). The same kinds of delinquency became less disturbing when the working-class districts became politically and socially structured *banlieues rouges*.

Similarly, when working-class neighbourhoods disintegrate and when the union, political or community networks that were to a greater or lesser extent linked with the workers' movement either decline or disappear, constant or comparable levels of violence are seen to be much more intolerable or dangerous than they used to be. When established forms of social life break up because the points of reference that once supplied an active principle of conflict have disappeared, the slightest sign of aggression can trigger or exacerbate demoralization, fear, or a definite feeling of being under threat.

Classical sociology often associated modern individualism and its damaging effects – and not least anomie and the threat of violence – with the dissolution of tradition and the old orders; it was very worried by the social damage done by capitalist industrialization, which it saw as the main source of the general breakdown of communities, culture and order, or at least of significant dangers. In the last three decades of the twentieth century, we lived through the death throes of the industrial society that sociology found so disturbing; it is time to recognize that, when we left it behind, we lost a conflicted relationship that was certainly characterized by blatant inequalities and injustices, but which also limited the failings and damaging effects of individualism, and discouraged individuals and groups from resorting to violence.

There is an important sociological lesson to be learned here. Nineteenth-century thought, from Tocqueville to Durkheim and the various schools of social and political philosophy, was tormented by the idea that there would be an upsurge of violence, anomie and disorder, and that this would spread as industry and the division of labour spread. It is now the disappearance of the central conflict of the industrial era that poses that type of problem by triggering, on the one hand, an increase in violence and, on the other, a general feeling of a loss of reference points that heightens and exacerbates worries about that violence. The fear of individualism that went hand in hand with the emergence of modern industry, and that could be blamed for all manner of threats and dangers, is now remerging, after the event so to speak, in the form of a modern thematics that emphasizes the isolation and emptiness of the modern individual. This is an indication that we are entering a new era in which there is no central conflict (though this may be no more than a temporary phenomenon).

Before and after conflict: far-left terrorism

Judging by these preliminary remarks, the space of violence appears to becoming greater, just as the space of social conflict, meaning the conflict between the workers' movement and the bosses, appears to be shrinking. In these circumstances, violence is an expression of the exhaustion of the conflict. To be more specific, there are now three main scenarios.

It is possible that the conflict is no more than nascent, or has not fully developed, and that neither its protagonists nor the civil society in which it is emerging think it likely that it will do so. It is, however, possible that the conflict is in a state of crisis, destructuration, or historical decline. The third possibility is that we have a combination of both those logics: there are two social conflicts within the same concrete experience, but one is no more than nascent or is slow to take shape, whilst the other is in decline and has had its day.

Far-left terrorism provides striking illustrations of all three scenarios, as can be demonstrated in the case of several countries. In the anarchist version seen in late nineteenth-century France between 1892 and 1894, it was an early expression of the weakness of an emergent conflict, announced the birth of a social actor who was slow to emerge, and preceded the formation of a trade-union movement capable of real mobilization. The 'era of bombs' ended, notes the historian Jean Maitron (1983), just as the *Bourses du Travail* and the unions were emerging as the first organized expression of the workers' movement in France, namely direct action syndicalism (also known as revolutionary syndicalism or anarcho-syndicalism). One of the major preoccupations of this syndicalism was to demonstrate clearly that it did not advocate terrorist violence. It did not reject various forms of radical action (sabotage, boycotts, and so on), but it had no murderous intent.

The far-left terrorism that appeared in several Western countries, and in Japan, in the 1970s and 1980s emerged when the social movement was in decline, and was an inverted expression of the end of the workers' movement and the Marxist-Leninist ideologies that saw it as the salt of the earth.[3] Its protagonists were still striving to fulfil its highest historical aspirations, and to continue an action that was in decline, and whose meaning could no longer be linked to general projects for the general conduct of collective life. In this case, the violence was all the more extreme, and potentially endless, in that there was a widening gap between terrorists who artificially spoke of the class struggle, and the accession to power of a working proletariat, or of workers to whom that discourse no longer had any real meaning.

Whilst it was certainly violent, the experience of far-left terrorism in Italy was not reducible to the image of a violence that was meant, however absurdly, to keep the banner of the workers' movement flying at a time when it has lost its centrality. The Red Brigades' or *Primea Linea's* descent into an increasingly blind terrorism in the early 1980s also owed a lot to the desires of an 'autonomous' youth that dreamed of playing with 'Comrade P. 38' (Calvi, 1982) and embodied new sensibilities and demands. The youth culture of the day in fact corresponded to Italy's entry into the post-industrial era, and was full of new expectations and new conflicts – women's movements, gay movements, ecological and student movements – that were too weak to exist in their own right and found no political outlet within Italy's institutional system of the day, even though it was very receptive to the 'extra-parliamentary' left. We have here a combination of a 'before' terrorism related to the decline of an old social movement, and an 'after' terrorism loaded with the confused aspirations of an actor who had yet to come into existence. As Alain Touraine puts it (1997: 58), 'A clear distinction must be made between the idea of a social movement and the idea of violence'.

The End of the Cold War

Only a few years after we saw the historical decline of the workers' movement, we witnessed the equally significant phenomenon of the end of the Cold War, which has to be linked to the name of Gorbachev and the symbolic date that confirmed that it was over, namely the year the Berlin Wall came down (1989). Once again, how can we fail to see that violence is the opposite of conflict, or that the two are not closely related?

The Cold War was a geopolitical conflict that structured the world for almost fifty years. During that period, the relationship between the Soviet Union and the United States of America was tense, and sometimes extremely tense, but it never became a direct military confrontation. This conflicted relationship did not lead to war between the two super-powers but, at most, to limited confrontations. Direct military confrontations were always avoided. Although their rivalry had a great influence on the major outbreaks of violence that occurred during this period, it does not explain any of them, with the exception of the Korean War, which was settled relatively quickly, and it did not turn the war in Vietnam into a world war. In some cases, the Cold War may have stirred up local tensions and violence simply because when these died down at a local level, it would suit the purposes of one of the two super-powers; it was therefore in the other's interests to play the tension and radicalization card. The important thing was that it prevented limited conflicts from escalating into major ones, and prevented certain states from pursuing the logic of war or violence too far. 'Any local conflict might have influenced the balance of power between the two great super-powers, and they could not be indifferent as to its outcome', notes Jean-Pierre Derriennic (2001: 42).

This is quite understandable after the event when we look at the situation in the post-1989 world. New fault lines have appeared. The nature of civil wars has changed since the end of the Cold War, and the new situation allows the privatization of violence, which now plays an instrumental and economic role. It also leads to a big increase in identity-based violence, as we saw with the murderous fighting that led to the barbarism of ethnic cleansing when Yugoslavia was dismembered. This was a country whose army had, in the days of the Cold War, made a contribution to international stability. What is more, the destructuring of the Soviet Union and, to a lesser extent, the break up of the Former Yugoslavia led to a kind of explosion in the arms trade. The almost viral distribution of arms fuelled wars or civil wars, terrorism, and organized crime or delinquency. In recent years, countries such as France have also seen a new upsurge of both organized crime and delinquency because access to weapons of all kinds has become increasingly easy. This is in part because the new political order means that there are many more guns in the market.

The end of the Cold War also signalled our entry into a new area in terms of nuclear weapons, which had until then been associated with the idea of deterrence. Nuclear deterrence actually introduced some rationality into a bipolar world that structured all its inter-state relations around the American and Soviet super-powers. For a good thirty years, nuclear weapons meant order and a certain restraint, even in conflicts that involved open war between their allies or vassals, but not between the big two. They have now become the symbol of the great danger of destabilization and crisis at the regional, local or world level, but that threat has much more to do with terrorism and the intervention of 'rogue' states than with the hypothesis of a war between the super-powers. Pierre Hassner puts it very well (1995: 55): nuclear weapons have 'become the ultimate example not of order, but of the gulf between the global and diffuse nature of the problems, and the partial and specialised nature of the bodies responsible for managing or controlling them'. It is tempting to add that it is difficult to see, now that the Soviet system has disintegrated and that the Cold War is over, which bodies are capable, at least to some extent, of taking effective action to deal with problems such as contemporary nuclear proliferation or the threat of nuclear terrorism.

During the Cold War era, nuclear weapons made it unlikely, or less likely, that wars would break out between states. They put controls on violence. The controls were of course both partial and uneven, but they were also real. They guaranteed a world order because, in combination with the principle of bipolarity, they guaranteed that extreme violence would not be used by either the two super-powers or all those countries that were, to a greater or lesser extent, within their orbits, which meant the vast majority of states. There was a danger that even a local shift in the balance would degenerate into escalating tension and lead to a major imbalance. The planet may well have left the nuclear order behind, to borrow a phrase from Phillippe Delmas (1995), but that does not mean that it has entered a post-nuclear era. There is now more room for localized conflicts and violence or what the experts call 'low intensity' conflicts, and it is becoming difficult to prevent them degenerating into a mass barbarism of which the massacres in Rwanda or the Former Yugoslavia may be no more than the first signs.

The end of the Cold War in itself owed nothing to any significant violence, and a great deal to the break up of the Soviet regime. It was not, on the whole, very violent, and its effects were, at worse, localized violence within the former Soviet empire, starting with the Caucasus and then Chechnya.

It is possible that the Cold War also acted as a factor that blinded us to the determinants and meanings of various experiences of violence from the 1950s to the 1980s, and that what seemed to be new – the importance of factors relating to local actors rather then distant outside influences – had in fact simply become more visible. Yet even though some careful analysts do take this hypothesis into account, researchers still conclude that the end of the Cold War did introduce considerable modifications (see, for example, Hassner and Marchal, 2003; Rufin and Rufin, 1996).

It would be a mistake to say that these inevitably took the form or more frequent and more serious outbreaks of violence. It is, on the other hand, true to say that the post-Cold War period has been characterized by conditions conducive to the opening up of what were once small-scale or non-existent arenas of violence.

Limited Conflicts

It is also possible to extend our overall sociological argument downwards and to look, not only at the major or macro-historical phenomenon known as the Cold War or the massive phenomenon of the workers' movement and the 'grand narrative' of which it was the hero, but also at much more limited situations such as those that explain the notion of urban violence. A 'March for Equality and against Racism' was, for example, organized in France in 1983. When it set out from Marseille and the suburbs of Lyon, the action was primarily a form of non-violent pressure. Attempts were certainly made to radicalize it, but they were the work of a very small minority. Its spirit was comparable to that of the struggle for civil rights that took place in the United States in the 1950s and the early 1960s. It ruled out violence, and was the very opposite or even the adversary of violence. It organized a peaceful protest and a democratic demand that political leaders could listen to, which is why the march's leaders were invited to the Elysée Palace by the then head of State, François Mitterrand. Once the hopes that it had inspired were dashed, it ran out of steam. The frequent riots and rage-fuelled behaviours that broke out, mainly in the suburbs of the city of Lyon, were expressions of anger and of the feeling that the marchers had not been granted any recognition and had been listened to. Young people's despair was fuelled by the fact that they had no political outlet for their non-violent demands. In Vaulx-en-Velin, for example, the riots, joy-riding and hatred had broken out before the 1983 march. That more violence occurred after it revealed that the young people of the working-class neighbourhoods were not really involved in any conflict. Similarly, and in the same small town in the suburbs of Lyon, the major riot of 1990, which is usually regarded as the most serious to have occurred anywhere in the country during this period, was followed by the emergence or resurgence of community associations which, like Agora, made the clear and explicit choice to turn the violence of the young into a social and political conflict. This meant that relations with the municipal authorities were sometimes strained, but no longer had anything to do with riots or attacks on people or property.

The fact that, in such experiences, violence gives way to more or less institutionalized conflicted action suggests that we may have to introduce what seems to be a paradoxical hypothesis, though it is at least a reminder that over-simplistic or over-deterministic arguments quickly become fallacious. This hypothesis sees violence as a basic element in the conflict, as its starting point, and as the initial precondition for the constitution of actors. In some cases, or for some actors, involvement in a violent episode such as a riot can, for example, be an initiatory moment that allows the expression or crystallization of a subjectivity that had previously been repressed, non-explicit, incoherent, or too afraid or too unhappy to speak its name. Young people from so-called difficult neighbourhoods will sometimes explain that they became politicized or involved in community projects after having become spontaneously involved, without asking too many questions, in riots triggered by some police 'blunder' (they may also, in some cases, turn to religion).

As we see once more, the idea that violence and conflict are opposites therefore has to be qualified. The two can in fact sometimes be more closely associated than in the paradoxical cases we have just mentioned. In some cases, the conflict is radical, and the violence is instrumental and merely an expression of the calculations of actors who see it as a resource they can control. That is why the idea that there is a contradiction between violence and conflict does not constitute a general theory or absolute rule. It is an analytical tool, an hypothesis that the researcher can use as a projector to shed light on one or another concrete experience; the findings are liable to vary from one case to another.

The pertinence of this sociological tool is, it seems to me, confirmed, if we compare two theoreticians of violence who have greatly influenced intellectual and political life – Georges Sorel, whose 'reflections' were contemporary with the rise of the workers' movement, and Frantz Fanon, a major figure from the period of anti-colonial struggle.

Against Georges Sorel – With Frantz Fanon

Georges Sorel

According to Georges Sorel, whom Hannah Arendt accuses (1970 [1969]: 12) of 'trying to combine Marxism with Bergson's philosophy of life', and whose 'fascist chatter' is criticised by Jean-Paul Sartre (2004 [1961]: xlix), it is violence that creates the protesting actor. Violence prevents the actor from becoming flabby or lapsing into 'trade-unionism' or a syndicalism that is prepared to negotiate. Because it creates the actor, violence furthers the action and allows the proletariat to 'perfect their organizations' (Sorel, 1961[1908]: 92); on the other hand, it forces the bourgeoisie to assume its vocation to be the dominant actor, and restores capitalism's 'warlike spirit' (1961: 92). We can overlook the way Sorel contradicts himself by evoking, on the one hand, the vitality of the bourgeoisie, which it rediscovers thanks to its recourse to violence and, on the other, its disappearance, which is apparently only a matter of time. We can also leave aside certain readings of

Sorel that insist on finding in his texts the opposite, or almost the opposite, of what his famous *Reflections on Violence* explicitly state.[4]

From the perspective that concerns us here, the important point is that Sorel outlines a theory of the collective subject that attaches great importance to violence on the part of both the protesting actor, but also looks as the relationship that both binds them together and brings them into conflict. Sorel's arguments are in fact very far-reaching. He associates a conflict-based violence with propositions that supposedly apply to civilization in its entirety: 'violence … appears thus as a very fine and heroic thing; it is in the service of the immemorial interests of civilization … it may save the world from barbarism' (Sorel, 1961 [1908]: 98). If we apply this theorization to the social movement and structural conflicts of industrial society, it is hard to accept. It proved to be historically inapplicable to France, even at the time when Sorel was writing, as revolutionary syndicalism was beginning to reject violence, and even social violence, at the end of the nineteenth century. Sorel's theorization collapsed with the major defeat suffered by revolutionary syndicalism in 1908; revolutionary syndicalism remained unusually radical and advocated direct action, but the great attempt to call a general strike ended with the implacable failure that Jacques Julliard (1965) describes so well. Finally, and during the 1914–1918 war, the labour movement underwent a mutation and began to move away from Sorel's anarcho-syndicalist ideas.

In more general terms, once an actor initiates an organised collective action that is both powerful and effective, as was the case with the workers' movement after the First World War, that actor is no longer afraid of negotiations and institutionalization; quite the contrary, even though they were by no means the only possibilities open to it. Throughout the inter-war period and until the 1970s, the workers' movement fought battles that were sometimes long and hard, but usually closed down the arena of violence which, throughout its history, has always been a sign of its weakness, of a crisis within it, or of its destructuration. Georges Sorel's approach provided an ideology for the social movement, and therefore for the emergent conflict of his day, but that by no means allowed him to theorize conflict as an established and structured relationship. As Arendt notes (1970 [1969]: 72), not without a certain cruelty, in her critique of Sorel, 'as soon as the workers had reached a satisfactory level of living and working conditions, they stubbornly refused to remain proletarians and play their revolutionary role'.

Frantz Fanon

Everything changes, however, when violence is no longer seen as a characteristic of an actor who is dominated in the logic of constructing a conflicted relationship with a dominant actor, but as stemming from a logic of rupture. When the protesting actor has no intention of defining the struggle in terms of a relationship with an adversary, and is determined to end that relationship, violence is unavoidable.

The thoughts of the late Fanon who wrote *The Wretched of the Earth* (published in 1961, the year of his death) deserve our full attention here. There is, of course, an outrageousness to some of his analyses and the tone is at times a little too rhetorical to be convincing, as when he describes the *lumpenproletariat* as an urban revolutionary vanguard. His argument is, however, very powerful when he explains that, in the Manichean world of colonization, the colonized must make the transition from being a non-man to being a man, and that this involves violence. According to Fanon, decolonizing violence creates the actor, or a human being who is the subject of his own existence. The theme is taken up and radicalized by Sartre[5] in his preface to the book. In Sartre's reading of Fanon, the colonized 'thing' becomes, a man through the very process of his liberation. According to Fanon, the first violence is that of the oppressor who exploits, dominates, and excludes the colonized, but who also denies his existence or despises his language, culture and history. The violence of the colonized is liberating and allows them, as Cherki puts it (2000: 3), 'to demonstrate their un-subjugation', to put an end to their alienation, and to invert the 'experience of shame and desubjectification'.

History demonstrates that independent nations and sovereign states do sometimes emerge from a situation of foreign domination or colonialism without violence being the main operator of the change. Fanon's approach may be more applicable to the action's starting point, to the colonized's decision to put an end to colonization and to the new self-awareness that transforms them into a subject, than to what happens next or to the armed violence of an established decolonization or liberation movement. History also teaches us that these movements can, in their turn, become oppressive forces and even authoritarian states, and Fanon was especially sensitive to that theme. Once again, a particular type of argument must not be turned into a general theory with an absolute validity: violence may be one modality of rupture, and may have a role to play in this type of situation, but there is nothing inevitable about it and it does not obey some absolute determinism.

When conflict is impossible, when what cannot be negotiated becomes central, when what is at issue is dissociation or the abandonment of a common political or social space, violence can, Fanon tells us, become foundational. In many situations, violence does make emancipation a real possibility; this appears to be especially true when separation is as important to those who are demanding emancipation as it is as unacceptable to those from whom that emancipation is being demanded. But, to stray away from the reference to Fanon for a moment, it has to be noted that violence is not the only modality of change. There may, that is, be an alternative. Non-violence is a choice that implies immense human, political, and strategic resources on the part of the protesting actors who adopt it, and on the part of those who oppose them, and, in many cases, those who are part of the same movement. This choice is only possible when the expectations are very high, when an unshakeable trust is established between the movement and its charismatic leader, and when that trust can take the form of an unassailable moral conviction. It also implies that the adversary can be swayed by it or, by, for example, the fact that there is a democratic or humanist current of opinion within the movement, or because it will respond to external pressures that are brought to bear to support the actors.

Comparing the thoughts of Sorel, who associates structural social relations and violence, and those of Fanon, confirms the idea that violence is a negation of conflict in the narrow sense in which we have defined that term. We must, however, emphasize the differences between the two thinkers rather than their similarities. The differences can only be abolished when the idea of social conflict itself is abolished by the call for a revolutionary rupture – a theme which is present throughout Sorel, who loathed reformist socialism – or support for a fascistic fusion of the national, the social, and the political. We know that, towards the end of his life, Sorel developed a great interest in Bolshevism and proved to be a great admirer of Lenin, even though he had a certain sympathy for the 'new right' of the 1910s, and even though his thought inspired certain fascists, and not least Mussolini. That, however, is a different story.

Conclusion

We are the orphans of two great conflicts, one social – the class struggle – and the other geopolitical and international – the Cold War. And in this new historical order, which dominated the end of the twentieth century, there seems to be much more room for violence.

Does this mean that we are doomed to live in a world in which, given the absence of any structural and structuring conflict, there is a growing danger that violence will break out against a background of unbridled individualism and the rise of all sorts of communitarianisms? Some take the view that we will never again experience conflicts as basic as those we have been describing, or at least not for a long time to come. Irene Taviss Thompson, for example, claims that we now live in societies dominated by 'pure' individualism, and that we have to learn to accept that there has been a 'shift from a conflict model to one in which the individual is embedded within society' (2000: 2). Others, and they are in the majority, take the view that this is an era of cultural and social fragmentation in which there are more and more forms of inequality, types of domination and, therefore, sources of conflict and forms of conflict (see for example, Martuccelli, 2001). From this perspective, conflict has not disappeared and is spreading and diversifying. It has been shattered into a multitude of oppositions, all of which are still meaningful, but we cannot identify any unity or centrality, or find it more difficult to do so. Conflict has therefore ceased to supply any principle of top-down structuration that applies to collective life as a whole, but nor does it make it possible to limit the arena of violence in an infinite number of situations.

We should not, however, turn the distinction between violence and conflict into an absolute rule. Which brings us back to Georges Sorel, who was always very wary of any generalization. We have to have a sense of proportion and recognize the complexity of the real world. Between the extremes of the axis that leads from completely institutionalized conflict to completely unbridled violence, there is an endless vista of situations that are less clear-cut, and more uncertain or vague. In such situations, the conflicted relationship between the adversaries does not preclude violence, but may lead to a peaceful conflict. The fact that the two logics (and an analytic distinction must be made between the two) may converge or even reinforce one another rather than clashing and colliding is not aberrant. Conflict can be devoid of the dimensions, expectations, and passions that can turn into rage or anger. Violence plays a role on the fringes of conflict, where it has little effect and cannot guarantee what Simmel calls the 'unity' of the parties concerned. It also plays a role when hatred or irreducible hostility is central to the conflict. But violence and conflict basically belong to different registers, and are contradictory rather than complementary.

Notes

1 A functionalist approach to conflict can be found in the work of Lewis Coser, who describes himself as a disciple of Simmel, and who has popularized his ideas (Coser, 1956). It is, however, also true to say that Coser's reading of Simmel has been criticized, notably by Christine Mironesco, who describes his theses as 'a betrayal of Simmel's thought' (1982: 30).
2 This analysis concentrates on the experience of the industrial societies of the West. It leaves aside societies in which truly proletarian social action is combined with political action and becomes subordinate to it in the context of a revolutionary crisis, and societies in which a totalitarian process leads to the use of extreme violence in the name of a working class whose actors, starting with the trades unions, are in fact enjoined to submit to it. A close examination of these experiences would not challenge my overall argument, but it would force me to make it more complex.

3 On this notion, which refers to the processes whereby an actor distorts and perverts a social movement's categories in order to bring about their radical transformation into the extremist ideology that comes with the transition to a more or less unbridled violence, see Wieviorka (1989).
4 See, for example Boime (1996); according to Boime, Sorel's violence can be seen as an extinction of social actions, and is the opposite of conflict.
5 At the time of publication and afterwards, many critics emphasized the distance between the author and Sartre who prefaced his book. According to Alice Cherki, for instance, Sartre 'justifies violence, whereas Fanon analyses it' (2000: 260).

2

VIOLENCE AND THE STATE

Does the State Lie at the Heart of the Problem?

The classic analysis makes a distinction between levels of violence. Pierre Hassner (1995), for example, suggests that we have to make a distinction between three levels of violence in the 1960s. The first was the international level, which in his view had to do with 'the bipolar balance of deterrence and, in Europe, the territorial division between the two blocs'. The second level was that of states, with their internal and diplomatic concerns, and the third level was that of intra-state societies, each with its own political system, structures and dynamic. This distinction, which I myself used in my work on the terrorism of the 1970s and 1980s (Wieviorka, 1989), has certainly not lost all its pertinence. But because it is completely centred on the state, it is now open to question as certain major transformations mean that we now require new analytic categories and can no longer reduce everything, or almost everything, to the state.

Thinking about violence at the international level used to mean, in classical terms, looking at those inter-state relations that were likely to involve violence and, basically, thinking in terms of war and peace between states or, as Raymond Aron put it in his masterly (1966 [1962]) study, between nations. Analysing violence at the level of the state meant looking primarily at political actors' attempts to take state power or, for example, civil war and revolutionary action, and studying, on the other hand, the historical processes that led to the creation of independent states in a postcolonial or post-dependency situation. And looking at violence in society, or within states, meant taking as our object behaviours whose frame of reference was provided by the state, if only because, to use a famous formula from Max Weber (to which we will return), the state supposedly had a monopoly on the legitimate use of force. From that point of view, any upsurge of non-state violence was effectively a challenge or threat to that monopoly.

In the modern intellectual tradition, and in the classical political, juridical and social sciences, the question of violence is inseparable from that of the state, even though one is obviously not reducible to the other. That perspective dominated theories of violence until recent years; the concrete phenomena of violence were usually apprehended within the framework of the state, which was complemented but not contradicted by the higher (international) and lower (social) levels, to use Hassner's useful distinction.

That point of view is, however, no longer adequate, or is at least becoming less and less relevant. A profound change has taken place since the 1970s, and it is perceptible at every level of the phenomenon of violence. There is obviously still a close connection between violence and the state, but it is no longer possible to restrict the analysis to the narrow framework of relations between the two. We now have to adopt a broader perspective.

The Great Disorder

Until the end of the Cold War, the world was, as we have seen, basically structured by the East-West bipolarity. And, thanks largely to the institutionalisation of the workers' movement, the nation-state looked like the formula that could organize and integrate political life, economic and social life, and culture.

Where inter-state relations are concerned, the image of a world organized around a central principle of conflict, and of states that could guarantee the internal correspondence and integration of politics, economics and culture, has given way to different representations. They no longer place the emphasis on the idea of one main division, but on two very different ideas. On the one hand, the world appears to be undergoing a generalized unification. In this perspective, its economic unification is a direct effect of globalization, whilst its cultural unification is an effect of that same globalization which, as a result of North America's hegemony, is supplying the whole world with the same cultural goods. It may even be experiencing a political unification, if we are prepared to take the view that the United States, which was once a super-power competing with another super-power (the Soviet Union), has become a 'hyper-power' that has no competitors. It has even been claimed that the world has, as Francis Fukuyama (1992) argued in a book that caused a big stir after the fall of the Berlin wall, entered into the 'end of history' as a result of the spread of democracy and the market. The world is also said to be dominated by logics of cultural and social fragmentation because the state is increasingly unable to control the savage and brutal forces of the market.

The notion of globalization that emerged from the 1990s onwards refers to the liberalization of trade, the internationalization of financial flows, and the combined global strategies of capital and the inventors of new technologies. The subsequent debate focussed on the notion of globalization itself, but also, or mainly, on its supposed effects. Globalization has been criticized because of its direct effect upon nation-states. It supposedly undermines nation-states, challenging their sovereignty and their leaders' ability to develop adequate economic policies. And, as Ghassan Salamé explains,[1] whilst the classic territorial state is disintegrating, the form of violence associated with it – war between states – is also becoming less important and giving way to other forms, such as civil wars and inter-ethnic massacres. They are such a feature of the contemporary world that they have completely destroyed the utopian dream of a world that will become less and less violent, and in which barbarism will steadily decline.

Neo-liberal globalization has also been criticized because of its social and cultural effects: it supposedly leads to growing inequalities, undermines identities and encourages some people to retreat into communitarianism or a nationalist retraction, and others (or the same) into radicalness and aggression.

These political, social and cultural criticisms were voiced by anti-establishment actors who began by stating their hostility to globalization and denounced, in more specific terms, its neo-liberal nature. Increasingly, they support counter-projects and alter globalist calls for a different form of globalization. Stressing the arrogance of the economic elites, especially when they meet for the Davos Forum, and raising the issue of how the international economy should be regulated, the protestors finally stressed one basic point, notably during the big demonstrations in Seattle (1999) and then in Porto Allegre and Genoa. So-called globalization also, and more importantly, masks a void and a great disorder: the exhaustion of the old world order on the one hand and, on the other, the decline of state forms of organization and integration, and of the development projects that were associated with them until the 1970s. For years, the planet seemed to be at the mercy of economic forces, but this disorder does not rule out the return of the state. Indeed, the terrorist attacks of 11 September 2001 encouraged the United States to become a warrior-state that could fight terrorism, and not only terrorism, as we saw from the war launched in Iraq in March 2002.

The term 'globalization' is now used to describe this context in what is ultimately a rather confused way, and this is the context in which we now have to look at violence. The great international disorder may indeed encourage certain states to turn to violence and war-mongering. These are the 'rogue states' denounced by the North American administration's propaganda, but according to the critical intellectual Noam Chomsky, the USA itself should also be on the list. Together with the withering away of classic forms of state integration, this context encourages certain actors at either the sub or super nation-state level to use what Hans-Magnus Enzensberger (1992) calls 'molecular' violence, or to become involved in what prove, on the contrary, to be metapolitical or religious struggles over issues that go far beyond of the continuation of politics by other means.

That is, for example, the case with the global terrorism that has, since 11 September 2001, been symbolised simply by the name 'Bin Laden'.

Violence sometimes allows groups with a culturally-based identity to claim to be resisting the globalized economy. Conversely, it can also be a resource that allows an identity-based group to play a part in globalization, and to not be destroyed or dissolved by it. This may be a form of self-defence or resistance, or a counter-offensive designed to allow it to become part of global modernity. It may allow the actor to declare war on one or another aspect of modernity, to find a place within modernity, or to break with it. The important point is that it is not necessarily the state which provides the framework that makes violent action conceivable. The frame of reference may be much wider or even global, as with Bin Laden's terrorism, not that this prevents it from being very localized in some cases.

In the contemporary world, social and cultural fault lines do not coincide with the frontiers between states, and are not necessarily internal to states. They may reinforce 'in' states or even whole regions, and divide them from 'out' states, whilst still having a very great influence inside the most highly developed states and regions. They may take the form of diasporic phenomena, and their actors may put forward demands that are not just addressed to one particular state, and may even intrude upon the political space of several states, as is the case with the Kurd question, which has been well analysed by Hamir Bozarslan (1997). They may also correspond to the rise of religions, and especially Islam; the map of Islam does not coincide with any map of states or even regions, as it is also present in both Europe and the United States. This, as it happens, is one of the reasons why Samuel Huntington's basic (1997) thesis about the 'clash' of civilizations seems somewhat unsatisfactory, as it underestimates the reality and presence of diaspora-related cultural identities or religious identities such as Islam within Western societies.

We can now go one step further and take the view that the great disorder that is described as the neo-liberal globalization of the economy – a notion that often includes its supposed effects in terms of social and cultural fragmentation – is contributing to the *globalization of violence*, or to *global violence*, or in other words to the rise of contemporary forms of violence that are fragmented and likely to become both local and global. The outbreaks of violence that accompanied the rise of radical Islam throughout the contemporary world, from Algeria to Pakistan, from the United States to Indonesia, and even to Europe, provide not only an image of a deterritorialized action based on networks, or even networks of networks, of a politico-religious vision of what the world should be, and of good's merciless battle with evil, but also of localized struggles and very concrete territorial issues, such as political and economic control over various zones. The latter image may, perhaps, bring us back to the state, to classic attempts to seize state power or to build an independent state, or to external pressures on specific states. These forms of violence may have both a global impact, as we saw with the terrorist attacks of 11 September 2001, and reflect local and therefore limited conflicts. This means that we cannot analyse them purely in terms of the state, but that does not make the reference to the state frame of reference redundant. Whilst Bin Laden's global terrorism is part of a global religious-political project, it is also certainly related to strategic calculations pertaining to the political future of certain states, such as Saudi Arabia.

Similarly, diasporas play a major role in the domain of the criminal economy and in supporting armed movements. There is nothing new about this role, but it has become more pronounced and more influential thanks to what Aline Angoustures and Valérie Pascal (1996) call 'net-working phenomena'. And when there is an outbreak of armed violence within a diaspora, it may, ultimately, be a way of bringing pressure to bear on a given state, or of taking part in conflicts involving the state. In the 1980s and 1990s, outbreaks of violence amongst the Kurdish diaspora occurred outside Turkey – amongst Kurdish immigrants in Germany, for instance. They represented an attempt to tip the balance of power in favour of the PKK (the Kurdish Workers' Party). Similarly, from the mid-1970s to the early 1980s, the Armenian diaspora was able to recognize itself in the clandestine actions of ASALA (the Armenian Secret Army for the Liberation of Armenia), whose networks in France went so far as to use blind terrorism in the attack on Orly airport in July 1983.

The globalization of violence therefore has to be seen as a phenomenon that does not fully conform to the model of an international system of states and possible armed conflict between states.

Taking State Power and Creating States

One other very significant development in the direct relationship between political violence and the state also occurred during the 1980s and 1990s.

The far left, the far right, and the nation

Between the end of the Second World War and the 1980s, political violence, sometimes in the extreme, radicalized form of far-left, far-right or nationalist terrorism, played a significant role all over the world. In Western countries, and especially Europe, the historical decline of the workers' movement led, as we saw in the previous chapter, to the rise of groups that continued to speak in its name in an increasingly artificial way because they were increasingly out of touch with the demands of actual workers. A number of variants on Marxism-Leninism then inspired self-proclaimed revolutionary movements – the Red

Brigades in Italy, the RFA in Germany, *Action Directe* in France – that turned to terrorism towards the end of this period. On the far right, small groups or networks that had, in some cases, links with the secret services began to plan violent action. They had little to do with the institutionalization of the radical right that began in the late twentieth century, when the neo-fascist party in Italy underwent a transformation and when the *Front National* in France enjoyed some success.

The period of both far-left and far-right political violence is now largely over, at least for the moment, though we cannot rule out the possibility that it might flare up again, as in Italy, where the spectre of the Red Brigades reappears from time to time. Nor can we rule out the possibility that we may be entering a new era in which conditions may once again give such phenomena the space to emerge. And neither can we rule out the possible return of Marxist-Leninist ideologies and the violence they inspire. The resurgence of guerrilla activity on the part of the EPR (*Ejército Popular Revolucionario*) in Mexico at the end of the twentieth century was one example, and it was in many respects reminiscent of the 1960s or the 1970s. Shining Path reappeared in Peru at the beginning of the twenty-first century, whilst guerrilla forces in Columbia continue to declare their allegiance to Marxism, albeit in a perverted form.

The political violence of the 1950s, 1960s, and 1970s could not just be labelled 'rightist' or 'leftist'; it could also correspond to meanings that had little or nothing to do with the left/right divide, and not least the idea of the nation. One major feature of the second half of the twentieth century was the growing number of national liberation struggles, some associated with Marxist-Leninist ideologies, and many of them taking the form of guerrilla activity, that gave birth, when they were successful, to new states or new regimes.

The association of violence with a national cause is still a basic reality in the contemporary world, but it is no longer as important in global terms as it was in the 1950s and 1960s. In many experiences nationalism is, even in the most powerful countries, still a powerful force, as it was in the past, but it is no longer bound up with the project of collective emancipation through violence. It speaks for sectors of the population that are worried about their social and cultural survival or that wish to distance themselves from other poor sectors that they see as a threat to the development of their own region; this nationalism can be observed throughout Europe, with the Vlaams Blok in Flanders, the Northern League in Italy, the FPO in Austria, the *Front National* in France, and so on. It usually oscillates between populism and far-right themes, and seems on the whole to resist the temptations of violence rather than inciting or promoting it. The more it becomes a matrix for political action within a democracy, the more it needs to look respectable, which rules out the use of violence or support for violence. It may still be associated with violence in sectors, on the fringes of nationalist movements, or in crisis situations; it then radicalises their position and quickly takes on overtones that are ethnic or even racial rather than nation-alist in any real sense. As its goal is not national liberation, as in experiences of foreign domination or colonialism, it is, rather, an expression of a desire to protect the nation from external threats and influences, and to purge it of anything that might taint its homogeneity.

Contemporary developments cannot, however, be reduced to images of a one-way process. We cannot pronounce the nation dead – the historian Eric Hobsbawm is wrong to describe the nation as a phenomenon that is 'past its peak'[2] – and we cannot say that the violence that results from nationalism and its embodiment in a state is a thing of the past. The Israeli-Palestinian confrontation in the Middle East over what is still one of the great issues in the contemporary world is enough to refute the idea that the link between nation and violence has come to an historical end.[3] The image of decisive forms of violence on the part of actors who aim to seize state power, or to create and then control a new independent state with all the classic attrib-utes of a state, has lost ground and importance. This also suggests that we must stop analysing violence solely, or mainly, in terms of its relationship with the state. That does not necessarily mean that this perspective is historically irrelevant.

The rise of identities

As the dominant expressions of post-war far-left, far-right, and – though a note of caution is required here – nationalist political violence fade, new manifestations of identity-based violence are coming to the fore, and many of them are either ethnic or religious. In some cases, identity seems to be a resource that can be mobilized in potentially violent ways for economic or political purposes; in others, it seems, rather, to provide the basis for an unrestrained barbarism that takes the form of ethnic cleansing or mass murder, and for a hatred and cruelty that go far beyond the classic political or economic issues.

The expression of cultural, religious, ethnic, regionalist or other identities often seems to correspond with the resurgence of traditions or long-established forms that have found new forms of expression or that have been revived in the contemporary world despite the progress of modernity. It is as though old meanings have been re-emerging. Although they do appear to be tradi-tional or even fundamentalist, most of these identities are in fact recent historic constructs. There is nothing natural about them and they recuperate and cobble together old raw materials to create new identities. They are being produced rather than reproduced, and are inventions rather than traditions (see Wieviorka, 2001; Wieviorka and Ohana, 2001). Whatever its manifes-tations, their potential for violence is therefore irreducible to the image of

33

some inheritance from the past, and Jean Baudrillard 1995: is quite right to say that: 'Rather than deploring the resurgence of an atavistic violence, we have to see that it is our modernity, our hyper-modernity that is producing this type of violence and these special effects. Terrorism is part of hyper-modernity'.

In some cases, this identity-based violence does quickly give rise to utopian projects for the seizure of state power or the creation of a nation-state. The reference to religion is in tune with the nationalism it accompanies or exacerbates, and is, basically, part of a political strategy at the state level. In others, the actors' projects or goals seem to relate to either an infra-state or supra-state level. Which means that we must revise our notion of political violence.

From Political Violence to Infra- and Metapolitical Violence

The meanings that once located violence at the political level are now constantly moving away from it, even though they still refer to it. They are being privatized and are therefore becoming more distant from the public sphere. In some cases, they move downwards; the outcome is infra-political violence. They can also move upwards, by giving the action religious dimensions that subordinate the political to a higher principle such as the good or the sacred; the outcome is metapolitical violence.

Infra-political violence

Since the 1980s, the growing privatization of the economy, especially in countries where it was strictly controlled by the state, has done a great deal to encourage the privatization of violence. The outcome is that the violence becomes less political. The protagonists are in fact less interested in state power, or access to a political system, than in keeping the state at a distance in order to engage in economic activities such as the drugs trade, the trade in stolen goods, child trafficking, the trade in human organs, and so on.

The picture is now disturbing. We see guerrilla groups evolving and controlling territories where they can become involved in the trade in narcotics, or take it over, as in Colombia. Others simply exploit resources that are not illegal in themselves but pay no allegiance to the state, and pay neither taxes nor customs duties. Other groups, and sometimes the same groups, appropriate a share of oil rents. In, for example, the Algeria of the 1990s, actors caught up in the spiral of terrorism and counter-terrorism proved themselves to be very effective smugglers for whom access to money was more important than a political project that looked increasingly hopeless. That is what an examination of the armed struggle in Algeria suggests. Various episodes involved clashes between Islamist groups, or between some of those groups and the armed forces. Their goal was to gain a local monopoly on extortion or smuggling. *Trabendo* can involve illegal goods as well as more conventional products, especially foodstuffs.[4] Mafias and similar groups are emerging, especially in the former Soviet Empire and the Former Yugoslavia, and are prepared to use force and weapons to defend and promote their interests. They are also prepared to attack the state if it looks too closely into their activities, or does not keep its distance. The Italian experience of the early 1990s, when senior representatives of the state were murdered, is a significant example. In countries where the practice of kidnapping on a very limited basis was, as in the Brazil of the 1970s, politically motivated (the phenomenon has declined in the first decade of this century), it is now becoming more common but for strictly criminal purposes. The same remarks could be applied to many other illegal and brutal ways of extorting money.

The privatization of violence can lead to a form of perversion if the police or armed forces, who have a monopoly on the legitimate use of violence, exploit their weapons and impunity to enrich themselves. This does not necessarily mean barbarism or the law of the jungle. But it does come close to that, and involves the use of behaviours of varying degrees of savagery to terrorize anyone who challenges the interests and power of actors who are using the violence they have perverted and privatized. One of the immediate effects of the privatization of violence and increased economic activity on the part of armed collective actors is that civilian populations become the tragic victims of forms of predation that go completely unpunished. One of the other effects is that, even when it was political to begin with, organized crime needs a certain political calm if it is to flourish. Mafias and gangs are not inclined to tolerate social or political protests inside the territories they control, as they might attract the attention of the media and may even lead to interventions on the part of the authorities. That is why what appear to be the quietest estates in France's *banlieues* are not necessarily the most law-abiding, but instead are those that are controlled by dealers or by organized crime.

The transition from political violence to economic criminality can occur in economically dynamic zones but, as Jean-Christophe Rufin notes (1996), it can also occur in areas that have been devastated.

> Disinvestment on the part of the great powers and economic disasters in the many countries that have been destroyed by war have encouraged guerrilla movements to do what they used to do discretely and on a modest scale openly and on a large scale ... The guerrilla movements of the 1990s tend to be based on real economies based on trade or even production ... The change in the international climate brought about by the end of the Cold War did not create the new mechanisms that fuel these conflicts *ex nihilo*. But it certainly helped to spread what were once marginal practices. (1996: 43–44)

Turning to a very different register, infra-political violence is, in democracies, also a characteristic feature of racist and xenophobic phenomena. During the early stages of its development, a far-right party with a racist, xenophobic or anti-Semitic ideology cannot openly advocate violence, or even claim responsibility for acts of violence and express support for them. The *Front National* in France is one example. Once it ceased to be a marginal group in 1983 it became a party that operated in the public domain and the democratic political field, and its desire for respectability precluded violence. In a democracy racist violence may flare up on the margins of the political, but once it goes beyond uncontrolled but minor outbreaks it inevitably becomes infra-political and is mainly confined to what the British call racial harassment or to unruly behaviour, and perhaps to crimes for which no political actor is willing to claim responsibility.

Infra-political violence should not, however, be reduced to meaning the decadence of perversion of the political, or the closure of the political field. It may also be an expression of the hesitancy of a political actor who is torn between delinquent or criminal behaviours and a more political violence. Even if it is not stable, it may take a 'pre-political' form or indicate the beginning of a trajectory that may, in the long term, reach a truly political level. In Milan, for instance, many young people wavered between delinquency and far-left terrorism in the early 1980s (Calvi, 1982); in Brazzaville, young *déclassé* men formed groups which looked at times liked political militias, and at other times like armed gangs (Bazenguissa-Ganga, 1996);[5] the social anger of American society's 'losers' can crystallize into the rancour that sustains far-right racist and anti-Semitic militias hostile to the federal State and international organizations such as the UN (Zecchini, 1996). The infrapolitical character of some forms of violence may reflect a sort of disarticulation; in a given situation it appears to be infrapolitical, but it can at the same time be associated with very different and highly political meanings. The resurgence of anti-Semitic incidents in France at the beginning of the twenty-first century did not, for example, appear to be politically-motivated in any real sense, but some incidents were informed by the Israeli-Palestinian conflict, and by an identification with the Palestinian cause.

Metapolitical violence

For a long time, modernity was associated with the image of progress and reason, and with that of the decline of particular traditions and identities, and especially religious traditions and identities. From that perspective, violence was certainly not destined to disappear; but it was destined to become combined with reason or at least to decline, and therefore to become, at least in its most decisive expressions, instrumental rather than expressive or identitarian, or to die down.

Contemporary developments completely refute that vision. Whilst instrumental violence is certainly a reality, the violence that sometimes accompanies the rise of cultural or religious identities has been a significant phenomenon since the end of the twentieth century. This phenomenon may also have one essential characteristic: it is metapolitical, or in other words, it rises above the political and becomes a vector for meanings that give it an intransigent and non-negotiable quality or a religious, ethical, or ideological import that makes absolute demands. In such cases violence recognizes no frontiers, and the goals it is pursuing are, from the actor's point of view, so vital that he may, in extreme cases, sacrifice his own life or destroy himself in an attempt to assert a plethora of meanings.

Metapolitical violence is not apolitical. It is a project in which political dimensions are at once associated with and subordinate to other dimensions defined in cultural, and especially religious, terms that can make no concessions.

The crisis in modernity, which fuelled countless discourses about post-modernity throughout the 1980s, does a great deal to encourage this type of violence, in which identity-based meanings that have nothing to do with any insertion into a political relational space find expression in ever-more acute forms as the actors mobilize on the basis of frustrations born of modernity. When international communications instantaneously broadcast images of Western-style happiness to the most remote places, when the consumption of material and cultural goods is a daily spectacle that is televised or that can be seen in the windows of shops to which one is denied entry, when access to money or the fruits of science and progress is denied or has been lost, even though it seemed to be just within reach, a feeling of profound social injustice, irreducible inequality, or major frustration can be sublimated into, for example, religious values, convictions, and faith. One possible scenario is that violence will take hold of the actor and mobilize him for political projects in which identity becomes a resource, and in which the political is subordinated to a higher principle, such as the demands of God or of the most sacred good. The great Islamist mobilizations of the 1970s and 1980s were products of this logic, which fuses the political and the religious, but religion was the dominant factor. Such mobilizations can take very extreme forms, as in the morbid cult of martyrdom that Farhad Khosrokhavar analysed from the 1980s onwards in his studies of Iran's young *basijis* (Khosrokhavar, 1992; 2001). Their self-destruction had nothing to do with the hopes inspired by a religious utopia, and everything to with their frustration and the correlative loss of meaning. Such mobilizations can also evolve into a 'colder' cult of martyrdom that is less directly bound up with the experience of a living community. It is this that makes 'global' terrorism so terribly effective, as we saw with the terrorist attacks on the United States on 11 September 2001. In all these cases, the cult of martyrdom seems to be fuelled by a deep despair. Whilst it takes violence beyond the political, and whilst religious belief makes it easier to do that, religious belief is not its essential precondition. Some of the Palestinian authors of suicide bombings on Israeli soil claimed, for example, to be acting not in the name of Islam, but in that of the Palestinian nation, or even a secular political force.

Metapolitical violence may find its point of anchorage in unsatisfied social demands. In its most radical dimensions, political Islam, for instance, has a social face. It is supported by 'depeasantified' peasants who are disappointed with the big cities where they thought they would experience upward social mobility, or by disinherited people who cannot transform their difficulties into a social movement, or who cannot make it a living reality. In Lebanon, Hezbollah, for instance, emerged from a mutation within the 'movement of the disinherited', as it was called by its founder Imam Moussa Sadr, who led it until he died in the mid 1970s.

The source of metapolitical violence may also lie in the radicalization of individuals and groups who once thought that they could be part of modernity, or who actually were part of it until they were expelled. Left by the wayside, these victims of progress are motivated by a feeling of deep injustice because they have lost their social status. The origins of metapolitical violence may also lie in a conviction on the part of educated elites of engineers, doctors, and so on, that they are living in a society that does not give them the professional and personal fulfilment to which they aspire, like the Japanese scientists, many of them highly qualified, who chose, in the early 1990s, to join the Aum cult and to use extreme violence (Trinh, 2001).[6]

These sources can easily work in combination with each other, and with other sources. When they are transmuted into a religious rather than a national project, or are harnessed by religious promises that no political project could realistically deliver, social rage, frustration and anger will then lead the actors to commit acts of extreme violence, which may be exploited, oriented, or even manipulated by leaders and organizations that do have real political skills.

It is contemporary modernity that produces this violence, and it is a mistake to see it as a form of resistance on the part of traditional actors. Metapolitical violence is overburdened with a meaning that can become plethoric. It therefore goes beyond the political, but can in fact revert to being political, especially if it takes power, as was the case during the Iranian revolution and, in a sense, when the Taliban were in power for a few years in Kabul.

The Violence of the Individual

Societies have changed since the 1960s or 1970s and the exhaustion of the class conflict that once structured them. Since then, a clumsy vocabulary has been developed and uses 'post' to signal that we have left one era behind. We cannot really find a name for the new era, which has been variously described as post-industrial, post-national, post-modern, post-colonial, and so on. And many of the most decisive transformations, which obviously vary from country to country, suggest that when we look at violence, we have to take into account the fact that there is less and less need for the state to supply a framework for the social life that it usually supplies. The decline of the state framework becomes spectacularly apparent if we look at political institutions.

Deinstitutionalization

All over the world we are witnessing the regression and weakening of the institutions that guarantee the social bond, irrespective of whether they are responsible for order and security, for socialization (the educational system), or are embodiments of the Welfare State. Deinstutionalization is often – and especially in former industrial societies whose main public institutions were established and strengthened just as the workers' movement was being institutionalized – seen as the product or the success of neo-liberal ideas that ask less of the state, and which have prospered because they have replaced ideology. It is in fact largely the outcome of the difficulties faced by those institutions, which were becoming less and less able to fulfil their missions or keep their social, economic, political or cultural promises. This phenomenon was most pronounced in the East or in former Soviet societies where the factory, in particular, was the place where all sorts of guarantees were organized. Everything was channelled through the factory: jobs, of course, but also housing, access to health care, primary schools, leisure, sports, basic consumer goods, and so on. That model has collapsed, leaving behind it the social tragedies that, for a time, provided the political fodder for national-populism and then neo-communism.

The decline of institutions is a major political and economic phenomenon, and a factor in the disintegration of the social bond, or what Robert Castel (1995) calls disaffiliation. It is also a cultural phenomenon that goes hand in hand with the crisis of authority. And when there is no authority, and therefore no compulsory norms and rules that apply to everyone, violence emerges in forms that are perceived to be delinquent or criminal.

The rise of modern individualism

Modern individualism has made huge progress since the end of the *Trente Glorieuses*, or the thirty years of economic growth from 1945 to 1975. Modern individualism represents a combination of two logics, both of which can have an effect on contemporary forms of violence. It is, on the one hand, an expression of a desire for an individual involvement in modernity, of a desire to have access, in eminently variable modalities, to money, consumerism, and immediate pleasure, but also to employment, education and health care. On the other hand, it can also be a source of creativity: everyone wants to construct their own life and to define their own choices, commitments and loyalties, without them being imposed by tradition or by the rules and norms of collective life, or of some particular group. Individual subjects may very well commit themselves to a collective action or chose a cultural identity, and then fully devote themselves to it without necessarily being subordinated or subservient to it. They can just as easily choose not to commit themselves or to withdraw from their commitments.

It should be added that there is nothing new about these twin aspects of individualism; in a sense, Emile Durkheim (1915 [1912]) evokes them when he makes a distinction between individuality, which pertains to the profane world, and personality, which in his view pertains to the sacred.

The rise of individualism encourages violence in at least two ways. On the one hand, violence may look like the best or only way of achieving legitimate ends, even though violence itself is illegitimate. In his day, Robert Merton (1957) clearly demonstrated that perfectly conformist individuals could be criminals and delinquents. They may, for example, want access to money. There is nothing illegitimate about that in our societies, but they can use theft as a way of gaining access to it. In Western countries, it is not difficult to establish a link between the almost steady increase of certain forms of delinquency, and specially predation, from the 1950s onwards, and the development of a consumer society. When the delinquency is accompanied by violence (which is not always the case), this violence is a response to desires that are stimulated by the media in particular and also to the promptings of a mass consumerism that has now become a global spectacle. It may, on the other hand, be an expression of a subjectivity that is prevented from speaking or silenced, or the product of a situation in which an individual does not have the concrete ability to produce his own choices or to become an autonomous subject and to invert the situation. That reversal can be either playful or destructive. To adopt David Le Breton's (1991) terminology, violence is, in such case, informed by a 'passion for risks' and ordeals that can, in extreme cases, become self-destructive. The system or situation makes it impossible for the individual to become the actor of his existence, and the individual turns that impossibility against himself. In such cases, violence is at once a quest for and a production of meaning, an attempt to produce for oneself what was once supplied by culture or institutions (which takes us back to my earlier point about the crisis in institutions). It may be a self-projection or the mark of an unhappy subjectivity, of an individual refusal to go on living when one's existence is denied or cannot find its place.

The rise of globalization makes everything to do with individualism much more acute than it was in the past, in both the dimensions we have identified.

Both dimensions further undermine individual fragilities. They make it more obvious to the actors themselves that it is very difficult to reconcile the instrumental or strategic efficiency, which is essential if they are to be able to become successful participants in modernity, with the construction of an autonomous subjectivity (see Ehrenberg, 1995). No one is unaware of what the modern world has to offer or promise, in terms of both possible consumption and self-realization, but it is very difficult to be both the consumer and the producer of one's own existence, or to be, on the one hand, efficient and rational and, on the other, autonomous and independent of the norms.

The decline of institutions and the rise of modern individualism therefore create conditions that encourage, if not violence in general, at least the rise of anomic and delinquent forms of violence, or forms of violence relating to the difficulty of constructing the self as a subject. These conditions make the state's role in protecting its citizens more and more difficult.

Intellectuals and Violence

Violence now seems to have lost all legitimacy within the political space, so much as that is has come to mean absolute evil. Violence is what a unanimous society must proscribe and fight, both at home and abroad. And yet in the 1960s and 1970s it could still be justified or understood by intellectuals, some of whom belonged to a revolutionary, anarchist or Marxist-Leninist tradition; it could be theorized and even supported to some extent, and could be tolerated within the political sphere. Some admired guerrilla fighters and took 'Che' as their hero, whilst other tended to extol social violence, and to encourage and inspire it. The thinking of Frantz Fanon, which centres on the experience of colonialism, theorized the idea of a violent rupture, and Sartre further radicalised the idea in his famous preface to Fanon's *The Wretched of the Earth*. A few years later, the same Sartre became involved in debates with 'Maoists' and encouraged them to take the path of violent action (Gavi et al., 1971).

Some reactions to the Iranian revolution, which was hailed by Michel Foucault, for example, may be a final expression of these currents of opinion and of this political and intellectual sympathy for processes and actors that resorted to violence. The legitimacy enjoyed by violence was all the greater in that it supplied a response, albeit a limited response in most cases, to the type of atrocities and authoritarian or dictatorial abuses of power to be found in Latin America until the 1980s.

Since then, the intellectual and political zone within which violence could be an object of sympathy has shrunk considerably. A very broad consensus now rejects and denounces it. Where violence is concerned, the philosophical, moral and ethical debate seems to be over. Western intellectuals have on the whole distanced themselves from it, rather as though the 1980s and 1990s had acted as a major purge. This development is inseparable from the decline of the figure of the classic intellectual who was tempted by political commitment and often ready to promote revolutionary projects.

The time when violence met with an absolute rejection as a result of the exhaustion of Cold War ideologies may also be over. Violence may once more find a legitimate space and escape the almost universal taboo it has been under for some years now.

It is easy to predict what the implications of this incipient reversal will be if it continues. So long as violence was taboo, and therefore absent from public debates because no political or intellectual actors were able or willing to break the consensus surrounding it, it was inevitably the object of perceptions and representations that easily distorted it by either over-estimating or under-estimating its importance. Some demonized it, whilst other minimized the importance of acts of violence. Terrorist attacks for which Islamists were not necessarily responsible were blamed on them. The Oklahoma City bombing of 19 April 1995, in which 16 people died, proved, to the stupefaction of all, to be the work of Timothy McVeigh, a far-right American extremist. Once it becomes the object of a new debate, violence can be discussed and examined in contradictory ways. The problems it reveals, and which it always perverts to a greater or lesser extent, can be looked at more soberly. Paradoxically, violence has to enjoy some legitimacy within the public space before we can discuss it seriously ... and deny it all legitimacy thanks to an intellectual and political debate.

On a Famous Remark by Max Weber

Classical sociology often associates the state with violence. A famous remark by Max Weber (2004 [1919]: 33) sums up this association in almost tautological fashion.

> The relationship of the state to violence is particularly close at the present time ... Nowadays ... we must say that the state is the form of human community that (successfully) lays claim to the *monopoly of legitimate physical violence* within a particular territory. For what is specific to the present is that all other organizations or individuals can assert the right to use physical violence only insofar as the *state* permits them to do so. The state is regarded as the sole source of the 'right' to use violence.

The definition is ambiguous; as Raymond Aron notes, it is unclear whether the concept outlined by Weber refers to a purely theoretical or abstract category, or to a concrete historical category that we can observe empirically.[7] Without going so far as to examine the historical changes that have affected modern states since 1919, and without necessarily turning Max Weber into the official theorist of the state-violence relationship (to which he actually devoted only a few pages in 'Politics as a Vocation' and *Economy and Society* (1968 [1956]: 56)), let us look at the current situation, and at the state's theoretical monopoly on legitimate violence.

The state outflanked

As we have seen, it is true that Western intellectuals have, for the most part, ceased to challenge the state's monopoly on violence, at least where the democracies in which they live are concerned. But can we be satisfied with Weber's formula at a time when the economy is being globalized, and when states seem to have been outflanked, both at home and abroad, by economic problems as well as social, political and cultural problems and by non-state logics that escape them because they are created by actors over whom they have little control? The contemporary state is finding it more difficult to claim to be the territorial, administrative, juridical and symbolic framework for economic life because flows, decisions, markets, and the circulation of people, goods, and information are now global and, to some extent, exist in illegal or uncontrolled forms that mean we have to speak of the globalization of organized crime, and not only of the drugs trade. The more it loses control of the economy, the more the state is forced to retreat and to give ground to informal activities, to the black market, or to clandestine labour that are, by definition, outside its control and especially its fiscal control. As the economy is privatized so too is violence, which becomes a way of pillaging the state and appropriating resources that should be under its control.

The state's legitimacy is further undermined by the presence, creation, or growth of transnational solidarities such as diasporas within the territories for which it is responsible; their functional space no longer corresponds to that of the state. It is weakened when it is subordinated to a more powerful legitimacy by, for example, international agreements, by transfers of authority that result in the establishment of international tribunals, or by the intervention of supra-national forces in situations where crimes against humanity have been perpetrated.

The legitimacy of the state rests, finally, upon an international recognition that may prove to be limited, or that may be challenged. When, for example, the Taliban took power in Afghanistan, they were not admitted into the international community; their state was reluctantly recognized by only a handful of others. In more general terms, the legitimacy of states that are regarded by others as dictatorships or as corrupt or rogue states (as denounced by the American administration), but also as especially weak or powerless states, is less assured than that of democratic states. The reason why the theme of the right to intervene has emerged since the 1970s, and why humanitarian actors now play such an important role all over the world, is that the sovereignty of those states masks practices of violence that they tolerate, implement, or cannot prevent, and that offend the world's consciousness or ethics so greatly as to legitimize interventions that flout their monopoly on the internal use of force (see Moore, 1998).

The state and its police

There is always a possibility that the state itself will, through the intervention of its agents, and therefore those who represent it, use or resort to illegitimate violence, even in the most democratic of countries. This may involve practices that contradict its official discourse, which is what happens when torture and all kinds of abuses of military and policy powers occur in democracies. Brazil is a particularly interesting case in point, as the growth of democracy went hand in hand with an increase in violence, including police violence (see Peralva, 2001; Pinheiro, 1996). States also often delegate the use of force to private actors who use it to further their own interests. At the same time – and this is a major problem in the United States and Canada – the social gains made by policy officers have given them enough time off and holidays to allow them to contemplate moonlighting in order to top up their wages. Many of them put their skills at the disposal of private security firms, which quickly leads to great confusion if they also use their professional contacts, or even certain attributes of their main function (such as their weapons). There are also many grey areas in which it is no longer very clear where the state's responsibility ends, and where that of other actors begins.

Take, for example, the example of security on France's public housing estates. Is it a matter for the police or for the housing authorities? The dividing line is unclear. Any examination of domestic security and policing leads us to question the validity not only of Max Weber's formula but also that of what has sometimes been called the Weberian state (Ocqueteau, 2002). Jean-Paul Brodeur's (2003) work (on the British and American research, see Brodeur and Monjardet, 2003) on policing clearly demonstrates that the social sciences have undermined what he calls a 'truism', first in British and American studies and then, much later, in other countries as well. Following Egon Bittner, he points out that it is not just the police who can legally and legitimately use physical violence. The medical profession can also do so, and parents can still quite legally use some violence against their children, though there are obviously national variations here (in 2003 'the Canadian penal code still recognizes the legitimacy of parents' recourse to violence against their children, and of teachers' recourse to violence against their pupils' (Brodeur, 2003)). Brodeur's work and Frédéric Ocqueteau's studies of France clearly demonstrate that the fantastic increase in the number of private security firms responsible for the surveillance or protection of property, people, and information does not simply reflect the idea that the police and their theoretical monopoly on physical force should be privatized. In modern democracies, new configurations and combinations of policing functions are emerging. The interplay between the state and the market is dense and complex. New private actors are beginning to take on public tasks and are either competing with or acting alongside the public authorities, and they have a real autonomy: 'The many different faces of security result from the challenge to the notion of a monopoly on legitimate force' (Brodeur, 2003: 11).

Who defines legitimacy?

This is in fact a serious problem, if only because what is or is not considered to be violence varies from one period to another and is often defined as such by public opinion or civil society before it is recognized as such by the State. So long as it is confined to the private sphere or similar domains, and so long as it is not made public, the state can, if not legitimate, at least tolerate violence, and sometimes even cover it up. Paedophilia, for example, is now regarded as a criminal offence in France but for a long time it was tolerated, even when the perpetrators were teachers working in state schools. If there was a hint of scandal, their hierarchy protected them at every level and hushed it up: the legitimacy of the institution meant that none of its agents could be charged with that type of offence. The state is less and less tolerant of the violence suffered by women, children, or the elderly. It is less willing than it used to be to allow institutions such as schools or churches to establish enclaves in which 'what is sometimes systematic violence can be used without the State challenging its legitimacy' (Brodeur, 1995). Private violence, or the institutional violence that goes on behind closed doors, decreases when protest movements make it visible and ensure that the public space recognizes it for what it is.

In more general terms, it has to be accepted that the legitimacy of violence can be a cultural and social phenomenon, and that it does not have to be defined by the state. Every culture and every society defines, at a given moment, what it will tolerate, accept, or reject, even if that definition does not conform to legal categories and does not derive solely from the norms that are established or recognized by the rational process embodied in the state and its bureaucratization. The definition of legitimate violence can be either conjunctural or structural, in which case it is part of a dense network of values that do not change quickly. For a long time, men who killed their wives' lovers were acquitted of murder in France. In the United States, black men who were without proof and usually falsely accused of raping white women were regularly punished extremely harshly. Society, or its most influential members, do not necessarily take the same view of crimes or serious outbreaks of violence, such as riots, as the state. As Philip Smith demonstrates in a stimulating article, society sometimes applauds what it sees as legitimate violence; at the same time, there is a danger that the state will lose the support of the public if its recourse to violence is out of step with society's perception of what is and what is not legitimate. Smith (1997: 111) adds that the interplay between society and state that defines the legitimacy of violence is the result of interactions that can give rise to unstable and rapid processes 'Consent for violence can come and go with a speed that is ... disconcerting.'

The thesis of the withering away of the state

Does the great disorder that goes by the name of economic globalization, and the cultural and social phenomena that go with it, mean that we have actually entered the age of the decline or withering away of the state? According to those who support that thesis, the state is growing weaker in places where, as in Europe, it is long-established. In regions where it is a recent 'purely imported product', as Bertrand Badie and Pierre Birnbaum (1979) put it, the State is often so corrupt and inefficient, and has lost so much legitimacy as a result of its own inadequacies, that it is possible to speak of the 'breakdown of the State' and to see it as a major threat to the planet's security. 'The most important threat to security today is not states' aspirations to power but their breakdown', states Philippe Delmas (1995: 9). Some prefer to speak of a decline, or of a return to the Middle Ages, to explain the weakening of nation-states and describe 'a plurality of communities and hierarchical and overlapping allegiances'. The theme was first outlined by Umberto Eco (1976) and has recently been taken up by Pierre Hassner.[8] Others are of the opinion that the demand for a State is being replaced, in both cases, by a demand for other agencies that can guarantee order and security. Ghassan Salamé, for instance, identifies the paradoxical phenomenon that arises, especially in countries where the 'transplant' of the modern state has resulted in corruption, inefficiency, and a loss of legitimacy, when there is a demand for insertion into an international order in which the protection would be supplied by powers functioning on the Empire model. He speaks of 'calls for an empire', and explains that an empire has 'a more flexible relationship with its territory than the Nation-State' (Salamé, 1996: 56).

Back to the empire ... a new Middle Ages ... The formulations may vary, but they are all expressions of the idea that the classical modern forms of the State are withering away, and that forms that were tried out in the past are being invented or reinvented.

This suggests that we have to examine the hypothesis that the state has undergone a mutation and that it is not simply in decline. It is not, first of all, clear that we have to conclude that all recent attempts to graft a State on to societies and peoples that were previously organized on a different basis have ended in failure. On the contrary, there any many arguments to support the idea, which is defended by Jean-François Bayart amongst others, that what we are seeing in Africa and Asia is the continued 'universalization of certain basic elements of Western civilization' (Bayart, 1996: 21), including, in some cases, the state. The weakening, decay, withering away, or rejection of the state does not explain everything, and several contemporary experiences suggest that the concept of the state is by no means historically obsolete. Olivier Roy, who has made a special study of the Middle East and Central Asia, demonstrates that the state is still an essential element in political reconstruction. His studies of the workings and rise of infra-state solidarity groups demonstrate that they cannot survive without the state: 'smugglers need borders' (Roy, 1996). Elsewhere, the most urgent task facing the UN in some of the situations where it finds itself in control is in fact the construction or reconstruction of states, as was the case in East Timor or Bosnia, and as is still the case in Afghanistan and Angola. What the jargon of the political sciences calls 'nation-building' is in fact more like 'state-building'.

It is impossible to paint a coherent and linear picture of how the 'State' formula will evolve, or of its ability to deal with the political problems of our era. One thing is, however, certain: we have entered an historical conjuncture marked by the obvious breakdown of the model for inter-state relations developed by classical political philosophy 'from Hobbes to Clausewitz, Weber and then Aron', as Pierre Hassner puts it (1998: 26). This era is also obsessed with the idea that the State is withering away or being transcended. Its withering away is no longer seen as the cause or source of violence, or as a justification for violence, or as it was in the 1960s or 1970s when attempts were made to explain so-called national liberation struggles or to promote revolutionary projects. In many situations, violence is of course an alternative, a response to state brutality, dictatorial power or neo-colonial oppression. But the State is still, as in the mainstream tradition of political philosophy since at least the time of Hobbes, the political formula that should ensure that physical violence does not take place outside of its field of action and control. The problem is that there is a growing discrepancy between the reality and the concept of the State. Violence breaks out and spreads when the State is, or is perceived to be, weak. It is all the more intolerable in that the State is expected to prevent violence. Citizens are more likely to feel that violence is spreading if they are, for historical reasons, convinced that the State has a vocation to prevent violence, that it was able to do so in the past, and that it is no longer up to its task. When the State has always been weak or of little relevance to them, citizens' expectations are lower. That is why the feeling of insecurity generates more political demands in a country such as France, where the State is expected to intervene in public life on a huge scale, than in Italy, where it has never been such a decisive reality, and is not expected to be.

The State still has a very important role to play in the contemporary world when it comes to defining and countering political violence that it does not control. Max Weber's famous formula about the State's monopoly on legitimate physical violence cannot, however, explain every aspect of its action in this area, and still less can it explain its inadequacies. At the same time, anyone who wishes to reflect upon contemporary violence must obviously refer to the axis that connects it to the State, but should not make it the alpha and omega of every analysis. Contemporary views thus – and this is no paradox – come close to those of pre-historians who, like Jean Guilaine and Jean Zammit (2001: 325), urge us not to ignore prehistoric man's experience of violence and not to restrict war to meaning 'a strategy that is closely related to the formation of the *polis*, state control and the coercive workings of the state'.

Notes

1 'Just as the emergence of the territorial state, two or three centuries ago, went hand in hand with inter-state wars, explained their existence and fed on them, the disintegration of the territorial state and the spread of civil wars are in reality mutually-reinforcing processes; one explains and encourages the other (Salamé, 1996: 95).

2 Cf Hobsbawm (1992 [1990]:196): 'The very fact that historians are at last beginning to make some progress in the study and analysis of nations and nationalism suggests that, as so often, the phenomenon is past its peak. The owl of Minerva, which brings wisdom, said Hegel, flies out at dusk. It is a good sign that it is now circling around nations and nationalisms'.

3 On this specific point, I refer the reader to my article on the question of violence and figures of nationalism (Wieviorka, 1997).

4 See Labat (1995) and Martinez (1995). According to Martinez the Armed Islamic Groups have a lot in common with small and medium-sized businesses, or with import-export companies that had been freed from state control. Three years after its outbreak, the 'civil war looks more and more like a bid for social promotion and personal enrichment'. This is an extreme view in which the political disappears completely.

5 For a study of similar experiences, see Marchal (1993). Similar phenomena have been observed in Haiti.

6 It will be recalled that Aum was a religious cult which planned and carried out a murderous attack using sarin gas on the Tokyo subway on 20 March 1995.

7 'Weber has not really distinguished between purely analytic concepts and semi-historical concepts' (Aron, 1970 [1967]: 244).

8 'We are back … to the contradictory character of international order in the present period. We are no longer in the interstate, Clausewitzian modern world. We are back to the medieval questions of legitimate authority … without a pope and an emperor' (Hassner, 1995: 56).

3

THE EMERGENCE OF VICTIMS

Traditional societies, and phases of modernity prior to our own, were familiar with various images of misfortune, the most obvious being poverty; the work of Bronislaw Geremek (1987 [1971]) provides some striking examples. Victims were, however, of little interest in their own right; their sufferings, or the fact that their physical and moral integrity had been scorned, negated, or destroyed, was not really important. Their lived experience, either at the time of the assault or afterwards (trauma, existential problems), if they survived, was much less important than what violence meant to the community as a whole. Victims existed only insofar as they made a contribution to the social order, or to a balance that was threatened by war or by natural disasters that reflected the will of the gods. The pain of sacrificial victims went unnoticed and their screams were muffled. The terrible nature of what they underwent was not perceived as such and, as many anthropologists have explained, their death was seen as a contribution to the common good, so much so that their martyrdom was denied or hushed up. The sacrifice they made had to look like something they desired or at least accepted without any recriminations (Lempert, 2000). And if, in all other circumstances, crime was something that could not be tolerated and delinquency was something that had to be combated, that was because they represented a challenge to society, threatened the social bond, and disturbed the social order, rather than because of the harm that was done to the victims. Victims were at most expected to lodge complaints, and help and inform the institutions responsible for the repression of crime.

And when justice did define punishments and when the state was established, the 'civil' code was much less important than the 'penal' code: when the criminal was sanctioned and when the delinquent made amends to society as a whole by undergoing punishment, the work of justice was essentially done. By administering the appropriate punishment, it demonstrated that it was helping to dissuade the majority from wrongdoing. There was therefore not a lot for the victims to demand. The wrongdoer was punished by the state, which in a sense took the place of the victim in order to obtain reparation. From the traditional perspective, but also in the classical phase of the modern era, the whole of society was affected when an individual became the victim of a crime or an act of criminal violence. It was society that had to be protected, and society required a formal acknowledgement, in the form of punishment, that the guilty would not go unpunished. Victims delegated the task of making reparations to the state and its justice. Or seemed, rather, to delegate it: they had no choice in the matter. In ancient law and jurisprudence, explains Denis Salas (2001: 13): 'the *infraction* repressed violence committed against the law of the prince; the *inquisitorial* system introduced a new actor in the form of the public minister who represented the victims in court; the *punishment* sanctioned the guilty party whose crime had offended the sovereign, and replaced private compensation. The victim was ousted to make way for the king, whose interests had to be defended by his minister'.

Birth of the Victim

The contemporary victim began to acquire a certain public visibility in the nineteenth century in at least two domains, one international and the other internal to social life. The victim emerged in part on the battlefield at Solférino, when Henri Dunant was inspired to found the Red Cross, and therefore to help war victims on a basis that inevitably transcended the viewpoint of states. It should, however, be noted that, at this time, 'war victims' meant soldiers and that the problem of protecting civilians scarcely arose. Subsequent developments were depressing. Simon Chesterman (2001) notes that, during the First World War, 5 per cent of war victims were civilians; in the Second World War, the figure rose to 50 per cent, and in the 1980s it rose to 90 per cent and obviously included large numbers of women and children. The first great international conferences such as the Hague Peace Conference had, before the First World War, introduced a distinction between civilians and belligerents in order to promote measures to protect … the belligerents, whereas the main goal is now to protect civilians (see Nabulsi, 2001).

The figure of the victim also reflected changes in the ways the violence inflicted on women and children was seen. It was, as George Vigarello notes (1998: 186), in the nineteenth century that women and children began to be seen as victims, that society discovered the moral violence that prolongs, accompanies or proceeds physical violence, and that it came to be accepted that pressures and threats mean that 'the territory of violence could be expanded to include a brutality that was not directly physical'. Doctors and lawyers, such as the forensic medical examiners Ambroise Tardieu and Alexandre Lacassagne in France, played a significant role in this movement.

Important writers such as the Comtesse de Ségur and Victor Hugo also played their own part by creating literary figures like the boy in the former's *Un Bon Petit Diable* (1865) and Cosette in *Les Misérables*, and even by writing what might be described as feminist texts. By the end of the nineteenth century, several Western countries had adopted laws to guarantee the protection of abused children.

The way in which the victim began to emerge as a specific object for policies in the late nineteenth century also reflected the birth of the Welfare State. A new emphasis was placed on 'assurance' against risks. When the authorities encourage or take responsibility for the introduction of protective systems or welfare insurance, when laws are passed on accidents at work, when the state recognizes that society must make provision to pay damages, and that compensation or reparations must be paid in certain circumstances, they introduce a logic that recognizes the existence of victims. As Renée Zauberman and Philippe Robert remark (1995: 8), 'the appearance of the victim as the autonomous object of public policies ... is a sort of extension, or new branch, of the Welfare State, but at the same time it comes into conflict with the logic of the penal State'. Whilst the penal state ousts or almost ousts the victim, the Welfare State introduces the victim.

But if we do have to speak of an anthropological reversal, it is mainly in connection with the massive transformations that put victims centre stage from the 1960s onwards.

Civilians, women and children

A change occurred in many countries at that time, if only with the introduction of laws – New Zealand was the first country to introduce a law compensating the victims of burglary in 1963 – or with various declarations or resolutions on the part of international organizations.

The changes that had begun a century ago now began to speed up or to be extended to all sorts of other domains as a result of collective mobilizations, some organized by the crime victims themselves or by associations speaking in their name, and by others, such as the World Society of Victimology, which claims to speak in the name of victims in general.

When it comes to war, the victims' point of view has become a central concern. The number of humanitarian organizations has risen considerably, and they have become more powerful. The case has been argued for a right to interfere in internal concerns in order to facilitate humanitarian interventions, which may, should the need arise, mean infringing upon the sovereignty of states. It has to be said once more that the violence of war now affects civilian populations on a huge scale, and that human losses and their correlates are not the lot of combatants alone.

This sensitivity to war-victims' sensitivities does not date from the last two or three decades of the twentieth century; its influence can be seen in psychiatry and then in psychoanalysis, in Charcot and in Freud, from the *Studies on Hysteria* of 1893 onwards, and then, more specifically, in his work on trauma and war neuroses. This sensitivity has, however, become so acute that it is now invading other disciplines within social science, and especially history, where views have changed considerably. War is no longer a problem within inter-state relations, the object of strategic analyses, or a domain within the history of nations and their conflicts. Reading Stéphane Audoin-Rouzeau's and Annette Becker's (2000) book on the First World War, war is now also seen as a form of violence that affects bodies, and that makes it difficult for combatants who have become victims to undertake the essential work of mourning. For survivors, it is a traumatizing experience.

At the same time, the revival of women's movements, feminist and non-feminist, made it more and more difficult to confine the violence suffered by women to private spaces. Increasingly, violence against women became publicly visible, and rape in particular came to be viewed as a serious crime. More recently, rape within marriage has also been recognized as a crime. These struggles were designed to do away with the shame that stigmatized the fact of having been a victim and prevented women from taking action. Whilst struggles for women's emancipation do not date from the twentieth century, it was in the aftermath of 1968 that women began to mobilize against the violence they suffered, namely rape, violence inside and outside the family, and incest. The law was changed in many countries as a result.

Irrespective of whether we are talking about violence in wartime, in social life, or in private life, the new emphasis on victims from the late 1960s onwards must also be related to the global role played by the electronic media, and especially television. Listen, for example, to Jacky Mamou's account of the birth of *Médecins Sans Frontières* (Mamou, 2001: 18–19). In 1968, he explains, a number of French doctors went to care for the tens of thousands of Ibos who were dying in Biafra. They wanted to talk about what they had seen but were prevented from doing so by the rules of the Red Cross, for which they were working. However, for the first time television showed images of young children dying of hunger, and the doctors themselves spoke out: 'The doctors screamed that there was no such thing as good victims and bad victims ... just civilians who were being killed'. This intervention gave birth to *Médecins Sans Frontières*, which succeeded in getting the attention of the media: 'Public opinion must be a shield to protect the victims. The media ... will make their actions highly visible'.

Public opinion is also increasingly concerned about the violence that is inflicted on children, and was especially horrified by the episode of the Dutroux affair in Belgium. The paedophile murderer's crimes did not just make such problems a public issue, they also revealed the institutional failings – and especially those of the Belgian justice and police systems – that allowed such crimes to be committed. The huge, and highly emotional, protest demonstration known as the 'White March' (20 October 1996) marked an important moment in the history of actors who have transformed victims' tragedies into a subject of debate and conflict. In the past, paedophile scandals were usually hushed up by the institutions in which they had occurred: the primary teacher was protected by the headmaster, who was himself protected by the education authority or the minister; the priest was protected by the hierarchy. The Catholic hierarchy was shaken by the huge scandals that broke when the North American press revealed the extent of paedophile activity in the Church in 2001. This is an indication that, as an institution, the Catholic Church is no longer untouchable, and can no longer look down on society from on high, as it once did in so many countries. Children new enjoy legal protection. The Convention adopted by the UN in 1989 asserts that they have rights, and institutions are no longer worlds unto themselves that brook no challenge. In debates about these issues, everything has changed to such an extent that it is now being suggested that what child-victims say should be treated with great caution, as the stories they make up can ruin the lives of individuals who are wrongly accused.

The emergence of victims can also be seen as one of the social movements that helped to shake Western societies after 1968. A co-authored study devoted essentially to the post-traumatic therapies available to the victims of acts of criminal violence contains, for example, an account of the history of American crime victims' movements (Young, 1988). Marlene A. Young reminds us that the crime rate in the United States rose in the 1960s, which is when the first studies of victimation were undertaken. An official agency was established to launch support and service programmes for victims in the 1970s, at a time when the government was expressing a growing concern about child abuse. The important point here is that institutional activity cannot be divorced from the emergence of collective protest movements. Women's movements denounced rape, and some opened centres for the victims. Shortly afterwards, battered-women's shelters and rape crisis centres were opened, most of them run by victims. Within this movement, women discovered and recognized themselves, and one another, for what they were. Ultimately, they were 'survivors' and this mutual recognition was a source of pride and dignity. The movement attacked a criminal justice system that had always turned a blind eye to this type of violence. The protests were accompanied by intense institutional activity, and by the development of programmes, services and research activity. This led to the concept of 'rape trauma syndrome'. This foreshadowed the Vietnam veterans' syndrome and the 'battered woman's syndrome', which in turn helped to define PTSD in 1980. Post-Traumatic Stress Disorder now features very prominently in the specialist psychiatric literature and is, for example, a category that is constantly referred to by the American Psychiatric Association. The movement's actors are not just victims, but also researchers and innovators working within the American legal system. The National Organization for Victim Assistance was established in 1975 and launched a series of annual conferences. The movement has diversified, and has sometimes been torn apart by serious internal tensions and even splits – one organization left NOVA in 1978 in order to concentrate exclusively on victims of sexual assaults. Some expect a great deal from institutions and federal aid, whilst others are developing mutual support networks, whilst still others, such as Mothers Against Drink Driving, are bringing political pressure to bear to demand laws and reforms. The movement is demanding justice for victims, making their shame and isolation a thing of the past, and forcing through legislative measures. As Marlene A. Young writes (1988: 325): 'Now, at last, the aftermath of crime was being understood from the victim's perspective – not from the perspective of a society that wants to keep victims at a distance.'

The emergence of victims' movements brings us face to face with two distinct questions, both related to the debatable theme of the weakening of the state. The first has to do with the internal working of our societies and their states: is the line that divides the private from the public being erased, now that victims have entered the public space en masse? The more victims speak out in their own names, and the more they demand public action against the violence they suffer in private, the more they challenge the distinction between the public sphere where the problems of collective life are discussed, and the private sphere where violence is not really regarded as such simply because it concerns only the protagonists – unless things get seriously out of hand and result in murder. The emergence of the figure of the victim is in that sense one of the contemporary symptoms of the institutional crisis we mentioned earlier. By making public the violence suffered by women and children, which had until now been minimized because it is private, recent developments simply move the problem from one sphere to the other. At a deeper level, they reflect a change in the way we see the State and its institutions, and in what we expect of them. What we are calling deinstitutionalization might also be described as reinstitutionalization. From that point of view, the future might not lie in the abolition of institutions, or in an unlikely return to their old ways, but in an extension of state control. It might also produce new and very different formulas in which institutions no longer stand apart from society and ignore private life, and become more sensitive to the needs of the individuals to whom they have a duty of care or who work in them. They might become user-friendly institutions rather than sanctified institutions. That tendency is already observable in the legal sphere, as we can see from recent developments. In an essay denouncing what she sees as the 'dead end feminism' taken by certain currents within feminism, Elisabeth Badinter notes (2006 [2003]: 10) that 'the new penal code of 1992 no longer speaks of "offences against public decency" but of "sexual aggression".' It is, in other words, less concerned with the collective order and more concerned with the integrity of individuals.

The second question has more to do with international relations, war, peace and the sovereignty of states. Does the State lose some of its sacred aura when the victim replaces the combatant in both the mind of the public and the work of historians who look at the past in the light of the questions and expectations of the present? Does the new emphasis on the victim destroy, for instance, the idea of sacrificing oneself for the fatherland that is enshrined in the thousands of First World War memorials in France? And does the right to intervene that is being promoted by many humanitarian organizations – and not just humanitarian organizations – mean that the State is, in their view, less important than the defence of the lives of citizens threatened by barbarism, and that the State is no longer the ultimate guarantor that protects them from violence, disorder or chaos? The foregrounding of the figure of the victim represents a challenge to the State, whose sovereignty is becoming less important than the defence of actual or potential victims, and which is in danger of being dispossessed or stripped of its essential attributes. It should also be noted that victims often turn to the State, even if they are not its dependents, to demand reparations, and do not necessarily bypass it. That is particularly true of the descendents of the victims of genocide.

Victims of crimes against humanity

What applies to the victims of criminality or delinquency also applies to the victims of crimes against humanity. The notion of 'crimes against humanity' is debateable because it elevates one variety of crime above the juridical and political norms of any collective life, and at the same time establishes norms and courts, and therefore the criteria and agencies to judge them. The same notion is the basis for the emergence of groups demanding recognition and/or, in some cases, reparations, which are not the same thing.

The first victims, in the contemporary sense of that term, to succeed in emerging were the Jews who, twenty years after the Second World War and the genocide directed against them, began to bring about an explicit reversal of roles. A particularly striking account has been given by Jean-Michel Chaumont (1997). It began, he explains, with a debate in which Elie Wiesel was the main protagonist. Its purpose was to demonstrate the unique nature of the experience of the Shoah, which was, argued Wiesel (1985 [1967]: 206), 'unique' and qualitatively different from any other genocide. It was messianic and not historic, Jewish, and therefore bound up with a singular identity. More importantly, Jews were able, thanks to

Wiesel, to put an end to their shame towards the end of the 1960s 'Why do we ... think of the Holocaust with shame? Why do we not claim it as a glorious page of our eternal history?' (1985 [1967]: 205).[1] This marked the beginning of a powerful trend for self-assertion in which the Jewish victims of Nazi barbarism demanded an acknowledgment of what they or their forebears had endured. Their memories then began to have an impact on how history is written; the nature of the Vichy period in France has, for instance, been re-examined by historians.

Other collective victims then began to crowd on to the political scene in Western societies, and they also inspired a new field of research in the social sciences: 'genocide studies'. Armenians demanded recognition of the geno-cide of 1915, first by using the terrorist methods of the ASALA and then by mobilizing non-violent resources. Blacks in America and Africa demanded reparations for the slavery endured by their ancestors, and for the traumatic effects they were still suffering. The victims who are now speak-ing out did not necessarily suffer an assault on their physical integrity as a result of genocidal violence or the barbarism of crimes against humanity. They are affected to the extent that they belong to a community or group; they, or their forebears in particular, were the object of crimes, mass murder, genocides, and other forms of extreme violence that destroyed their histor-ical points of reference and their cultures. Hence the use of neologisms such as 'ethnicide'. What they are asking for is not self-evident. And nor, as Jacques Derrida has shown in the lengthy debate published in *Le Monde des débats* in December 1999 (republished in Derrida, 2000b), is what they may be able to give, namely forgiveness. Do the victims expect some recog-nition of the tragedy they suffered, or do they expect to be paid compensa-tion or reparations, perhaps in the tangible form of financial reparations? The claimants argue that they have every right to do so, but they are in fact the victims' descendents. Can they speak in the name of their parents or ancestors, and what can forgiveness mean when it is granted by a relative or descendant of a victim who is dead or has been killed, and who is therefore a relative victim rather than an absolute victim?

And what are we to make of those who admit to what has happened and make reparations? Are they guilty and can they expiate sins or crimes when those who committed them were merely their ancestors or the former owners of the power or resources they now hold? In discussions of mass murder, the subjectivity of both parties soon comes to mean that of the persons concerned or involved, yet in many cases their relationship with the tragedy in question is purely historical or memory-based. It is mediated by religious, ethnic, cultural and political identifications, but it is also largely the product of highly personal choices and decisions. They choose to demand recognition, or prefer to forget. They choose to demand repara-tions, or to take the view that nothing can expiate the sin. And so on.

Our entry into the era of victims raises countless major political, ethical, juridical and intellectual problems. It puts centre stage actors who, as such, had no place there in the past and who are, in extreme cases, shaping strange social movements. These are movements in which the living speak in the name of the dead and the disappeared, but their demands are not necessarily restricted to a demand for recognition of what happened in the past: the 'mothers of the Plaza de Mayo' in Buenos Aires recall the crimes of the military dictatorship that took away their husbands, children and relations. But some of the demands put forward by these women, and still more so the associations of the children of the disappeared, are living calls for democracy and justice in today's Argentina.

The more 'victims' speak out and demand recognition, the greater the danger that the classic framework of the nation-state may be demolished. The victims are raising issues that do not necessarily respect national boundaries. They also appeal to international organizations and sometimes organize on a diasporic or transnational basis, and this helps to undermine the states and institutions in question. The undermining of states and institutions is, as we shall see later, an essential corollary of the rise of victims.

The science of victims

Once the figure of the victim exists as such, it is not surprising to see the emergence of a specific body of knowledge, or to find that the victim is becoming the object of discourses that aspire to be scientific.

Criminology, sometimes in association with psychiatry, paved the way but there have long been doubts about how it did so. For some while, the infant science of victimology was primarily interested in the processes whereby an individual becomes a victim and in their effects on that individual, and emphasized the idea that there is, almost by definition, a basic link between the victim and the criminal. For the founding fathers of this branch of the study of crime, the victim and his or her torturer formed a couple. As Hans Von Hentig, who was the father of 'victimology', remarked in 1948 'we observe that the victim and the author, the killer and the killed, and the swindler and his dupe do have common features' (cited in Damiani, 1997: 35). There are in fact two schools of thought within this emergent discipline.

The first continues to explore the idea of a relationship between the victim and the criminal. From that point of view the two are inseparable, and this view would appear to be confirmed by the fact that, in statistical terms, 'chance victims' whose 'victimization' (some authors use 'victimation' – the vocabulary is still not settled) is pure coincidence are much rarer than victims who in some way collaborate with the criminal, either willingly or unconsciously.

The second is an extension of the first but adopts a psychoanalytic or psychiatric point of view by looking at the basic personality traits or psychic mechanisms that make some people more likely than others to become crime-victims, and especially the victims of sex crimes (including rape and incest). Some studies stress that today's aggressors were often yesterday's victims, which blurs the distinction between the two figures.[2] The kidnapping of Patricia Hearst in 1972[3] and then the terrorism of the 1970s illustrate the confusion of the two. What Frank Ochberg refers to as 'Stockholm syndrome' is observable when, during and after a kidnapping, the victim takes the side of the kidnappers against the outside world, which may mean the police in the case of a criminal offence, or the country or regime denounced by the terrorists in the case of a political incident. An original variant on this thesis has been put forward by Bernard Lempert in connection with the acts of violence committed in some cults. If we wish to understand these acts, which may include the murder of some cult members, we have to see that they have been committed by individuals inside the cult who have reproduced abusive processes that work by transposing old family models. 'Cults are in part the child of the family, and the experience of abuse within the family of origin has something to do with the radical nature of such groups' (Lempert, 2002: 10). In this case, it is not a personal trauma that turns a victim into an abuser; it is the reproduction of a family structure. The argument therefore belongs to the category that explains the present in terms of the past, even if it means inverting the roles.

The confusion of victim and criminal, or the idea that today's abuser was yesterday's victim, is not restricted to the psychological mechanisms we have just evoked. It can also take the form of a logic of vengeance. This logic is much more conscious and is often legitimate in cultural terms, or even part of an endless cycle in which every vendetta leads to another. What applies at the individual level can also apply at the collective level. Neil Kressel, for example, uses this type of analysis to explain the massacres and mass rapes committed by the Serbs in Bosnia at the beginning of the 1990s: 'No single factor contributed more to the Serb war criminals' willingness to ignore moral prohibitions than their reactivated anger at how their people had suffered at the hands of the Croats during World War II' (Kressel, 2002 [1996]: 32).

'It is only by identifying with the criminal that we can attempt to establish the extent to which the victim is guilty', explain the authors of a 'short study in general victimology' (Audet and Katz, 1999). 'It is because we adopt the criminal's point of view that we think that the girl who is on her own and wearing a short skirt is asking to be raped, that the unlocked car is waiting to be stolen, and that leaving an apartment unlocked is an invitation to burglars. If we identified with the victim, we would see things very differently'. In order to explain the tendency to identify with the criminal, they make a distinction between Von Hentig's 'first victimology' and a 'second victimology' which is not so much interested in the relationship between victim and criminal as in society and its ability to recognize the status of the victim, and to provide the help and assistance that any victim needs (Audet and Katz, 1999: 13–27).[4]

The science of victims, which is essentially the creation of lawyers, psychiatrists and doctors, can make an important contribution if we wish to define what a victim is, and to distinguish between different types of victim; it allows us to approach the central problem of trauma, to further specify the notion of harm, and to outline and discuss concrete ways of caring for victims, making reparation to them, or indemnifying them.

Does a better understanding of violence from the victim's point of view lead to a better understanding of violence in general, and of crime and delinquency in particular? The earliest studies of so-called 'victimation' were made in the United States in the mid-1960s at the request of President Johnson, and their purpose was to advance our understanding of criminality. A representative sample of a given population was interviewed, using a two-part questionnaire. Part One was concerned with 'victimation' or the number of crimes and felonies of which the participants were the victims over a given period, and Part Two with the victims themselves. The goal was to reduce the discrepancy between the 'black figure', or in other words the official figures recorded by the police or justice department, and the reality of the crimes and delinquency actually experienced by the population, who did not necessarily report all crimes to the police. In the case of France the earliest studies date from the 1980s, and there are now international studies and comparisons. Studies of victimation are now a matter of routine in several countries.

This type of methodology in fact raises a lot of problems. Contrary to what their precursors expected, these studies provide useful information about victims or, to be more specific a wide range of 'victimations', rather than about crime or criminals. They also tell us a lot about what is expected of the authorities in terms of security and intervention.[5]

Violence as a Negation of the Subject

We are beginning to get a clearer idea of what is at stake in the anthropological turn that occurs when victims emerge within the public space. It marks, on the one hand, an institutional mutation, if only because it displaces the line that divides public space and private space; on the other, it transforms a category that was invisible, or almost invisible, in the public space into a major figure of contemporary modernity. It gives individual, and sometimes collective, subjects a new voice.

The crisis within the State and the political

The emergence of victims, and still more so the impact of their emergence, cannot be divorced from what they often reveal: the failings and dereliction of the political, and the decay of states and political and juridical systems that can no longer fulfil their classic functions of guaranteeing order, cohesion and the social bond, and which are thrown into confusion by the growing demands of all kinds of victims. This is the worrying aspect of the era of victims, as Zauberman and Robert (1995: 22) stress when they suggest that

> It might be thought ... that this interest in victims owes a great deal to the feeling, which emerged in the 1970s, that all the solutions that were intended to 'treat' delinquents and 'reintegrate' them into society had ended in failure. Once it was decided that *nothing works*, radical critics of the criminal justice system, those who defended equality (the *Justice Model*) against the arbitrary nature of indefinite sanction, and neo-realists intent upon promoting the neutralisation of delinquents and intimidation, all helped to distract interest away from the delinquent, and thus created a sort of vacuum which gave rise to the new interest in the victim.

This crisis within the State, the political, and institutions feeds on what it helps to produce. It gives rise, for example, to the feeling that the authorities cannot do anything about crime and delinquency, and that other answers must therefore be found. Some feel a vaguely reactionary nostalgia for a mythical past in which order ruled, whilst others lose all faith in the criminal justice system and expect, rather, to be paid compensation by the State or the insurance companies, or seek compensation by taking out private prosecutions that may be settled out of court. This attitude reflects the growing trend to appeal to the courts and not the State. The more the victims mobilize in one way or another, the more the media report their actions, expectations, and demands. As the deinstitutionalization increases, more and more people lose confidence in the State and the political class.

As the authorities prove incapable of providing a political, policing, or juridical answer to violence, victims become more vocal. And as these victims become more vocal, the State becomes less capable of acting as the guarantor of order.

That is why it is not absurd to associate the theme of fear with that of victims. But we still have to ask how far the State is to blame. Does it have to take full responsibility? Or do we, as David L. Altheide suggests (2002), also have to blame the media which have, since the 1990s in the case of the United States, supposedly been creating an image of a world that is out of control, or in which there are no controls? The media tell us, he explains, that we are incapable of playing a part in social life in our own right, that we are dependent upon the news they distribute, and over which we have no control. And their main message, which overrides everything else, is fear. From this point of view, it is not so much order and the State that the media are replacing, as God and morality. In a secularized society, Altheide goes on, we no longer fear God but we do fear crime. He then notes that the term 'fear' began to appear in the media from the mid-1990s onwards. The same is true of the word 'victim'. There is supposedly a link between fear, which is everywhere in the media, and the fact that victims are speaking out: 'Victimization (or victimhood) as a status relies on pervasive fear because this is what makes victimization meaningful and plausible to audiences' (Altheide, 2002: 41). Another author allows Altheide to illustrate the thesis that: 'The precondition for the emergence of the victim identity was the consolidation of the consciousness of risk. In the UK and the USA, the growing fear of crime and the growing perception of risk have contributed to the sentiment that everyone is a potential victim' (Furedi, 2005 [1997]: 100).

This point of view extends the critique by associating the ubiquitous presence of victims not just with the decadence of the political and the failures of the State, but also with the media system and the way it constructs our categories. It leads to the idea that a victim is an individual who must be protected and who lives in a world that really has become dangerous because there are no state – or other – controls to take away the fear.

Politics, the media ... do we have to extend the critique still further, given that the victim theme is, at a still deeper level, an expression of a general cultural shift, or a deep cultural crisis? That is the view taken by, amongst others, Robert Hughes (1993), who also denounces the ubiquitous presence of victims with contemporary sensibilities, but sees it not just as a political phenomenon but also, or primarily, as a cultural phenomenon. Everyone, he explains, wants to be a victim because 'complaint gives you power' (Hughes, 1993: 9). This creates 'an infantilized culture of complaint' in which 'the expansion of rights goes without the other half of citizenship – attachment to duties and obligations' (1993: 10). This decadence goes hand in hand (or so Hughes thinks) with the rise of subjectivity. The emphasis is always on subjectivity. He goes on to cite Goethe's claim that 'epochs which are regressive, and in the process of dissolution, are always subjective, whereas the trend in all progressive epochs is objective (1993: 10). He therefore relates the victim theme with that of subjectivity and its growing importance in public debates. That seems a reasonable argument, but the idea that the rise of subjectivity is associated with the idea of decadence seems much more debateable. The theme of decadence usually appears when the landscape changes, and reflects, as Marc Bloch used to say, the fact that it is difficult to come to terms with anything that is new and surprising.

Recognition of the subject

Why reduce the subjective dimension of the victim theme to the negative hypothesis of decadence? The emergence of the victim figure also means that the public recognizes the sufferings endured by an individual or group, the lived experience of violence, and its subsequent impact. It signals the presence of the personal subject in the collective consciousness, in politics, and in intellectual life, and bears witness to a greater sensitivity to not only the problems of the workings of the social and socialization, but also the problems of subjectivation and the dangers of desubjectivation. From a victim's point of view, violence inevitably results in a loss or an attack on her physical integrity, but it may also result in a denial of subjectivity, ravage, and in the destruction of the subjective points of reference that allow that victim to find her bearings. She will therefore feel that she has been depersonalized, that her personality is disintegrating, or that there has been a break or a discontinuity in her life-trajectory. Being a victim also means, in many cases, feeling ashamed or guilty and experiencing all sorts of problems that may have long-lasting effects on one's life.

Victims, their descendents, and their families do not all speak out, and they do not necessarily voice the same demands for recognition. In some cases, they want the specificity of their experience to be recognized, be it individual or collective. They may, for instance, want to be recognized as having survived a genocide. In other cases, they are, on the contrary, asking for a recognition of their normality despite the fact that their experience has marked them out as different. A girl who has been raped may want to be reintegrated into society and not to be treated with compassion because she has been defiled or made to feel dirty. Violence both belittles its victims and makes them stand out. Its victims may suffer in two ways: they can be made to feel inferior, or made to feel different. The mechanisms that allow them to hope they will recover their capacity for subjectivation are therefore complex and multiple, as they must by definition take both dimensions into account. But all these mechanisms emphasize the need for each victim to become a subject once more.

The recognition that there is a dialectic between victim-subjects and the public institutions or policies that respond to them also implies that certain political or institutional changes do not come about, or do not really come about, precisely because the victims concerned remain silent or do not speak out loudly enough. Two examples from very different domains come to mind. The first concerns road accidents, which kill a very high number of people in France (almost 8,000 in 2001 alone). The number of deaths would surely have fallen before 2003 if the victims' families and relatives had been capable of speaking out, forcing a debate, demanding changes, sensitizing public opinion, and changing behaviours. The second example is historical. Our conceptions of history sometimes change because victims, or their descendents, force history to take their memories into account. The history of the Second World War, and of the Vichy regime in particular, owes a great deal to the action of Jews who have ensured that it is now very different to what had been said about it in the 1950s and 1960s. Similarly, it is because Armenian communities actively mobilized that France officially recognizes the Armenian genocide of 1915. The Algerian war, in contrast, is still a painful subject that is difficult to talk about, presumably because of the fragmentation and the passions that typify its 'victims'. These include the descendents of Algerians who supported the FLN, of Algerians who refused to do so but also wanted their country to be independent and eventually came to live in France, and the children of *harkis*, *pieds-noirs*, war-time conscripts, and so on. In this case, the mobilization of memories is not just too painful but too contradictory to have any great influence, or any unified influence, on history.

The victim thematic therefore paves the way for a thematics of the subject. We must, however, look carefully at how this happens, as there is nothing natural about it.

The dangers of 'victimism'

Being a subject in fact means more than saving one's skin, body and life, individual or collective, or one's physical and moral existence. It also means constructing a personal experience, being in control of one's choices, and making use of one's ability to innovate and invent forms of cultural expression. Nowadays, as Paul Gilroy (1987) clearly emphasizes, the victim does not appear as such in this light. The victim's identity is in a sense negative, corresponds to only half the subject, tells us nothing about his or her positive identity. A victim is defined by something of which he or she has been deprived, by something that has been destroyed, or by a loss. That is why, when the public stage is invaded by so many victims, it may suggest an image of tensions that are dragging the debate into the past, and recognition of the past, without necessarily doing anything to help to create new issues or new relationships – except, as had been said of the 'mothers of the Plaza de Mayo', by invoking the name of past victims to influence the future and to ensure that public policies or international agreements make it impossible, or more difficult, for what happened in the past to happen in the future. A remarkable article by Jean-Paul Ngoupandé, the former Prime Minister of the Central African Republic, expresses this idea in forceful terms. He explains that Africans were certainly victims of the slave trade for centuries. But today, 'We [Africans] are the main gravediggers of both our present and our future' (2002). It is time, he says in substance, for them to stop claiming to be victims; 'we take most responsibility' (2002) – for the decay of states, the lack of security, the extent of the AIDS tragedy, and the endemic corruption. In his view, the thematic of the victim simply plays into the hands of the logic of self-destruction; being a victim means wallowing in one's impotence rather than becoming an actor.

In more general terms, there is the recent trend within intellectual and political debates to denounce the excesses of what Pascal Bruckner (1999) calls 'victimization', and what Elisabeth Badinter (2006 [2003]), whose views are quite similar, calls 'victim feminism'. Does modern individualism lead to an 'illness', to a systematic tendency on the part of both individuals and groups to 'think of themselves as persecuted peoples'? 'No one wants to be held responsible, everyone wants to look like a victim, even if they have not lived through some ordeal'. Bruckner finds this 'scandalous' because they usurp the 'place of the real disinherited' (1999: 14–17). The emergence of the victim has, he argues, resulted in widespread abuse of the term 'victim', to an inability to recognize that we are responsible for our own lives, and to a disastrous confusion. Everyone is a victim and no one is guilty, because being guilty means that you were once a victim. Certain currents within feminism, which choose to define women primarily as victims, represent an extreme example of this perversion, and Badinter is bitterly critical of it.

This type of remark is quite acceptable, assuming that it is a critique of the abuses and excesses of 'victimism' and not of the concrete figure of 'real victims'. It does nothing to refute the central idea that is being put forward here, namely that the emergence of the victim means that we have to look at violence not only in terms of its author, and the subjectivity of the author (which may have been destroyed, negated, or instrumentalized; we will come back to this point), but also in terms of the subjectivity of those it harms and affects. It then becomes clear that we will not put an end to violence by recognizing and making reparation for the wrongs and the damage it has done. We can do so only if and when the victims themselves turn themselves into constructive actors or actors who cannot be reduced to their negative identity or their loss, and who actively create the conditions that will allow others to become true subjects and true actors.

We must therefore recognize once more the historical novelty of a major phenomenon, namely the conspicuous public presence of the figure of the victim. We must assess its impact and draw the sociological lessons than will allow us to understand the phenomenon of violence. The presence of this figure implies a demand for justice which would otherwise not be satisfied or would be inadequately satisfied. It also implies a recognition of a lived experience that the courts previously tried to cover up or minimize. It will help to promote justice, including a trans-, supra, or international justice that can, especially where crimes against humanity are concerned, transcend the relativism of the values specific to particular societies and particular civilizations. Mireille Delmas-Marty (2002: 65) expresses this in very strong terms when she looks into the possible historical basis for the notion of crimes against humanity, and asks whether 'we should not be asking the victims to find shared values even though they come from very different civilizations. Even if countries where rape and torture are not criminalized as such and are not subject to legal sanctions, it can still be assumed that the victims still feel that they have been humiliated, and that their dignity as human beings has been diminished'. What is more, the presence of the victim obliges us to open up and transform the official version of history. It upsets the accepted versions that overlook certain things, usually because they are designed to promote the viewpoint of the victors. It encourages politicians not only to admit that mistakes were made in the societies they govern, but also to take them into account in order to avoid future injustices, collective crimes, and various forms of barbarism. Victims may, finally, find it easier to embark upon a process of self-reconstruction when their voices are heard than when there is no space for their recognition.

On the other hand, the public presence of victims can give rise to or encourage some terrible aberrations. Whenever victims invade a particular domain, there is a danger that they will also pervert it. Victims or their relatives may persuade the courts to take decisions that are based on their convictions rather than strict proof, and whilst their tragedies and sufferings do shed light on the crimes they have suffered, these are not necessarily enough to establish the truth, and may even obscure it or sway judges and juries, either directly or through the intermediary of the media, which are always quick to stir up our emotions. Victims may bring pressure to bear on history not in order to enrich it or to correct it, but in order to prevent it from asking certain questions or to determine what can and what cannot be said. They then begin to compete with historians, and to exploit the immense legitimacy lent them by the barbarism they have suffered. An historian who rejects the interpretation of some massacre given by the descendents of its victims, or who insists that it should be placed in a different category, exposes himself to serious and sometimes violent accusations, as Bernard Lewis and Gilles Veinstein learnt to their cost when they criticized the use of the term 'genocide' to describe the Armenian tragedy, even though they never denied the reality of the massacres and collective crimes inflicted on the Armenians in 1915.

Victims can pervert the political and weaken the state still further by destabilizing political debates and relying on emotional arguments rather than a rational analysis of the facts. There is also a danger that their intervention into public life may blur the line between different registers, not only between private life and public life, but also between juridical life and political life when, for example, the victims' viewpoint turns a trial into a political operation. The trial of Eichmann, the Nazi criminal kidnapped in Argentina by the Israeli secret services and put on trial in Israel, is a good example here: by putting the emphasis on the words and presence of the victims and not the documents, and by turning the courtroom into a real theatre, the prosecutor tried to touch Israeli hearts, to further integrate the nation, and to establish more powerful links between Israel and the

Diaspora. The presence of the victims – Annette Wieviorka (1992) calls them 'witnesses' but her comments have a lot in common with my own remarks about victims – turns trials like this into moments when justice, politics and history fuse, merge and become muddled up. And if, finally, victims define themselves negatively and in terms of their destruction because they cannot escape their public or media image, there is a danger that they will not be able to project themselves into the future and construct, or reconstruct, themselves as subjects. A social or cultural movement that traps itself into a 'victimist' self-image, and historical actors who, as the historian Salo Baron puts it, reduce their historical experience to a 'tearful' story, tend to go in circles, cannot construct anything, and can only project themselves into the past.

We have entered an era of victims, and we must both take their views into consideration and refuse to make them the alpha and the omega of all political juridical or intellectual debate. Victims are part of our collective life. They can help us, and even encourage us, to arrive at a better understanding of violence, which is what they have suffered. But we also have to realize that they can blind us to its meaning and prevent us from understanding it.

Notes

1 In 1967, a symposium brought together four Jewish personalities – Emil L. Fackenheim, Richard H. Popkin, George Steiner and Elie Wiesel – to discuss 'Jewish Values in the Post-Holocaust Future'. The speeches and debates, which were subsequently published in the journal *Judaism* 26 March 1967) are seen by Chaumont as having a foundational value.
2 More specific references to this work and, more generally, to what the author calls the 'advent' of victimology as a science will be found in Damiani (1997).
3 Patricia Hearst, the daughter of a famous American multimillionaire, identified with the group that kidnapped here and demanded a ransom for her release.
4 The authors also speak of a 'clinical victimology' and an 'anthropological victimology'.
5 This is the main lesson to be learned from studies such as those carried out in France by CESDIP. See Zauberman and Robert (1995).

4

VIOLENCE AND THE MEDIA

There is nothing new about the idea of a link between violence and the media. Criminals, for example, have been explicitly trying to get their names in the papers since the nineteenth century. To move to a very different register, it is clear that the media's role in propaganda and counter-propaganda has played a decisive part in mobilizing combatants ever since the First World War. In the letter that opens his famous exchange with Sigmund Freud, Albert Einstein notes (1985 [1932]: 346–7) that even the 'intelligentsia' can yield to 'the psychoses of hate and destructiveness' and specifically adds that intellectuals also can be greatly influenced by 'the printed page'.

And yet the 1960s once more mark a turning point, as it is then that the question of violence becomes the object of debates, which were both frequent and complex, polemics, and public policies. The media, now seen as autonomous actors and sometimes as a system, were much more likely to find that the very basis of their existence was being called into question. They began to be criticized because of the effects they had, and to be blamed for certain phenomena that were deemed to be disturbing. The change in the criticisms made of them also relates to the growing importance of television, which was very much part of everyday life in the United States from the 1940s onwards and then became commonplace in Eastern-bloc countries and Western Europe.

The media, or some of them and especially the audio-visual media, were initially criticized in studies that tried in one way or another to establish a causal link between their practice and various expressions of violence. They were accused of being, if not guilty of encouraging it, then at least partly responsible for the spread of terrorism, certain crimes, aggressive behaviour on the part of young people, and so on. And even if they did not cause violence, surely they influenced its intensity and the forms and ways in which it was manifested, and helped to shape and define its repertoire?

This type of criticism has not disappeared. On the contrary, it has been extended, sometimes in the form of broad denunciations of the media, which are accused of being new and autonomous forms of power – the 'fourth estate' – or at least of being in the service of the economic and political powers in general, of being ideological apparatuses that guarantee the reproduction of social domination, or of using a symbolic violence that guarantees the alienation of those who are dominated but who do not even have the categories that might allow them to realize it. But just as it becomes more and more necessary to include the media in any analysis of contemporary violence, arguments that are primarily designed to blame violence on the media become less and less satisfactory.

Terrorism and the Media

There is nothing new about international terrorism either. It is clear, however, that a new period in the history of the phenomenon began when aircraft were hijacked to Cuba, and then with the first hijackings carried out by militants from the Popular Front for the Liberation of Palestine in 1968. Other attempts to hijack planes were followed by the massacre of the Israeli athletes in Munich in 1972, and by other acts of extreme violence on the part of radicalized actors speaking in the name of a Palestinian national consciousness.

A symbiotic relationship?

A climate which was, in several Western societies, dominated by the fallout from the movements of 1968, and the rise of *gauchisme* and its terrorist offshoots, gave rise to a thesis that postulated the existence of a 'symbiotic' link between terrorism and the media. They had, various specialists explained,[1] common interests because the terrorists had, thanks mainly to television, an instant audience that amplified the impact of their acts and because, at the same time, they produced a spectacle that the media could use to satisfy their audience. Indeed, they had the best possible ingredients – including deaths, emotions, and images of destruction – and operated at the point where politics intersected with 'the news in brief'.

This thesis attracted all the more interest in that it stressed that there was something new about this wave of terrorism which, unlike early forms of the same phenomenon, worked on an international scale and appeared to profit greatly from means of communication that had not previously existed. The basic idea was that a symbiotic relationship implied certain expectations, or a certain demand for which terrorism had the ideal response. Even though they might not admit to it, viewers at home expected to feel these emotions. There was then, a cultural dimension to the 'diabolical pact' between terrorism and the media. There was an appetite or desire for violence, and terrorism allowed the media to satisfy it. Speaking of images of violence in general, Yves Michaux (2002: 101) rightly notes 'the complicity of our curiosity, our morbid and unhealthy interest in the pornography of disaster, and our need for entertainment and escape, even if it does take macabre and odious forms'.

There is something seductive about the thesis that there is an instrumental relationship between terrorists and the media and that they have a vested interest in each other's existence. But it does not stand up to analysis. The first reason is that, as research carried out in the mid-1980s demonstrated (Wieviorka and Wolton, 1987), there is not just one relationship between the two: there are several. If, for example, we adopt the viewpoint of the terrorist actors, we can identify four scenarios: *total indifference* – the terrorists are simply not interested in how the media cover their actions; *relative interest* – this can be observed when terrorists do not try to gain access to the media by carrying out spectacular actions, but do not rule out issuing communiqués through a sympathetic press; *media strategies* – in which the terrorists foresee how the media will react, and use them as much as possible; *rupture* – the media are seen as enemies, just like other actors, in which case the terrorists will try to silence them, or at least to challenge their neutrality and independence by intimidating them or bringing massive pressure to bear. This takes us a very long way from the idea that they have interests in common.

It also has to be pointed out that those who do most to create the media spectacle of terrorism do not necessarily work with a schema of the 'symbiotic relationship' type. On closer examination, we will find that we have to make a distinction between several scenarios. In some cases, the initiative lies with the terrorists; in others it lies with the journalists, who may actually stage the event they later show on television, even using professional actors in some cases. In still other cases, the media amplification is mainly the work of third parties – magistrates, politicians, police officers and so on – who feed the media with, if not spectacular images, at least pieces of information that will stimulate or reawaken public interest.

The production of terrorism

Images of terrorism and news reports about it are products of a process that sets in motion all sorts of actors, some inside the media system, and others outside it. Inside the system, journalists do a job which, whilst it may look as though they are simply transcribing various events, always involves a multitude of tasks and activities. Some will be on the spot or in direct contact with sources close to the event, and will set up their cameras and microphones, or even themselves, in some observation post or other; they will write articles or provide the raw materials for the 'story'. In sum, they will get as close to the news as they can. The same journalists, or others, will analyse and describe the events, compare sources, which may differ, gather further information by consulting their colleagues and interviewing the public, choose from the images that are available to them, and, if need be, look for others in the archives. The editors will have yet to decide where the story will fit into the news hierarchy, and which heading it will come under (International? Law? General News?). They will play a role in deciding which images should be used, and will ensure that, if need be, an expert, politician or soldier is called in to provide further clarification. The editorial staff may or may not also have a general watching brief, even though acts of terrorism are unpredictable, and may ask whether or not a particular story should be followed up by a specific journalist. They will, or will not, have thought about how to react to possible demands not only from the terrorists, but also from the political, military, police, or legal authorities. An agency news release, a newspaper report, a news flash, and the television news quickly become complex products that will also set in motion the many actors who work outside the media system. Many people have an influence on what the media say: magistrates, politicians, lawyers, policy officers and, in some cases, military spokesmen and diplomats, informants, witnesses, key figures with specialist knowledge who speak up spontaneously or are invited to do so, the victims and their relatives, the terrorists and their relatives if they wish to release information about themselves, intellectuals ... There is always a danger that what the media say will be distorted. Some people will manipulate them, whilst others will not wish to tell all. Some will confidently put forward hypotheses that cannot be verified as though they were certainties, and others will ask for certain things to be kept quiet. It is not in the interests of all those involved in the production of news about terrorism to ensure that it is as objective and complete as possible; some are not under any obligation to do so. Their relationship with truth and secrecy, interests of state, ethics, public opinion, and the authorities is not always the same. What is more, their relationship with time may not be in synch with the media's; the only constraint on the media is the need to keep up to date, whilst other actors will have their own agendas and will work to different timetables. The production of terrorism-as-news is also influenced by other factors, the most important being the way a government reacts. It may or may not be in control of the situation, be in crisis or have the resources to deal with the situation. It may attempt to control the media, or in certain cases, will impose a media black-out.

News about terrorism is the product of a whole host of activities and a complex web of mediations. It simply cannot be reduced to the spontaneous argument that postulates the existence of mutual interests or some sort of quasi-automatic exchange of mutual favours between terrorists and the media. That is why it is unacceptable to say that the media are responsible for terrorism, or that they are responding to a supply of violence which they themselves demand. Nor is it acceptable to say that they are one of the sources of its most devastating effects because they amplify it. Terrorists can be highly effective without the help of the media. It is not the media that explain what makes terrorists, how they come into being, or what their political expectations are. At most, they are, at one point or another, included in their strategic or tactical calculations.

It is true that terrorism and terrorist events are what the media show us. But, no matter how seriously journalists take their work, it is difficult to speak of objectivity in this context. The representations that are made public by the media are inevitably out of step with the actual phenomenon. That is why competition is so important, as we saw at the time of the attacks of 11 September 2001, and as we have seen since then. The images put out by the Kuwaiti channel Al-Jazeera provide a counter-balance to those put out by the American channels, which are themselves dominated by CNN and, more recently, Fox News.

When it comes to terrorism, what the media broadcast is manufactured by the media. It is of course based on real events, but it is selective and shown in a particular light. It is inevitably approximate and exaggerated to make the news more dramatic, but there is also something missing, or lacking, and that is, to a greater or lesser extent, deliberate. When we watch television, we rarely see images of the actual horrors that take place, and it is no accident that we did not see the corpses or body parts of the 3,000 or so victims of the 2001 attacks on Washington and New York. As Yves Michaux underlines, the media do not show violence in its nudity, horror, and obscenity. The media images therefore have something in common with pornography, but they take the form of a decent spectacle that has been both standardised and aetheticised: 'We do not have violence on the one hand and the media on the other; we have violence as it is shown by the media' (Michaux, 2002: 95). In a word, 'when we cannot complain about the falsification or the disinformation, we can complain about the aestheticization, the way everything is packaged for our consumption' (2002: 100).

It is not only the way the media show violence that has to be seen as a representation. The way it is perceived by the audience is also the object of processes, interpretations, and transformations, and they too are highly mediated. Depending on which national culture we live in, we see events, historical phenomena, discourse and characters differently, as was demonstrated by a classic study (Liebes and Katz, 1990) of how the characters in the American soap opera *Dallas* were perceived differently in different countries. What is true of vast communities is also true of smaller groups: the way an individual receives televised images of violence at any given moment depends upon his or her family environment and personal trajectory, and, in many respects, the specific context. He may be having a meal and listening to the TV news with half an ear. He may, on the other hand, have decided to watch the news carefully. She may be alone, or may be with someone. What is more, we do not form our ideas directly, or on the basis

71

of what the media tell us. They are also shaped by discussions and filtered by 'gate keepers' and opinion makers, whose importance was demonstrated long ago by Paul Lazarsfeld (1972 [1932]), and they act on the basis of our political leanings, ideologies, prejudices, and opinions. In many cases, the media simply reinforce rather than modify them.

There is, therefore, always a considerable distance between the raw terrorist event and what we all see of it. Which suggests that we have to stress the idea, and perhaps even the principle, of the distinction between the objectivity of violence and its subjectivity.

The Objectivity and Subjectivity of Violence

Terrorism is no more than one example, but it is the example that, because of the debates that began at the dawn of the 1960s, does most to help us accept the principle of a distinction between the objectivity and subjectivity which lies at the heart of contemporary modernity, and whose general implications go far beyond questions relating only to violence.

It is an expression of a great tension that is itself never anything more than one of the modalities of the great divide between universalism and relativism that characterizes the modern era. The more we take the view that violence is what we perceive to be violence thanks to the media and other mediations, the more we have to accept that our perception is subject to temporal and spatial variations, and that it varies from individual to individual, from group to group, and from period to period. We must, in other words, take into account both individual subjectivity and national particularisms. We therefore tend to take a relativist view. Violence is not, however, reducible to the idea of the representations or norms that define it within what is inevitably a relative frame of reference, at a given moment, and for a limited number of people. It is also, or primarily, a very real assault on the physical and moral integrity of its victims. It is a tangible phenomenon that affects the people who are killed, injured, damaged, or destroyed, and whose property is looted or stolen. Whatever the culture or personality of the observer, it is a phenomenon that anyone can perceive, and there is therefore something universal about it.

The more we try to give an objective definition of violence, the closer we come to universalism. That perspective may involve attempts to develop quantitative tools that are acceptable to all and allow us to use statistical methods. It may also be part of a more philosophical approach that attempts to define common criteria for the definition of violence, or some of its modalities, that has a supra-national validity. In an attempt to give a precise and universal meaning to terms such as 'genocide' or 'torture', jurists may, like the International Criminal Tribunal for the Former Yugoslavia, put forward criteria that define crimes against humanity in legal terms by noting that 'unlike common law, it is not just the physical integrity of the victim that is under attack but the whole of humanity'. Such crimes 'transcend the individual because, when the individual is attacked, the whole of humanity comes under attack and is negated' (Delmas-Marty, 2002: 63).

Just as universalism and a concern for objectivity go hand in hand, so too do relativism and a desire to recognize the subjectivity of individuals. Any discussion of violence is therefore faced with the problem of reconciling the two registers. Do we have to conclude that they are incommensurate, or should we try to reconcile them? This is not merely a theoretical question, and it may quite quickly become a concrete question. How, for instance, do we reconcile the views of researchers in the social sciences who find that, objectively, cartoons contain a lot of violence, and the findings of opinion polls showing that the general public does not take the same view (Potter, 1999: 76)? And are we in fact certain that the researchers and their content analysis are purely, or completely, objective?

A combination of extreme or abstract universalism and absolute objectivism looks at violence without taking into account the actors, be they its protagonists or its victims, or the observers and journalists who report it, or even the public. It ignores the lived experience of all these individuals, and takes no account of the historical conditions or the context in which the violence occurred. It tries to rely on the statistical data. Unconditional relativism makes it impossible to analyse anything, as it assumes that an experience can be understood only on the terms of those who have experienced it or who are describing it; violence is simply what the speaker says it is, and everyone is perfectly entitled to accept or challenge what he says.

When it comes to violence, the objective approach is always open to question, or even serious challenge. The available statistics on delinquency in a given country, for instance, certainly provide us with information about the phenomenon. But there is always the suspicion that they also tell us about the legal and police apparatuses that produce them, and about the ideology of the administrators who draw up the categories used. The data are always confused. By the same criterion, a strictly relativist point of view makes it impossible to make comparisons, or even to conceptualize violence.

If we wish to avoid both the universality of approaches based upon the pseudo-objectivity of 'facts' whose social production is concealed, and the impasse of pure relativism, a radical divorce between the two registers is unacceptable. How, then, are we to conceptualize their articulation? It is not enough to take the linear view that there are such things as 'facts' or 'realities' that are distorted by various elements, starting with the way the media handles them, and that the longer and more complex the chain of intermediaries, the greater the distance will be between objectivity and subjectivity. This argument overlooks other factors that distance us from events, such as the influence of prejudices or the inability to comprehend or understand an unacceptable reality. It lays all the blame at the door of those who are responsible for the distortions, if any, and has nothing to say about the authors of the violence. One answer to this problem, though it has to be admitted that it is not brilliant in intellectual terms, is to refuse to take sides, and to always try to look at both sides of the argument, to take both viewpoints into account, and to try to introduce the subjective-relativist view when the discourse of objectivity is dominant, and vice versa.

In public life, it is possible for the distance between the two viewpoints to become so great that it becomes a gulf; it is also possible for it to become so small that it disappears. In some cases, the violence is surrounded by silence because only the victims and perhaps their relatives will attempt to talk about it. The objective nature of the facts then disappears because the facts themselves are not made public. The victims then feel that they have once more been abandoned. This is what happened at the end of the Second World War. Most of the Jewish survivors of the death camps wanted to speak, and to talk about the specific agonies they had suffered because they were Jews. In France, they were met with a wall of indifference or at least silence that began to break down only in the 1970s (Annette Wieviorka, 1992).

At the opposite extreme, the changing discourse of the French left on urban violence exemplifies how the gap between facts and representations can be narrowed. In the early 1980s, the left refused to relate the general increase in the feeling of insecurity to the rising rate of delinquency recorded by the police and the courts. It then came closer and closer to the right-wing view that postulated the existence of a direct link between the facts and this feeling of insecurity. It has to be said that, in the meantime, political pressure had been brought to bear on the left by opinion polls and press campaigns urging it to listen to an increasingly worried population. What is more, the objective definition of violence had changed and, thanks to the work of Sebastian Roché (1994) and Hugues Lagrange (1995), amongst others, the notion of anti-social behaviour (*incivilité*) emerged. The feeling of insecurity was mainly a response to a minor form of violence (insults, threatening attitudes, minor acts of vandalism, spitting, and so on) that scarcely figured in the statistics for delinquency. By introducing the theme of anti-social behaviour into the public debate, research in the social sciences revealed a previously unknown, but objective, source for the feeling of insecurity. The research findings thus came much closer to lived experience. It is, however, also true that the same research has never stopped criticizing the official figures for delinquency, explaining that it was not necessarily because the phenomenon was growing that the figures were rising, but also because police methods changed in the 1980s. The introduction of neighbourhood policing, for example, encouraged people who had previously not reported the delinquency that affected them because they felt that they were being ignored by a police force that was indeed becoming more and more distant from them.

The Violence of Images

Birth of a debate

On 12 December 1963, the *New York Times* published a letter in which one of the daily's readers claimed that 'The shooting of President Kennedy was the normal method of dealing with an opponent as taught by countless television programmes. This tragedy is one of the results of the corruption of people's minds and hearts by the violence of commercial television'. The letter is cited at the beginning of the co-authored volume edited by Otto N. Larsen (1968: 8).[2] This was one of the books that, in the late 1960s, launched – on a grand scale – what is still an important contemporary debate. At the same time, and still in the United States, Paul L. Briand Jr noted in his preface to the staff report of the National Commission (Baker and Ball, 1969), established by President Johnson to look into the causes and prevention of violence, that the media claimed to influence what people bought and consumed; why should they have no influence on violent behaviour? He even supplied his own practical solution to a problem that was beginning to worry public opinion: nursery school teachers underwent training for their diplomas and were expected to go on further training courses, and the same standards should apply to television. After all, he added, it is thanks to television that children learn that medication relieves pain, that deodorant produces social acceptance ... and that violence offers the shortest and simplest solution to their problems. He was also critical of the fact that television used double standards. The media argued that they should not be subject to any censorship, he explained, but in fact censored themselves by refusing to say anything about the cancers caused by tobacco or the deaths caused by the 'cars that kill'.

Since the 1960s, television has been the object of criticisms that basically accuse it of encouraging violence on the part of certain people and especially children. The debate has spread from the USA and Canada to all Western societies. It reached France relatively late in the day, for the very simple reason that television itself was slow to develop there and was for a long time subject to strict political controls. It was a public service and there was no advertising. As we shall see, these criticisms also apply to important aspects of the market economy.

As soon as they were formulated the criticisms opened up a different front to that opened up by the idea, which we have already discussed, that terrorism and the media had common interests. Unlike the criticism of terrorism, the criticisms addressed to the violence of images do not identity the evil with a particular political actor, and turn it into a much more diffuse phenomenon. Television – and it is television that is the target – supposedly encourages violence by showing it and putting it on display, either in fictional form or on the news and in documentaries. Television is the prime culprit. When, in contrast, it is television's role in encouraging terrorism that comes in for criticism, terrorism is the prime culprit; television simply signs a devils' pact with it. It will be noted in passing that the debate got somewhat carried away about television and virtually ignored radio, even though its role also deserves examination. Jean Hatzfeld (2008b [2003]: 84) recalls that Radio Rwanda and Radio Mille Collines played a major role in triggering the Tutsi genocide of 1994, and pertinently cites Serge Daney, a distinguished film critic and a columnist on the daily *Libération*. At the time of the Gulf War (1991), and when the way images influenced that event was being discussed, Daney contradicted the received opinion of the day by asserting that:

> Radio is far and away the most dangerous of the media. It wields a unique and terrifying power, once the state or its institutional apparatus collapses. It casts off everything that might attenuate or sidetrack the force of words ... it penetrates unhindered to the individual's deepest core, anywhere and at any moment, immediately, with the necessary and critical distance inherent in the reading of a text or image. (Ibid., p. 84)

His remarks are unqualified and somewhat partial, but they do have the great virtue of reminding us of the influence of radio, which is usually overlooked in criticisms of the media, which concentrate on television on the one hand and the press on the other.

Thousands of studies

The debate now seems to be very wide-ranging, if we try to follow it by looking at the vast literature that sustains it. The publications surveying studies and specialist work on the theme as well as articles and books on the subject run into the thousands, not to mention the activities of the parliamentary commissions and similar bodies that have looked into the question in certain countries, and especially in the United States. Since the 1950s, a impressive range of work was published, including academic studies and studies commissioned by associations, governments, television channels, or institutes associated with them, and the rate of publication speeded up greatly from the second half of the 1960s onwards. These studies attempt to quantify the violence of television programmes, which involved the perilous exercise of arriving at a precise definition of the phenomenon under observation, to propose indicators of levels of violence and to calculate how much time various categories of viewer spend in front of the screen. They attempt to make a quantitative study of the violent content of certain programmes and ask, for instance, how their violence is or is not sanctioned (an NTVS study, for instance, shows that in 73 per cent of the violent scenes surveyed the authors go unpunished, and that in almost one in every two programmes the harm done to the victims is overlooked).[3] Other studies try, in every conceivable way, to establish a link between images of violence and aggression (which is often confused with violence), aggressive behaviour, and 'anti-social' attitudes. Psychological-style experiments have been carried out in laboratories to measure the aggression of those taking part before and after they have watched images of violence; statistical studies have used questionnaires to look at children in nursery schools who have been exposed to television programmes including images of violence, measuring the children's blood pressure, hormonal stress levels and other physiological effects after they have watched violent programmes.

On the whole, and as a remarkable synthesis published nearly two decades ago demonstrates (Martinez, 1990), most of these studies reach a positive conclusion: there is indeed a link, even though most researchers think that it is an exaggeration to describe it as a direct cause-and-effect relationship. Some researchers are very cautious and make a distinction between, for example, adults, in whom there appears to be no link between violent images and aggression, and young people, who appear to be more vulnerable if they come from working-class or very poor backgrounds. Some studies are very sceptical about the link – not to mention those, which have in fact been abandoned since the 1970s, that attempted to demonstrate that images of violence had a positive effect and reduced aggression because they had a 'cathartic' effect.[4] If, however, we measure, not acts of violence, crimes and delinquency, but in many cases more aggressive attitudes or statements of intent (for example, willingness to give other people electric shocks), these studies do not necessarily shed any light on why individuals act out what they have seen. In some experiments one group of young people watches violent images on television, whilst a second group watches a variety show. Their respective levels of aggression are then measured. All the findings suggest that the young people in the first group display significantly higher levels of aggression than those in the second. These are not, however, studies of crime or delinquency, and whilst they do make an important point, it is not the idea that there is a direct link between images of violence and violence. What they do demonstrate is that, by encouraging a certain aggression, such images would have a direct effect if the young people in question were living in a social and personal void, and if there were no mediations between television and their behaviour, or between their heightened aggression and acting out.

This phenomenon emerges more clearly from current research carried out under my supervision. When young working-class people of North African origin who are not under the wing of a school, community association, or place of worship watch television and see the extreme images of anti-Semitic violence broadcast by an Arab satellite channel, they do sometimes behave a aggressively towards Jews or throw stones at synagogues. This happens less often if they, and other young people, are involved in community activities that can mediate between the images they see and the way they behave. That is why the idea that the violence of images is 'toxic' leads not so much to the assertion that there is a direct or immediate link between violent imagery and actual violence, as to the more common argument that it has an impact on young people's personalities and worldviews. In most cases there is no suggestion that watching a film or television serial leads to violent behaviour, or that the link between the two is one of cause and effect. It is, rather, suggested that there is a diffuse but real effect, rather as though the violence of images, and television in general, shapes culture, and especially youth culture, and creates, at best, conditions that encourage those concerned to act out what they have seen. A study carried out at Columbia University in New York (Johnson et al., 2000), based on follow-up interviews with a panel of 700 viewers over a period of seventeen years, established a link between the number of hours spent consuming television and violent behaviour, irrespective of which programmes were watched. But if that link can be established without taking the content of the images into consideration, do we not have to take into account that it inevitably included a high percentage of violent images?

The debate is present throughout academic life, but often extends beyond academe. It is also present in political life and in the media, and becomes more focussed in response to political events (such as the American presidential election of 1996, when the violence of images was a central theme), or whenever some event reignites it, as when, a murder committed by a teenager is obviously inspired by a film, a video game, or a recent television programme.[5]

In several Western societies, the climate of the late 1990s and the early twenty-first century was marked by a growing demand for a return to greater authority, by increasingly strident appeals to a moral order, and amongst other things new expressions of worries about violence and pornography on television. The fear of crime easily fused with the idea that controls had to be placed on what the media supplied because they would otherwise corrupt young people and encourage violence. In this context, the countless empirical studies that are published every year appear to verify the hypothesis that there is a link between images of violence and violent behaviour, even though the diagnosis is often somewhat vague and imprecise. Elihu Katz, who was one the pioneers on the sociology of the media, put it well when he noted in 1988 that the research findings had yet to clearly demonstrate the power of mass-media effects. He then recommended that researchers should continue to debate the eternal question of how to reconcile the findings with our intuition that they do have an effect (Katz, 1988), as reported by Martinez, (1995: 23)). Blandine Kriegel's report on 'violence on television' clearly demonstrates how difficult it is to adopt a clear-cut position. We find in both clear assertions ('the extent to which television is responsible for the way young viewers behave ... and to which violent images trigger certain behaviours ... has also been found to be proportional to the length of time spent in front of the screen. No one can deny this' (2002: 18)) and very nuanced comments ('the effect of violent programmes on behaviours is still minor'). On the whole, no one will completely deny the existence of a link that has yet not been demonstrated with any certainty. Most of the time, these studies and reports will assume that such a link has been established and will then set about explaining it, usually after having expressed some doubts.

Various suggestions will then be made. According to some, television's images of violence give simple answers to any situation. Television provides a simple and effective solution to problems that cannot be solved in any other way, and the solution is all the more seductive in that television supposedly has the effect of lowering inhibitions; it removes the taboo on violence and renders obsolete the commandment that tells us 'Thou shalt not kill' by constantly showing murders and killings. Images of violence, this explanation goes on, leave us dumbfounded, paralyse our ability to think, and make reflexivity impossible. They offer role models – personalities, types of behaviour, values – with which some people will identify; they teach them to be cold and emotionless, and to act in such a way as to use violence as a mere means to an end. They influence minds that are still malleable to such a degree that, in extreme cases, young people acquire a taste for violence.

A new culturalism is, in other words, at work, and the electronic media lie at the heart of its apparatus. This, to use the specialist jargon, is the 'acculturation'[6] or 'cultural incubation' thesis. The most extreme images of violence shape personalities typical of a culture whose characteristic features are, broadly speaking: an inability to tell right from wrong because taboos can easily be transgressed on screen; an inability to distinguish between reality and fiction, which is especially obvious in cartoons; a belief that violence is something that goes without saying, that is unavoidable and fatal; insensitivity, which is also the best defence against the real violence one wishes to avoid. Olivier Mongin (1997: 139) argues that 'the more we watch, the more we become insensitive and the more protected we feel ... paradoxically, the most extreme forms of violence are the most painless: they desensitize the viewer. As the on-screen violence becomes insane, the viewer wrongly believes that he has succeeded in eradicating violence where he is concerned'. If we accept the arguments of Divina Frau-Meigs and Sophie Jehel (1997), we can add that these processes conceal America's economic hegemony, Europe's inability to resist it, and also Europe's acculturation to the American model – and it is true that, as Monique Dagnaud emphasizes (1999), a high proportion of violent images are from the many American fictions that have been imported into Europe.

The main criticism, in short, is that images of violence shape worrying cultural models based upon the destructuring of the points of reference we need if we are to live in society. This criticism is open to many objections, as societies often use very violent images to provide points of references that play an important structural role. The image of Christ on the cross is one example.

Some versions of this type of explanation put the emphasis on the learning effect in very general terms. Others stress the way television supposedly encourages the imitation of specific events. Such explanations in fact exonerate it of some of its responsibilities; what is being imitated may well be a very real event, but the media are simply doing their job by reporting it. It has, for instance, often been noted that when the desecration of graves in a Jewish cemetery in Europe gets media coverage, a lot of other graves may then be desecrated. Explanations that lay all the blame at the door of the media overlook the content of the news they broadcast, even though it can have a tangible effect. Similarly, attempts have been made to demonstrate that when the media show images (either fictional or documentary) of, for example, a star who commits suicide, a wave of similar suicides follows – but the studies of this particular issue have been done clumsily, and have easily been refuted by other researchers.

From other perspectives, television is accused of paralysing subjectivation, and especially that of the young. Young people are left alone with the television, and the family institution is of little help to them. They themselves will choose what they watch, without any supervision or guidance. Television does not help the young to construct themselves as subjects; on the contrary, it leaves them to their own devices. One study (Roberts et al., 1999) of the role played by electronic media (television, video games, and so on) in the lives of young Americans notes that there is a very definite tendency to individuate the way the media are used. The authors argue that the proliferation and miniaturization of communications devices are changing the context in which the media are used; what was once a family experience is, for many young people, increasingly a private experience. A critique of the electronic media with the idea of a crisis or mutation within the family institution.

There is, then, no shortage of explanations. They are, however, too partial and one-dimensional to be satisfactory. They are also so different and stem from such conflicting paradigms as to rule out the idea that synthesizing them will supply us with a general theory.

As Todd Gitlin (2001) reminds us, we – both adults and children – live permanently in a world of images and sounds that overwhelm us. The average amount of time children spend in front of the television is, according to some studies, almost six hours a day in the United States, and half that in France. An American child who spends between two and four hours a day in front of the television will have seen some 8,000 murders and 100,000 acts of violence by the time he leaves primary school. Images, including violent images, are a massive phenomenon that is as, or almost as, grounded in everyday life as school or work, and these images' impact on individuals' behaviour, psychology, and personality is likely to be considerable. Their role in these lives is so great it is absurd to assume that their influence always works the same way, or always impacts upon an infinite variety of forms of experience in the same way. And if, by the same criterion, we take as our starting point the different forms of violence that are at work in our society, rather than images of violence, and ask ourselves which of them have anything to do with the influence of the media, we can readily conclude that the media have very little influence: do, for instance, delinquency, crime, or the acts of violence that are committed in time of war owe anything to the media? Obviously not. The problem then becomes not so much, or not only, criticizing the media for their influence, as developing education for dealing with both the media and violent imagery without assuming that they are synonymous.

And in order to develop polices to combat violent imagery, we have to ensure that they articulate not only more or less compatible points of view, each determined by one or another of the available explanations, but also – and perhaps above all – perspectives derived from other logics, such as the logics of ethics and economics.

Ethics and economics

Despite the impressive number of studies and analyses that supposedly demonstrate their harmful effects, the debate about the violence of images is organized around them to only a limited extent. It owes much more to the expression of moral preoccupations that are all the more powerful in that they arise in a context in which all great institutions appear to be out of their depth or in crisis. When schools appear to be struggling to carry out their mission and also seem not to know what to do about television – and teachers are often hostile to it or unable to adapt to it or use it – when the Churches seem to have run out of steam, when authority appears to be coming under attack from all sides, and when fear of crime becomes one of the primary characteristics of collective life, violence becomes a nagging social worry, and locating its source becomes a major preoccupation. The problem is then not so much the reality of violence or the rise in violence, as what they appear to mean: a crisis affecting the social bond, the undermining of moral values, a loss of interest in the younger generation on the part of older generations, and so on. Increasing pressure is brought to bear in an attempt to make politicians tackle the issue, especially when a young viewer who has just watched *Scream* acts out what he has seen. Whether or not this is an exceptional phenomenon is of little importance; the point is that there has to be a response to what is basically a moral demand.

Such demands are now determined by social categories that might be expected to be in favour of a certain liberalism, at least where moral issues are concerned. They are in fact voiced not only by sectors of the working class and other groups that have always been inclined to appeal to the moral order, but also by relatively liberal and modern strata who are beginning to worry about their children, now that they know that they are circulating pornographic cassettes or playing electronic games which can be very violent.

The critical discourse on the violence of images therefore gives rise to certain doubts and criticisms. Does it reflect a failure to understand the young or a fear of young people rather than a tangible reality? Are Martin Barker and Julian Petley (1997) right to suggest that the media show us what public opinion expects to see because it is being manipulated by moral campaigners?

As a result, this moral pressure comes into conflict with the principle of freedom of expression, which is applied in very different ways in different societies. To what extent can we say, show, and distribute everything, even in the mass media? Does not freedom of expression call into question other rights and other freedoms? Does it not imply, for instance, an assault on human dignity? And does not respect for human dignity have to be an absolute rule, or at least as great an imperative as the First Amendment to the American Constitution? Does not the application of moral principles mean the arbitrary assertion of certain conceptions, an order and forms of power?

These worries have become significant and have fuelled a moral panic about the electronic media for reasons that have to do with the general triumph of the market economy, which upsets rules, norms, and ethics, and imposes the law of profit and the highest possible profitability. At this point the critique goes beyond the specificity of the media and even the electronic media, and attacks the excesses of cultural industries that programme violence with no concern for anything but their own profits. James Hamilton, for instance, applies to television an argument he has already used about industrial pollution, and especially chemical pollution: 'The pursuit of individual self-interest by consumers, producers and distributors of violent programming leads to undesirable social outcomes' (Hamilton, 1998: xvii). From this point of view, violence is a marketing choice that generates 'negative externalities', or in other words costs that have to be borne by society, or at least by those who are not responsible for them, usually in the norm of higher rates of aggression and crime that call for remedies comparable to those used in the struggle against pollution: broadcasts containing violence should be restricted to certain time slots, and information should be provided about both the violent content of the programmes concerned, and about the adverts that will be shown during them.

One especially interesting point about this critique lies in an unexpected aspect of the marketing involved in violent programming. The violent content is, Hamilton explains, aimed in particular at adults aged between 18 and 34, and violence is programmed for their benefit. Many of the actual consumers are in fact much younger and are much more likely to be influenced by the violence, even though they are not being targeted by the advertisers and the programmes' producers. The 'negative externalities' (the aggression of younger viewers) are, in other words, a cost that becomes absurd and all the more unacceptable in that they are of little benefit to the advertisers, who are aiming at a different, and older, target audience. And as neither those who make the adverts shown during the programmes nor the channels that show them factor this cost into their programming strategies, there is only one answer: the authorities have to intervene. Ultimately, the problem comes down to politics. Which, as Georges Balandier was saying as early as the 1990s, raises the question of democracy: 'Democracy's modern sickness is the way the cathode-ray tube anaesthetizes political life' (Balandier, 1992: 11).

The contextualization of violence

But does not this type of argument use too loose a definition of 'violence'? Does it not confuse, not for the first time in this public debate, phenomena as different as murder, wars, delinquency, terrorism, and minor crime stories, not to mention the 'aggression' that figures in so many of the American studies mentioned above?

One elementary distinction may help to advance the debate. A distinction can be made between televised images (and the films and electronic games that young people are so fond of) that give violence a fairly obvious meaning and inscribe it in a political, historical, social, or cultural context that is clear enough to make it comprehensible, and those that turn it into a phenomenon that appears to have no context or that is only loosely related to some context and therefore loses all meaning.

This distinction, which is vigorously formulated by Olivier Mongin in his (1997) analysis of developments in contemporary cinema tends to simplify the argument greatly, to think of violent images in terms of an axis. At one end of the axis, violence can be shown in such a way as to distance the viewer from it and to promote a 'clear awareness' (Desbarats, 1995, cited in Mongin, 1997: 12) of what is going on. At the opposite end of the axis, the violence that is shown appears to be inevitable or unavoidable because it illustrates the behaviour of heroes whose sole characteristic is that they are incarnations of violence with no human or historical depth. There is a great difference between representations of violence that make us think about it reflectively and ground it in an experience in which the conflict, otherness, or confrontation are such that it is possible to negotiate with it on an intellectual basis, and representations in which it sweeps everything before it, looks natural or superhuman, or in which it is 'an unshakeable given'

(Mongin, 1997: 118). Those differences must have an influence on possible recommendations for media policies. Showing a war, a battlefield, strategies, and goodies and baddies is not the same as showing only the aesthetics and cruelty of transgressing prohibitions, or pure butchery without any hierarchy of values, whatever they may be.

According to Olivier Mongin and other media observers and analysts, the contemporary trend is towards a loss of meaning, values, and points of reference. One argument that is often used against Hamilton's criticisms of programmed violence on television is that television also shows films like *Schindler's List*. This is a great film which both shows the horror and brutality of the Holocaust and contextualizes its violence, but this argument in favour of the media is weak because 'Of the 5,000 movies with indicators for violence shown on broadcast and cable television in 1995-96, only 2.8% were from four-star films' (Hamilton, 1998: xvi). This observation is quite in keeping with the changes mentioned in earlier chapters of this book. The end of the Cold War, the decline of the workers' movement, and the related demise of 'grand narratives' have had an influence on the production of images, both fictional and documentary, and have destroyed meaning. Globalization encourages the distribution of images that can be viewed all over the world. Such images therefore erase specific points of reference and values, and promote a universal culture that is poor because it is shared by all.

Such an approach helps us to get away from arguments that move in linear fashion from images of violence, which is itself defined too vaguely, to violent behaviours. It introduces the idea that the reason why the debate rages, at least periodically, is that in the media, violence is increasingly made to look like an absence of meaning. It appears to be a pure *jouissance*, which may be aesthetic. It seems to be gratuitous, and the destruction borders on the absurd because it is not part of a clearly defined conflict or broader relationship. This pure violence appears to be comprehensible only in its own terms. It cannot be read in terms of a classical grid or a grand historical narrative, such as that of how the West was won or that of the Second World War. It is disturbing, whereas films about cowboys and Indians do not provoke the same reactions in the United States. The responsibility lies mainly with the broadcasters and distributors.

From this point of view, where images are produced is one thing, and where they are received is another. Those phenomena in which the violence is most unhealthy and most disturbing are heightened when images are produced in a given country, such as the United States or Japan, where they can still be grounded in national debates, or in the experience of particular people, including young people, but are intended to be seen in different national contexts where the reference points that allow viewers to relate them to those debates and problems are either less visible or non-existent. *Taxi Driver* was shown in the United States in 1976. French and American viewers saw it in very different ways. France had not just emerged from a war in Vietnam and, unlike American society, which had talked a lot about Vietnam from an internal point of view, French society had not, as Benjamin Stora (1997) has shown so clearly, been able to discuss its experience of war in Algeria, which was still a fresh memory, in similar terms.

The trend for violence for the sake of violence appears to be reinforced by the way television is consumed, and not least the now widespread practice of zapping, which definitely encourages the non-contextualization of the images that are received. In this context, individualization means having to decide, if one can, the meaning of images that have no meaning, or of images we see in conditions that render them meaningless. The viewer is responsible for the story he thinks he understands. The viewer's responsibility is even greater when it comes to video games. The young people who play them are often alone with the screen, and make up their own stories. Violence always plays a huge role in them, and that is inevitable. The viewer is omnipotent and in complete control of the story he is making up. The story is set in a fantastic and imaginary world in which reality, such as historical reality, can be evoked, but in which it can also be dismissed or ignored at any moment.

This dissociation of registers may be a general phenomenon specific to contemporary modernity. It might be argued that violent images were more embedded in the social, the political, and emotional registers than they are today. More importantly, we can advance the hypothesis that there is now a definite tendency to divorce the violence from any context. Violence seems to becoming violence for the sake of violence. There is no longer any reason, or less reason, to relate it to the narratives of political reason, social relations or the passion of affects. The same comments may also apply to the very different phenomenon of pornography. The spread of pornography is a further sign of dissociation; in pornography, sexuality is dissociated from love and morality. The story of their divorce provides the best summary of *The Sexual Life of Catherine M* (Millet, 2002 [2001]), and may explain the book's success.[7] This is why the worries that give rise to debates about violent imagery are increasingly concerned about the media presence of pornography. This is also why the theme of violent imagery quickly becomes a debate about its effect on the sexuality and brutality of young men who become involved in the gang rape of girls. The aggression and the absence of moral points of reference may be further expressions of the same dissociation, and the existence of images in which anything is possible may be undermining discourses that attempt to introduce barriers, rules, and respect. The effect of the media may be to blur the distinction between what is possible and what is desirable and to do away with the need for sublimation. In the media, anything can be done very easily and without any transition.

Is there such a thing as pure violence?

Useful as it may be, an approach that makes this distinction between two types of violence does raise certain doubts. The first is that the more disturbing of the two, namely violence for its own sake, can also be imputed, in terms of the worries it creates towards the failings of a receiver who is unprepared or ill-prepared to receive it, or who does not have the categories that would allow him to understand the violence for what it is. It may in fact be less 'pure' than one might think. This is why certain specialists, including Serge Tisseron (2003), take the view that the fight to reduce the impact of violent images requires a pedagogic strategy, and that it is both desirable and possible to recontextualize them. If schools try to educate children and explain violent images in a context that allows them to be understood and discussed, violence becomes comprehensible and we get away from perceptions that see only its most extreme or purest forms.

Perhaps we should go yet further and displace the argument, which is not without its pretensions to objectivity, that makes a distinction between violence that can be contextualised and pure violence. The feeling of meaninglessness and decontextualization that may be experienced by adults is not necessarily universally valid. It may be an indication that they are outside a culture that is widely shared by others, and especially by young people, and may signal that adults know nothing about the interpretive codes or reading grids specific to other generations or other social milieus. Those codes and grids may relate to ways of constructing stories in which the meaning is deciphered or found in a manner they are not familiar with. 'Meaningless' is always an accusation that gives rise to doubts and suspicions, and there is no reason why we should abandon our own critical senses here. We should be careful or wary about stating that such and such a film or programme includes pure violence or violence for its own sake, and check that our comments apply to the entire audience – young people or children – in question. Which brings us back to the debate between universalism and relativism that we mentioned earlier, and to the suggestion that we need to think much more seriously about violence for the sake of violence. That is the topic of Part Two.

Notes

1 One of the most sophisticated works supporting this thesis is that by Friedrich Hacker (1976).
2 At the same time, the report of the 'Task Force on Mass Media and Violence' (*National Commission on the Causes and Prevention of Violence*) looked into the correlation between televised images of violence and violent behaviour, and noted that the question had been debated in the United States since 1954. As early as

the late 1920s, American researchers were claiming that there was a correlation between juvenile delinquency and cinema going (see Dagnaud, 2003).

3 National Television Violence Study, *National Television Study: Executive Summary 1994–1995*, and Scientific Papers, 1994, 1995, Studio City (CA): Mediascope, 1996, cited in Hamilton (1998: 19).

4 The idea is that exposure to televised violence reduces aggression because it has a cathartic effect, because these images have some kind of purifying power.

5 Monique Dagnaud (2003: 6) mentions several such cases of murder or slaughter. One involved the murder of a teenage girl in France on 4 June 2002. The case involved several young people and the murder was modelled on the film *Scream*. It was argued that television or films provided an explanation.

6 The pioneering figure here is George Gerbner (1988).

7 On pornography, see Baudry (1997).

CONCLUSION

THE LIMITATIONS OF CLASSICAL SOCIOLOGY

If violence was reducible to reactive behaviours and was just a matter of instincts, nature, or pure reactivity, the social sciences would not have much to say about it unless they surrendered to social Darwinism or Spencerian theories, and turned the 'struggle for life' into a central analytical principle. They could then, at most, look at the political and cultural conditions that either encourage or discourage violence. That is why classical sociology's main contributions to the study of violence are to be found in arguments that look at the protagonist of violent action and try to find a meaning, orientation, or goal that has been internalized by the actor.

Expressivity and Instrumentality

When it was at its apotheosis, classical sociology was, thanks to Talcott Parsons, who did more than anyone else to bring about its intellectual integration, able to outline the now familiar distinction between instrumental and expressive action. This distinction contrasts instrumental violence, which is a resource that is mobilized for certain purposes or as a means to an end, with expressive violence, which delivers a message and whose very existence has a content that is enough to define it without reference to any instrumental rationality. Expressive violence is therefore a crude message, a set of meanings whose sole purpose is to translate, directly and without any mediation, a state of mind or affects such as anger or hatred, or even a culture, values, and an identity. It confuses means and ends and, in extreme cases, becomes an end in itself.

This distinction in a sense brings together the main approaches described in classical sociology. As we shall see, it can be of real use, and can shed some interesting light on certain historical experiences. But, for basic reasons that have to be pointed out from the start, it fails to clarify some decisive points. It really allows us to understand violence in only two main types of situation or experience. On the one hand, it makes it possible to approach phenomena of violence using the general framework of a social (or other) system within which the behaviours of the actors are functional, normal, and rational. Violence then appears to be one option amongst others, or the only option that remains open to an actor who is especially weak or destitute. On the other hand, it suggests that violence has a meaning that exists in a pure state and that it expresses that meaning, even if it becomes mixed up with all sorts of other elements, many of them emotional. It also suggests that the meaning does not really have to be established or theorized. The actor calculates (instrumental violence) or is trying to say something (expressive violence). That aside, violence remains an imponderable, at least for the social sciences, and seems to come within the remit of explanations that either naturalize or pathologize it to an extreme degree. It is this gap in the understanding of violence that we now have to look at.

Hot and cold

Expressive violence is hot and expresses feelings that crystallize around particularly paroxysmal situations. Fear, anger, a feeling of dereliction or abandonment may come into play, sometimes in confused ways, and may focus on individuals or material goods, some with great symbolic weight. The focus is all the less instrumental in that it may seem irrational, given the actor's interests, or ill-adapted to the goals he or she should be pursuing. In extreme cases, expressive violence comes to seem absurd or even self-destructive. It may also seem to be purely ludic, Dionysian, or orgiastic.

Hot violence is unstable. It breaks out unpredictably, or almost unpredictably. It also dies down very quickly. It is radical and non-negotiable, and may be followed by a sort of apathy that is just as absolute, rather as though there could be no situation in between, for example, riotous outbursts and withdrawal, discouragement, a total lack of mobilization, and idleness. It is as though it were the only alternative to passivity and dereliction, as though the exasperation and active rage it expresses could never be mediated by any institution.

Instrumental violence is very different. It is cold, structured to some degree, constructed discursively, and works in an orderly, controlled fashion. Cold violence looks like rational behaviour, and may be associated with a school of thought, a doctrine, a policy, or an ideology that inspires the actor and allows him to implement strategies and tactics with the support of a more or less methodical mode of organization. In extreme cases, it requires a machine or an organization to ensure that it is efficient. The more its workings resemble the model of the state, the more its logic resembles that of state coercion, and the more it seems to be striving for rational efficiency.

When, for instance, political violence turns into civil war or terrorism, it can be the product of structures similar to those of a state apparatus, as we can see from the organizational charts of Italy's Red Brigades in their glory days at the beginning of the 1980s (Della Porta, 1984).

A useful distinction

In practice, the behaviours of actors are never sociologically pure forms, and are always combinations of greater or lesser complexity. The analytic distinction between hot and cold violence is not always clearly observable in reality, where the phenomenon's two modalities are always entwined and to some extent confused. And yet it is in many respects a precious tool.

The distinction can, first of all, be used to differentiate between things that current discourse amalgamates into a single category. It has, for instance, been suggested that the category of 'lynching' should be exploded in order to demonstrate that it corresponded, in late nineteenth- and early twentieth-century America, to two types of practices that were relatively distinct, at least from the point of view of the actors if not that of the victims, who were all Black. Popular lynchings were disorganized, ferocious, and not very fussy when it came to their choice of victim; they always occurred in economic situations that were difficult for poor whites. This was hot violence. 'Bourbon' lynchings were organized and 'polite'. They were essentially a racial call to order orchestrated by affluent and influential citizens who took it upon themselves to 'punish' a black man, who was usually accused of having raped a white woman. This was cold violence (see Stoetzel, 1963; Myrdal, 1944). It will be noted in passing that hot violence may, if we can generalize on the basis of this example, be characteristic of working-class strata, and cold violence of social categories that are less impoverished, less inferiorized, and better educated. We must, however, be very careful here, as there is a great danger that we will lapse into the failings and elitist prejudices of those who believe that barbarism is by definition found in the countryside rather than the cities, and amongst the poor rather than the rich.

The distinction between expressivity and instrumentality can, on the other hand, help us to analyse historical experiences in which violence can only be understood as a combination of both dimensions. This interpretation explains how violence can become so excessive. As Wolfgang Sofsky (1996) remarks, emotional violence is commonly episodic, extravagant, uses crude methods, and has limited goals, whilst rational violence is constant, intensive, and calculated. Rational violence makes up for its lack of energy by appealing to the emotions, whilst emotional violence makes up for its lack of rationality by making calculations. A combination of the two gives the forces of destruction immense power. We should in fact make a distinction between different scenarios here. In some cases, expressive and instrumental violence can complement one another, or can be combined with some degree of success. As the historian Simon Doubnov's remarkable (1988) descriptions demonstrate, pogroms in Tsarist Russia represented a combination of popular violence based upon pre-modern hatred of Jews that was anti-Judaic rather than anti-Semitic, and cold political actions encouraged and even mainly organized by the government, or by political actors protected by the government. The violence succeeded, in this case, because it was based on the ability of 'cold' actors to manipulate 'hot' actors, and to orchestrate or simply trigger their violence. Similarly, the genocide in Rwanda, which was planned several months before the first killings occurred in April 1994, cannot be explained solely in terms of a Hutu political plot to exterminate the Tutsis. It was possible only because, basically, the hatred and jealousy were simply waiting for a favourable opportunity to turn into barbarism, as the stories and reflections of Tutsi survivors collected by Jean Hatzfeld (2008a [2000]) demonstrate much more clearly than most reports.

In other historical experiences, the distinction between expressivity and instrumentality does allow us to arrive at a better understanding of violence. In these cases, violence is not a combination of two different types of logic; they are neither complementary nor integrated. On the contrary, it is the clash between the two or their failure to come together that gives rise to the excesses. When an attempt is made to combine the two, the violence spirals out of control. The excesses of far-left terrorism in Italy in the early 1980s are a particularly eloquent example. At this time, the terrorist organizations, and especially the Red Brigades, which had been structured and organized for at least ten years and were promoting what was intended to be instrumental violence, found that thousands of angry young people who wanted to become actors and who also wanted, in many cases, to play at being 'Comrade P. 38', were bringing more and more pressure to bear in order to be admitted into their ranks. These very 'hot' young people, who were in a hurry to join the armed struggle, destabilized the Red Brigades and *Primea Linea*, and forced them to use an increasingly frenzied and disorganized violence. The organizations then went into decline. They were ideologically exhausted, and the confessions of the *pentiti* and the great successes of the forces of repression also took their toll. The 'hot' took over from the 'cold', or collided with it. The hot violence went on for a surprisingly long time, precisely because of the structured, political forms it encountered and threw into confusion, and which tried to resist and contain it by absorbing and channelling it. When the two collided, the terrorism took an extreme form. It knew no limits, was capable of being cruel, and became demented rather than political.[1]

The distinction between expressivity and instrumentality can also help us to understand how a single historical experience can be transformed over time. In historical terms, the transition from very expressive violence to an instrumental violence that precludes or even rejects and represses all expressive spontaneity is a particularly significant example. The pogroms and destruction of *Kristalnacht* (1938), for example, mark a turning point in the history of Nazism. This episode was in fact the only significant outburst of populist anti-Semitism, though it was of course manipulated and orchestrated by organized actors under the command of Goebbels. Even so, 'hot' violence exploded on to the streets in an uncontrolled fashion. After this, there was more apparently spontaneous involvement in outbreaks of anti-Semitic violence, as Hitler resolved to exercise much tighter controls over the management of the Jewish question and adopted much more methodical practices that were so far removed from popular 'heat' that the destruction of the Jews had to be kept 'secret' (Laqueur, 1982). The 'hot' drove out the 'cold' to such an extent that, at least on German soil, the genocide of the Jews seems to correspond to the bureaucratic logic that is, according to Zygmunt Bauman (1989), the final outcome of modernity.

The opposition between expressivity and instrumentality, and attempts to correlate the two categories, do prove to be useful when applied to violence. And yet the distinction, which is a condensation of many of the contributions made by classical sociology, is not really satisfactory. It fails to grasp the most intriguing and mysterious aspect of violence, and ignores one aspect of the phenomenon that cannot be contained within the theoretical space it marks out.

What Traditional Approaches Fail to Take into Account

Hot violence – Philippe Braud (2004) calls it 'choleric' – is spontaneous, impulsive, and unstable, and those characteristics make it formidably difficult to analyse. Is this violence the immediate expression of a meaning and does it, in its own way, shape significations that may be social, cultural, or political, as the word 'expressive' suggests? Or does it unleash elements that are neither social, cultural, nor political? Does it unleash instincts that are part of human nature, or an aggression whose deepest origins have nothing to do with the situation in which it finds expression?

At this stage of our analysis, we can do little more than note that these questions remain unanswered. One thing is, however, quite clear. 'Expressive' violence is in fact never a pure expression of some meaning. There are always elements that seem to us to be absurd or gratuitous, but there are no grounds for thinking that the meaningless element automatically has to do with animality, the economy of the instincts, or human nature. 'Instinct' does not explain, or does not fully explain, the cruelty that is so common in mass murder, and which is so horrific if we think of the eye-witness accounts of those who have survived a genocide or the 'useless violence' of the Nazis as described by Primo Levi in an especially powerful chapter of his last book

(1988 [1986]). That violence could become disproportionate at any moment in the day-to-day life of the extermination camps. And nor can it be explained in terms of the general meaning that might be ascribed to it by those who identified with the Nazi plan to destroy the Jews. We will come back to this point again at greater length.

Nor can we reduce behaviours such as those we have just evoked to the image of pure instrumentality, or to a utility whose individual, or even collective, dimensions can be clearly outlined. Discussing the horrors that were reported in connection with three recent experiences (Bosnia-Herzegovina in 1992–95, Rwanda in 1994, and Guatemala in 1981–83), Jasna Adler (Violences aujourd' hui, violences de toujours: 188) takes the view that the mass rapes and sexual mutilations were staged with an unimaginable cruelty that had a purpose:

> The goal was to destructure the group to which the victims belonged ... to destroy everything the group's solidarity was based on, be it a family group or a village group. Its feeling of identity and dignity was destroyed. It was a way of sending a message to the whole community, be it Bosnian, Muslim, Mayan or Tutsi... My hypothesis is that this was a way of achieving a well-calculated and clearly defined goal.

This hypothesis is fragile: it implies that the authors of these crimes were convinced of their impunity, which now looks somewhat irrational. It dismisses the idea that violence can be an end in itself, and overlooks the fact that such crimes can be a source of sexual pleasure. The killers can indulge in the pleasure of negating their individual victim. She does not deserve to live because she was raped because she is part of her community or quite simply because she belongs to the world of the living. Adler's hypothesis tells us nothing about the barbarity that was so unbridled as to exclude its victims from humanity. It turns cruelty into a rational behaviour and ignores its excessive dimension. As one female Tutsi survivor put it (Hatzfeld, 2008a: 18):

> I think that once you have seen your mother being chopped with such wickedness, then suffering so slowly, you forever lose a part of your trust in others, and not only in the interhamwe [Hutu militias]. I mean that a person who has looked for such a long time on such a terrible suffering cannot live amongst people in the same way as before, because she will be on her guard.

Simplistic ideas notwithstanding, even the most controlled instrumental violence can never be completely reduced to an image of calculations that allow the actor to methodically adjust the means to the ends. Anything worthy of the name 'violence' inevitably signals a certain transgression of what a body of actors regards as legitimate means, no matter whether we are talking about individuals, groups, or wider ensembles that function on an international scale. Violence is a resource that is different to any other, to the extent that it implies the idea of non-legitimacy and marks a break from what is acceptable within a given social or political space. Even when it is instrumental it implies an infringement of established rules and norms, even in situations where the objective appears to conform to those rules, to correspond to legitimate ends, and to pose no threat to the general principles that organize collective life. In a text that has already been mentioned, Robert Merton (1957) demonstrates this clearly with reference to delinquency and criminality. Delinquency and criminality commonly employ non-legitimate means and use some violence to achieve ends that are in themselves socially legitimate. Crime and theft can, for example, be explained in terms of a real conformism, or a desire to gain access to dominant values that seen inaccessible by means that are normal and accepted by the community.

It is because, and even then it is in theory instrumental, violence is always to some extent transgressive that it can spiral out of control even when it appears to be calculated, cold, and rational. It can know no bounds, despite the resistance and obstacles it may encounter in the shape of, for example, the forces of repression. In such cases it appears to be eminently rational, because it is based upon elaborate calculations, the use of appropriate tools, such as weapons, explosives, and means of communications, and a real ability to imagine what the enemy is calculating or how powerless the victims are. At the same time it is profoundly inhuman, and may become demented, fanatical, and completely intent upon doing evil. It appears to be almost drunken, but there is still a rationality to it. It works because it relies upon an instrumental or technical rationality, but is used to further projects and goals that are, to a greater or lesser extent, out of touch with reality. In some cases, the goals become all the more demented as it becomes more and more unlikely that the actor will achieve them. The history of modern terrorism from the anarchist and populist episodes of the nineteenth century onwards is, for example, based upon a combination of two contradictory logics. We have, on the one hand, a real elaboration of complex strategy and thinking, and perhaps a recourse to technology and science, and, on the other, an artificial or even oneiric reference to a social figure an actor claims to represent, such as down-trodden people, an oppressed nation, an exploited class or a despised religion. Terrorism is never as murderous and as blind as when it combines rational calculation with a disjunction between the protagonists of the violence, and the lived experience of those whose cause they claim to represent, or as when it is capable of being instrumental whilst remaining completely ideological. Terrorism becomes extreme and knows no limits when its excesses take its action beyond its initial ideology.

Because of the dynamics it involves, which are irreducible to any clear or simple meaning or any recognizable social, political, or cultural markers, expressive violence escapes its definition because it permeates downwards. And instrumental violence escapes its definition because of the excesses that are potentially present in any significant historical experience, precisely because it is by definition transgressive. It is used by actors and causes whose passions, ideologies, political and metapolitical aims, or utopias are such that there is an unfathomable gulf between very distant ends and means that are used on a daily basis. The gulf is so great that, in extreme cases, a reversal takes place. As Hannah Arendt warns us, we have to be wary of political violence: 'Violence is by nature instrumental' (1970 [1969] 51) … 'Where violence is no longer backed and constrained by power, the well-known reversal in reckoning with means and ends has taken place. The means, the means of destruction, now determine the end – with the consequence that the end will be the destruction of all power' (ibid: 54).

The classic approaches to violence are ultimately unsatisfactory. The light they shed on it is useful, but it is not enough. Some suggest that violence can be reduced to rationality, but its rationality is always overtaken by elements that can only be described as irrational. That explanation is not satisfactory in intellectual terms. When explanations for behaviours cease to be logical, it is very tempting to immediately introduce the notion of insanity, nature, or some infra-social or supra-social principle; and perhaps we do have to do that, but not before we have made a much greater effort to conceptualize violence in sociological terms.

The other classical approach is to explain violence in terms of the state of the social or political system, or in cultural terms. It is, in short, explained by determinations which, ultimately, mean that we do not need to study the actual actors. All we have to do to predict possible outbreaks of violence is to understand the conditions in which the actors function, even if this means relying on the idea of an elementary mechanism, such as frustration, in order to both analyse the system and understand the actors.

The analytic tools developed by the social and political sciences always seem to put to one side some aspects of violence, which appear to be a sort of residue or remainder, a minor or marginal element. They do not help us to understand the extreme aspects of violent behaviours or the moments of frenetic madness. They take no interest in phenomena such as the loss of meaning or savagery. Unless they can naturalize or pathologize them, they do not have much to say about sadism, cruelty, violence for its own sake, the excesses of mass murder, or episodes in which the actor is both destructive and self-destructive.

That is why it is time to invert the argument. We have to look at the most disconcerting aspects of violence, which the classic approaches deal with badly or superficially, as minor, peripheral, or secondary aspects. If violence is such an important phenomenon, and if understanding it is a central issue, then we have to recognize that its most mysterious and elusive aspects are the most decisive. Given the factual information, it is not difficult to reconstruct the calculations of, say, the military, terrorist actors, or organized crime. Analysing the individual and collective processes that result in acts of violence that cannot be fully explained in terms of calculations is much more complex but also much more necessary, given that they can include a perversion of meaning, cruelty, and ideological excesses that are, in strictly instrumental terms, pointless.

The reversal implied by such an intellectual stance is easily formulated. It means that we have to centre our analysis on elements that have hitherto been marginalised, and look at the subjectivity of the actors, at what cannot be defined in terms of calculations, the influence of a culture, or mere reactions to events. This reversal is what is at stake in Part II and it is, in broader terms, what the author sees as this book's conclusion. Ultimately, it leads to a proposition that appears to be paradoxical but is not. It suggests, in other words, that it is the most extreme forms of violence that lie at the heart of the phenomena, and that it is by looking at its most astonishing and least comprehensible modalities that we can in reality come to terms with its essential features, if not its essence.

Note

1   On this experience, see my (1989) study, which is based on discussions with a number of Italian terrorists.

Part II

THE MARK OF THE SUBJECT

INTRODUCTION

The classical approaches are, on the whole, reluctant to concentrate on the act of violence and therefore concentrate either on analysing the conditions that encourage action or acting out, or on studying the actor, who is reduced to being a sociological variant on *homo economicus* who is defined solely by his calculations, strategies and, ultimately, interests. They take no interest, or very little interest, in the meaning of the action or orientations that the violence might be expressing.

If they did so, they would soon find themselves in difficulties. The initial characteristic of action is usually that it appears to be distorted or transfigured, when compared with what it would be if violence were not an integral part of it. There appears to be an element of excess, but there is also something lacking. Then there are the extreme cases in which there is so little meaning that it is tempting to say that they are meaningless, and to see the violence as the mark of nature, as a purely biological phenomenon, or even as madness and dementia.

It is too easy to explain behaviours we do not understand by naturalizing them, relating them to some metaphysical explanatory principle, or medicalizing and pathologizing them. But it is also true that, leaving aside its most instrumental dimensions, violence does seem to drift constantly away from meaning and, in many respects, from the dictates of reason. So much so that, in many experiences, the protagonist seems to be someone who is acted upon rather than an actor.

We are now going to look specifically at the least comprehensible and most mysterious aspects of violence. We will therefore reject two symmetrical ideas because they are both too reductive. The most elementary observation, such as listening to the discourse that sometimes accompanies violence, means that, in most cases, it cannot be said that violence expresses meanings simply and directly, or that it is no more than one of the resources in action's repertoire. That does not necessarily mean, however, that we can immediately relegate its protagonist to the realm of non-meaning, rather as though he had simply surrendered to barbarism, to an absence of humanity, or to the animal element that is supposedly there in all of us. Once we have mapped these extreme points, which mark out the space of the analysis, we face the much more difficult task of exploring the processes and mechanisms that shape the individual or collective protagonist of violence and his acting out. We have to regard the protagonist as a subject, or at least a potential subject, and then look as best we can at how he transforms himself. The outcome may, depending on the individual case and the context or situation, be a loss of meaning, non-meaning or the expression of unbridled cruelty, or of logics that are dominated by a boundless subjectivity.

5

VIOLENCE, LOSS OF MEANING, AND EXCESS MEANING

How are we to theorize the relationship between violence and meaning, or in other words the significations that orient violence and which, without ever being completely external to the actor's consciousness, are never completely reducible to it? If we emphasize the idea of the frustration associated with a changing situation that has, for instance, become unbearable or too unfavourable, we ultimately reduce violence to a reaction on the part of an actor who wishes to establish or restore an equilibrium that is in his favour. The state of the system or sub-system (which may be political, economic, social, and so on) in which the actor operates, and the transformations that are undergone by that system or sub-system, are assumed to supply the explanation for his violence. The explanation does not lie in the actor's own efforts or in a process involving his ability to define his position within relations of one kind or another. Those who inscribe violence within the continuity of a culture, or see it as a personal attribute, also reject the idea of the construction or perversion of a meaning by and through violence, as the violent actor is never anything more than what his culture, education, or personality tells him to do. The subjectivity of violence is neither denied nor minimized, but these approaches tend to see it as something that is shaped outside the situation in which it is used, and claim that it has little to do with the relations within which the actor operates; at best, they are conditions that either encourage him to use violence or discourage him from doing so. And if we refuse to see the instrumental character of violence, we obviously associate it with a meaning because the actor regards it as a resource that allows the pursuit of determinate objectives. But even then, the singular nature of the resource is not even taken into consideration, rather as though violence existed on the same level as money, material resources, or solidarity networks. This approach suggests that violence is something that can be fully controlled by the person who resorts to it, and for whom it is no more than a technical tool that is completely unrelated to the emotions, passions, desires, and drives, or to the individual or collective personality of the actor. It suggests, in a word, that violence has nothing to do with anything that escapes pure rationality.

The common feature of most of the classical approaches to violence is that they hardly ever introduce, except in a marginal fashion, the processes of *subjectivation* and *desubjectivation* that inevitably characterize its protagonists, as we shall see. This remark leads to the more general suggestion that we should in fact make the *subject* central to our analysis. If we wish to pursue this theoretical project further, and demonstrate its utility or even its necessity, we must first systematically look at various instances in which violence is incomprehensible unless we refer to one or more processes in which its meaning is either lost or becomes excessive.

Loss of Meaning

The deficit

In certain experiences, violence appears to correspond, in a rather elementary way, to a mere deficit of meaning: in such cases, the actor is all the more violent in that the system of relations within which he could or might give a meaning to his action is in decay, in the process of disappearing, or is so ramshackle and so ill-constructed that social, political, interpersonal, or intercultural relations are still immature or in their infancy. We have in fact already dealt with this question in Chapter 1 by showing that violence is often not a modality of conflict, but the opposite of conflict or something that breaks out when conflict is impossible because it is blocked, because a crisis overwhelms it, or because it is coming to an end and its actors are decadent or, at the opposite extreme, because it has yet to come into existence.

In this context, violence is something that no longer makes sense, or that does not yet make sense, except from the protagonist's point of view. It indicates that the subject has little social, political, or cultural content. A social relationship involving at least some conflict allows, or will allow, the actor to assert himself as a social, political, or cultural entity confronted with another actor; that is possible only because the other is recognized in his humanity, either as a collective or as an individual. When that relationship is absent, falls apart, or is slow to come into being, the actor must either disappear and be dissolved as such, and then recreate some other meaning or relationship, or must exist in a purely artificial manner by asserting what is now an imaginary meaning that exists only for him, by bringing the relationship to life in oneiric fashion, by transforming the other into a non-human figure such as a barbarian, monster, or superman, and by recognizing not adversaries, but an enemy or enemies.

What we are calling 'meaning' relates to the actor – the way he conceives and manages his own experience, his trajectory and his situation – and not to the situation, its state, or its transformations. In that sense, the notion of a loss of meaning is distinct and far-removed from all those notions that, in one way or another, explain violence in terms of a crisis in a system, such as a crisis in the social or political bond. This brings us closer to certain of Hugues Lagrange's analyses. In his analysis of the juvenile delinquency typ-ical of working-class areas, he rightly notes that, if it were correct, the hypothesis that 'the social bond has been destroyed' or that 'sociability has been impaired' could be validated empirically. Yet, 'If the neighbourhoods that are in trouble really do represent a challenge to social cohesion, that should be observable not only in metaphorical terms but on the basis of the most characteristic indicators of the breakdown of the social bond: crime and delinquency' (2001: 9), which is not the case. In this case, the violence has much more to do with what we are calling a loss of meaning. It allows, for instance, the young people of the *banlieues* who turn to violence to 'invert the stereotype that presents them as losers'. Violence 'allows them to compensate for the fact that they have no future and cannot assert them-selves, and takes away the feeling of emptiness'. Taking his cue from Marc-Olivier Padis, Lagrange remarks of that emptiness that it leads to risk-taking behaviour and to 'a search for physical ordeals as a form of self-assertion' (Lagrange, 2001: 6, 12; Padis, 2000). The notions of a loss of meaning and a crisis in, say, the social bond are not contradictory, but we cannot automat-ically move from one to the other, or from a would-be objective analysis (which may be backed up by statistics on rates of unemployment, incomes, and so on) to a more subjective understanding of these practices.

The loss of meaning finds expression in a lack or a deficit, but violence is rarely the only thing that compensates for it. Indeed, an actor who turns to violence in such circumstances feels a need to justify it, both to others and to himself. In his view, his violence is not meaningless; on the contrary, it is or can be meaningful. That is why the notion of a deficit or loss of meaning can be applied not only to collective violence, such as social or political violence, but also to delinquency and crime. The literature on criminology contains countless descriptions and analyses of cases in which a crime (such as murder or rape) signals that meaning has broken down, sometimes long before the crime was committed. In a book that is, from this point of view, particularly rich, James Gilligan (1996) mentions the case of Ross L, who met a girl he had known at school in a service-station where his car had broken down. She offered to drive him home. He accepted the offer, killed her in her car, and then mutilated her eyes and cut out her tongue before dumping her body in a roadside ditch. When he was arrested, he denied nothing, showed no guilt, and expressed a feeling of complete innocence. What was his explanation? He did not like the way the young woman had looked at him. James Gilligan, who spent a lot of time talking to Ross L, realized that as a young man he had always felt that he was being put down and made to feel that he was worthless. Before he reached puberty, he was beaten up by other boys, and used as a passive homosexual object, as a 'non-man'. His crime put an end to the shame he had associated since childhood with a negation of his physical and moral integrity. If I destroy their eyes, he explained to the psychiatrist, they can't make me feel ashamed, and if I pull out their tongues they can't mock me any more.

This type of crime associates past shame, the experience of being despised and of being the victim of violence, with a murderous act. This is a classic theme that takes us back to the received wisdom that today's criminal was yesterday's victim. The murder means that meaning was lost or destroyed in the past, that an old debt that has become unbearable has been settled by an act that also liquidates the shame that went with it. This may also explain why, in some cases, this type of criminal makes no attempt to avoid being caught, and even appears to want the police, the judge, the jury, and the media to know and understand what he has done (see Silberman, 1978: 78).

Whilst violence may signal a loss of meaning, it does not necessarily silence the actor. On the contrary, it can give the actor the opportunity to express himself. In more general terms, processes that lead to violent behaviours are often accompanied by discursive production, especially when they are not restricted to isolated gestures but are repeated over a period of time. Despite the loss of meaning, collective violence is often associated with various narratives. Two types of narrative are especially interesting: myths and ideology.

Myth and violence

Myths and violence can go hand in hand. This is especially true when the actor is in a situation in which he finds it increasingly difficult to reconcile in practice elements of meaning that are not only becoming removed from reality, but also prove to be more and more contradictory and less and less easy to reconcile. Violence then becomes the concrete expression of a myth, and the two are inseparable. From this point of view, a myth is a construct that allows the imaginary integration of contradictory or incompatible meanings. In such cases, the violence and the myth are two sides of the same coin. This idea suggests a return to Georges Sorel, whose famous *Reflections of Violence* has already been mentioned. This is well known for its analysis, which comes close to being an apologia in many respects, for the myth of the general strike.

It is in fact no coincidence that someone at the time of the birth of the workers' movement should take a positive view of violence, see it as a decisive element in working-class action, and be the first to understand the import of the general strike as a myth, 'a body of images capable of evoking instinctively all the sentiments which correspond to the different manifestations of the war undertaken by Socialism against modern society' (Sorel, 1961 [1908]: 127). It is quite possible, Sorel explains, that the general strike is, for the workers, nothing more than a mythical prospect, but that does not detract from its importance, which resides in its power to mobilize. The workers' movement later unambiguously rejected violence and abandoned the dream of a great general strike that would allow workers to organize the entire social field and the State by taking power away from the bosses, civil servants, and parliamentarians and by rejecting organized political forces. According to Sorel, the mythical imagination goes hand in hand, for the working-class actor, with a violence that can challenge the violence of the State. It is, as Stathis Gourgouris puts it (1997: 144), 'an irreducible expression of collective convictions' or a 'radical language' that must not be confused with a utopia. A myth must be in excess of reality in order to make historical action possible but, unlike a utopia, it is not a projection of the present or a teleology. The association between myth and violence suggested by Sorel's *Reflections* also rules out utilitarian analyses of violence. It will be noted that they were a major source of inspiration for Walter Benjamin, whose critique of violence departs from the instrumental conceptions at work in Aristotle, Kant, Carl von Clausewitz, or Engels: 'In Benjamin, pure violence no longer remained trapped in the circularity circulation of means and ends' (Hanssen, 1997: 246; see also Benjamin, 1996 [1921]).

The experience of ETA in the Spanish Basque country is a very good illustration of the idea that there might be a correspondence between myth and violence. In the late 1950s, ETA began to wage an armed struggle and claimed, in Franco's Spain, to speak simultaneously in the name of the Basque nation, political emancipation, and the workers' movement. ETA symbolised all three meanings in a situation in which the Basque nation was indeed oppressed, in which the workers were indeed subjected to harsh repression, and in which the dictatorship was all the more politically vigilant in that Basque nationalism had been on the Republican side during the civil war. As ETA came more and more to symbolise these three registers of domination and oppression, the less it needed its guns to speak on its behalf; well-planned symbolic actions involving little violence were all that were required.

After the death of Franco in 1974, Spain began to make the transition to democracy, and all three registers were transformed. The Basque nation was granted a great deal of autonomy in various domains (recognition of the Basque language, administration, the police, Basque media, and so on). The workers' movement was in decline and was not the driving force behind Basque society, which was no longer industrial, and the workers no longer saw the terrorists as their representatives. Spain's democracy was not a dictatorship and Marxism-Leninism, which was often central to ETA's discourse, was running out of steam. Each of the significations that once gave ETA its pertinence and reflected the highest aspirations of the Basque population had been modified and weakened. At the same time, the end of Francoism signalled the disappearance of the principle that once guaranteed the integration of ETA's actions; no matter whether it spoke in the name of the nation, the labour movement, or its political aspirations, ETA had always opposed the Franco regime.

The paradox is that, as this development became clearer, ETA's violence not only became more and more murderous, it became more and more blind, and knew no limits. Its victims included members of the Basque population itself. In this case, terrorism was a loss-of-meaning phenomenon; the discourse of the actors remained the same, but society was changing. In order to go on existing, their discourse trapped itself into a myth that spoke of a nation that was still as oppressed as it had always been, of a people who were, in social terms, Spain's victims, and of aspirations to political emancipation that Spanish democracy could only frustrate. A far from negligible proportion of the Basque population still clung to this mythical construct, which, as Alfonso Perez-Agoté (2002) has demonstrated, functioned as a self-fulfilling prophecy by proclaiming that democracy had not changed anything, and acted as though nothing had changed. The myth became increasingly divorced from the lived experience of the population, its expectations and its perceptions. And the more it became divorced from the real world, the more those who wanted to keep it alive needed to unleash a violence that knew no limits.

A mythical discourse by no means prevents an actor from developing strategies designed to give a new consistency to the original project, which was, in this case, dominated by nationalism, even though, as we have said, other social and political dimensions also played an important role in it. In ETA's experience, its efforts were always devoted to showing that the Spanish state was actually oppressing the Basque nation, mainly through its repressive practices and the way Basque militants were treated in Spanish prisons. Its terrorism triggered a repression whose harshness and occasional excesses were seen as proving the need for Basque violence. The more the mechanism proved to the 1960s revolutionary militants that they were right when they theorized the idea of a cycle of 'action/repression/action', the more ETA's discourse seemed to be grounded in reality and not myth: after all, its activists and supporters were being subjected to the terrible violence of a Spanish state that was brutal, anti-democratic, hostile to the Basque nation, and insensitive to the social difficulties of the moment.

In this example, as in other related experiences, the relationship between myth and violence is therefore not one-dimensional; there are all kinds of configurations, and there can be many variants of both terms. This means that at times the relationship is stable and relatively clear, whilst it is more confused, contradictory, unstable, and likely to unravel at others.

Ideology

Myths offer an imaginary reconciliation of elements which, in the real historical or social world, cannot be integrated. Myth is, however, not the only discourse that allows actors who are caught up in the maelstrom of the loss of meaning to sustain, at least where they themselves are concerned, the illusion of meaning. Ideology can easily play the same role. In that case, the actor outlines a representation of the real that is also intended to supply, should the need arise, a theory of the changes he wants to see, and he identifies with that theory. When it is nothing more than a false idea, ideology is to be understood in a 'modest' sense, to use Karl Mannheim's (1936 [1929]) expression. When it is much more than a false idea, or a general vision that is both historical and political and can, in some cases, abrogate the legitimacy that science can give it, it is, to use Mannheim's terminology, 'total'. Ideology, as defined in the second sense, is central to the totalitarian phenomenon, as analysed by Hannah Arendt (1985 [1951]). It comes to mean the pursuit of an idea, or the logic of an idea, that frees its advocate from any need to relate to concrete experience and reality.[1]

The links between ideological production, as defined in the second sense, and violence emerge clearly from the experience of the far-left terrorism that emerged in several Western societies in the 1970s and 1980s, though it was only in Italy that it became a mass phenomenon. This terrorism wanted to keep two flags flying high, but they corresponded to realities that were ceasing to be relevant. It claimed to speak in the name of the workers' movement, at a time when it was approaching its inevitable demise, at least as a central social movement, and when the classical industrial era was drawing to a close. It wanted to sustain the projects and utopias of Communism at a time when the end of the Cold War was in sight and when its promises were exhausted. Being the orphans of both industrial society and the Cold War, those who still wanted to speak in the name of the workers' movement and Communist-style perspectives used a discourse that was increasingly artificial and divorced from the real world. They trapped themselves into variants of an ideology that justified a terrorist violence that was all the more barbaric in that there was no conflict between them and the population in question. In this case, the loss of meaning resulted in a combination of discourses that became ever more demented and acts that become ever more murderous and blind.

The discourse of the protagonists of violence can, especially in certain political experiences, thus come to look like an abundant or even superabundant ideological production, and can even come to resemble logorrhoea.

Ideology then serves to justify acts, or future acts, even though it seems primarily designed to preach to the converted, or those in whose name the actor is speaking, and to disturb and weaken the enemy. In such cases, the actor's discourse is not subject to any reality-testing: 'Once it has established its premise, its point of departure, experiences no longer interfere with ideological thinking, nor can it be taught by reality' (Arendt, 1985 [1951]: 471). The actor is constituted both by his discursive production and his practice of violence; he claims to speak of truth and justice and, at the same time, translates his thoughts into action, and combines power and knowledge in an non-discriminatory way.

The example of far-left terrorism in Italy relates to an experience whose primary references are social. In that case, there can be no denying the ideological nature of its discourse, as it can be shown that the social figure to which it referred – primarily the workers – no longer conformed in any concrete sense to the terrorists' representation and, moreover, that the vast majority of them were opposed to the violence they were supposed to want. But when we are dealing with a cultural rather than a social entity everything becomes complicated, because the discourse that accompanies the violence can easily constitute not so much an ideology, or an abusive and self-justificatory representation of the real, as an imaginary construct that is certainly free-floating, but which can still provide the basis for membership of a community that can grow and convince a population. National movements are often dreamt up by intellectuals who resort to violence in order to awaken their nation before it has come into existence. A nation is, as Benedict Anderson (1983) puts it, an 'imagined community', but those who actively outline its contours and content, and who take up arms to give that political and cultural entity a form and then to liberate it, are not ideologists, even though their 'nation' is a figment of the imagination. That is why, once again, we must be wary of both over-simplistic and over-generous arguments, and be especially careful not to confuse ideologies of a political and social nature with similar discourses that refer to phenomena which are themselves abstract or imagined, and which it would be difficult to reduce to concrete groups or collectives.

A Plethora of Meaning

These remarks about the links between nationalism and violence in fact lead us to a conclusion that applies only to certain experiences and which complements the idea of a meaning-deficit: when it goes together with a loss of meaning, a discursive product does not necessarily take the form of a mythical or ideological aberration that artificially abolishes the distance that divides the real from the aspirations of the actor. When they go hand in hand with violence, discourses and narratives can take many forms other than that of the mythical or ideological reconstructions that allow the actor to reconcile in imaginary and self-justificatory ways things that can no longer be reconciled in practice. The violence is a product of a meaning-deficit, but the emergence of a new meaning can indicate a change of perspective, open up new horizons, and install the actor in a new discursive and practical space.

In a sense, myths and ideology reify the problem the actor is faced with. The actor may, for example, wish to keep the banner of working-class revolution flying high even though the workers' movement is in decline, and may claim to embody hopes and convictions corresponding to a situation that no longer really exists, even though they have undergone major transformations. But when the original points of reference lose their pertinence or utility others can be created or at least used, and the gap can be filled by a new and different meaning.

A social movement supported by a population that is homogeneous in religious terms can, for example, become both violent and increasingly religious. We saw this in the Lebanon, with the movement that was launched in the 1960s under the leadership of the charismatic Imam Moussa Sadr (see Rabinovitch, 1984). It aspired to being a movement of the disinherited. The protagonists were, in this case, certainly Shiites, but the actor was defined in social rather than religious terms. The movement became more and more radical, initially because the Lebanese political system was scarcely in a position to meet its demands – 'and if our demands are not met, we will use force', exclaimed Moussa Sadr – and then because it became caught up in the turmoil of the civil war and the Israeli-Arab conflict when it found itself on the front line in Southern Lebanon. A social figure that announced that it might one day resort to force despite itself became an armed religious actor, one of the components of the Shiite Islamic nebula in Lebanon, and developed a logic of war against Israel. It became, essentially, Hezbollah. This schematic analysis could be extended to many of the other experiences that led to radical Islamism. In some cases, the origins of Islamist movements, and some of the ways in which they develop, do lie in social demands that have not been met by the State or some political power, and that have not been handled in political terms.

This type of transformation leads, then, from the social to the religious. Another process, which belongs to the same sociological family, leads from the national to the religious. The Palestinian movement, which was initially strongly nationalist, with some social or socio-political overtones, has since the 1980s been tempted by forms of extreme violence such as terrorism or martyrdom which claim to be essentially (but not exclusively) Islamic: the excessive violence goes along with the assertion of convictions that go beyond the earlier meaning, rather as though a national action that would otherwise fail had to be given a religious significance. In a situation that is deteriorating and that has been at a standstill ever since the peace process launched in Oslo in 1993 ended in failure, Palestinian despair makes the appeal to a religious meaning seem necessary to some of the population. That meaning seems higher than the meaning that formerly put the struggle on a national basis, but it also seems powerless, too limited, and doomed to fail in historical terms.

When it shores up a meaning that is faltering and supplies points of reference for actors who would otherwise experience the loss of meaning, religion can signal the transition to a stage of extreme violence. Religious belief can in fact come to terms with unrestrained violence by giving meaning to an action that does not restrict its space to the real world as it exists *hic et nunc* by allowing it to combine hopes and convictions for both this world and the next. Those hopes and convictions have a greater import than anything that can be expected of political violence, and hint at the absolute that transforms them into *metapolitical* violence, to use the expression suggested in Chapter 2. The plethora of meaning that a religious faith can supply gives the actor an unheard of, limitless power and a legitimacy that can withstand anything because it is not conferred by any earthly court; it authorises the actor to forbid, or to forbid itself, all concessions and all negotiations, to accept no limits, to dismiss all nuances, and to see anything that threatens or resists as obstacles to be destroyed or enemies to be eliminated.

We must not, however, reduce the excess of meaning that can be supplied by religion to the image of an action that cannot be controlled, that is devoid of all rationality or all political or instrumental concerns. The characteristic feature of the major contemporary phenomena that combine violence with religion or sectarianism, and not just Islam, is that their leaders can be very rational and rigorous, and that they articulate a metapolitical meaning with calculations and strategies that make their action an element in political or geo-political struggles

Self-Destruction

The loss of one meaning and its replacement by another become paroxysmal when the violence is self-destructive, irrespective of whether or not it is also destructive. The theme has sometimes been touched upon with reference to contemporary urban violence in order to suggest, amongst other things, that when young vandals destroy buses, even though they allow them to get out and about, or socio-cultural facilities that have been established for their benefit, they are committed to a logic of self-destruction. This interpretation is in fact too superficial, and often betokens a refusal to look closely at the events, situations and problems that result in violence. The stoning of the bus or the torching of the youth club is almost always part of a bigger story: the bus driver got angry with them or made racist comments. They were fined for travelling without tickets, and that went down badly with the young fare-dodgers' friends. The youth workers had been there for too long, had stopped listening to the young people properly, or were suggesting inappropriate activities …

On the other hand, and to expand upon the above comments on the plethora of meaning and religion, one contemporary phenomenon obviously does have to do with a combination of violence against others and self-destruction: the Islamic cult of martyrdom, in which the individual who kills himself adopts a set of significations that justify his action on two levels. Viewed one way, he may think or wish that his action will make him meaningful to the survivors; viewed another, that it will take him to the better world of the beyond.

Here we can identify at least three types of experience and three distinct logics. The first gives its protagonist a strong identity that has its roots in the community or nation, and a feeling of despair or a conviction that the projects with which he might have identified will end in failure, and a conviction that they can be realised in the next world. Iran's *bassiji* are one example, and Farhad Khosrokhavar has demonstrated the great complexity of their behaviour. Some of these very young men, especially during the phenomenon's final phase in the early 1980s, committed themselves to the war against Iraq in the full knowledge that they would probably not survive. They were looking for a 'worthy' death and, given that they were on the front line, they found it by spreading terror in the enemy's ranks. And they found self-fulfilment in that experience; their suicides fulfilled the promise of a better world that, as they knew, the revolution could no longer keep (Khosrokhavar, 1995; 2001). Over-simplistic arguments notwithstanding, these young martyrs no longer believed in the revolution that had overthrown the Shah's regime. They were acutely conscious that it was over and that it had failed. They thought that, by sacrificing themselves, apparently for the sake of the revolution, they would find themselves in the site of its utopia. For them a morbid religiosity was the only way of expressing their creativity. 'Death was synonymous with salvation' (Khosrokhavar, 1995: 18) and their cult of martyrdom became what Khosrokhavar (2005 [2002]) calls 'martyropathy'.

A second logic once more combines a strong identity anchored in a community, despair bound up with the current situation, and a desire to strike blows at an enemy in order to weaken him and promote the actor's cause. The difference between this and the previous example is that the despair is not fuelled by the fall-out from the hopes and discourses that characterized the period that has just ended, and that the sacrifice is experienced as an urgent military necessity, as a challenge to any enemy who believes himself to be all-powerful. The suicide-bombings carried out on Israeli territory by young Palestinians, especially since the beginning of the second Intifada (October 2000), display all these features. Unlike Iran's young *bassiji*, their authors' primary aim is to influence the political and military in the here and now and not just to project them into what they believe to be a better world, even though they too are inspired by religious convictions. Their nationalism is more powerful, or more despairing, than that of the young *bassiji*.

A third logic, finally, corresponds to actors who have removed themselves from a concrete community in order to join deterritorialized networks, and who are therefore no longer supported by the warmth of the population from which they came, and therefore by the meaning they could give to their action. The authors of the attacks of 11 September 2001 removed themselves from the social and political relations of their society of origin, where they might have been able to enter public life, and distanced themselves from that society's internal problems. Precisely because it could not be inserted into a specific, delineated political space, their extreme violence looked like a struggle that acknowledges no frontiers, or a battle between good and evil on a global scale – which is why some descriptions of Osama Bin Laden's networks refer to a 'global terrorism' whose ideal is related to what Khosrokhavar (2005: 3) calls 'a transnational neo-*Umma*'. These actors acted coldly and prepared their murderous sacrifice over a very long period. Their determination was proportional not only to their despair, but also to the hatred they felt for a modernity in which they had long been immersed, given that they lived in Western Europe or the United States, had been to university, and had taken flying lessons (see Wieviorka, 2002).

Even a rapid evocation of these three logics easily demonstrates that self-destruction cannot be reduced simply to a loss of meaning. It actually implies a plethora of meaning, and a combination of despair, hatred, and a very disappointed relationship with modernity, as well as feelings of communitarian, religious and perhaps national belonging, and perhaps also the hope that the terrorists will find salvation, recognition, happiness, pleasure, and even sexual pleasure, in the next world. The actor exploits an intense subjectivity, and moves from one social and political space to another. Although they are oneiric and situated in the beyond, his actions are very meaningful to him and represent a total commitment, so much so that, in some cases, it surprises even the specialists who are responsible for predicting this kind of violence. The reason why the 11 September 2001 attacks on New York and Washington disconcerted even American anti-terrorism experts is that, in the 1960s and 1970s, international terrorism was the work of individuals and groups who knew they were taking considerable risks, but who had not condemned themselves to certain death. The cult of martyrdom mobilizes a fantastic plethora of meaning. Its actor bestrides two fields: the here and now, and the beyond. He asserts himself as a personal subject within a double temporality, and his violence is a form of hypersubjectivation. And as Khosrokhavar's work clearly shows, hypersubjectivation is not alien to modernity or, more specifically, modern individualism. In the three logics we have identified, the martyr is a subject. He expresses a frustrated desire to be an individual, and is not just what a community tells him to be. In a sense, he even expresses the destructuration of the concrete community he comes from and whose norms have been turned upside down by modernity, thanks to what television, for instance, shows about how sexuality or consumerism functions in the West. The contemporary Islamic martyr finds his vocation 'because the aspiration towards individuality is articulated with membership of a real or imagined community' (Khosrokhavar, 2005: 52).

This takes us a long way from two contrasting ideas that both deny that violent action has meaning. The first is the idea of nihilism. From this perspective, which provides, for example, André Glucksmann, with the key that allows him to understand the terrorism of Bin Laden's networks, self-destruction relates not so much to an invasive despair as to a confused feeling of omnipotence, as it abrogates the right of life and death over all sorts of people and of the total destruction of the meaning of the lives of other people and the actor. The nihilist slogan is, according to Glucksmann (2002: 44), 'nothing to lose, nothing to save' or, as the back cover of his book has it, 'I kill, therefore I am'. Which leads to a suggestion that shows that Glucksmann sees elements in the American mass media or great literature that can help us to understand 'globalized nihilism'. 'We must', he exclaims, 'use Dostoyevsky to sub-title CNN'. If our approach is justified that explanation is quite inadequate and superficial, and shows no understanding of the actors' behaviour or the processes that give rise to it. The least than can be said is that these actors do believe in something – and that is the very opposite of nihilism.

The second idea, which merits further discussion as it sustains some important theoretical and historical debates, is that of the absence of meaning. It means that, for the violent behaviours in question, there is no actor and, *a fortiori*, no subject, but merely agents or pawns who obey orders and submit without any qualms to some authority. They are no more than its executive agents. And it is the non-meaning hypothesis that we will examine now.

Note

1 See Arendt (1985 [1951]); on the relationship between sociology and ideology, see Wieviorka (2003).

6

THE NON-MEANING HYPOTHESIS

The thesis that associates violence with a complete absence of meaning or with 'non-meaning' rather than with a loss of meaning or, symmetrically and perhaps at the same time, a plethora of meaning, or with either a deficit or an excess of meaning, exonerates the author of acts of violence from all responsibility and relieves him of all guilt. There is nothing new about the debates that this approach can inspire. Evoking Primo Levi in his preface to the French translation of Christopher Browning's *Ordinary Men* (2001), Pierre Vidal-Naquet recalls that 'there is nothing new about this problem as it was raised by Etienne de La Boétie (who died in 1563) in his famous *Discourse on Voluntary Servitude'*.[1]

The real debate developed, however, around Nazi war criminals, not so much at the time of the Nuremberg trials of the immediate post-war period as from the 1960s onwards, and especially when Adolph Eichmann was put on trial in Jerusalem, and in 1963 when Hannah Arendt's on-the-spot press reports were republished in the very controversial *Eichmann in Jerusalem* (Arendt, 1977 [1962]).

The banality of evil

In 1960, Adolf Eichmann, who was one of those responsible for the 'Final Solution', was kidnapped by the Israeli secret services in Argentina, where he had found refuge after the war, and put on trial before an Israeli court. Hannah Arendt covered the trial for the *New Yorker* and her reports, republished in *Eichmann in Jerusalem: A Report on the Banality of Evil*, gave rise to several controversies. It is the central controversy that is of interest to us. When she speaks of the banality of evil in connection with Eichmann, Arendt is suggesting that the extreme violence of the Nazis who destroyed the Jews of Europe, especially in the case of the intermediaries and those who simply obeyed orders, may well correspond to nothing more than a culture of obedience or passivity. She notes (1977 [1962]: 25) that 'he was perfectly sure that he was not what he called an *innerer Schweinehund*, a dirty bastard in the depths of his heart; and as for his conscience, he remembered perfectly well that he would have had a bad conscience only if he had not done what he had been ordered to do'.When interviewed by the police, he stated that 'he would have killed his own father if he had received an order to that effect' (ibid: 22). She then adds (ibid: 49): 'The longer one listened to him, the more obvious it became that his inability to speak was closely connected with an inability to *think*, namely to think from the standpoint of someone else. No communication was possible with him, not because he lied but because he was surrounded by the most reliable of all safeguards against the world and the presence of others, and hence against reality as such'.

From this perspective, the executioner or criminal is defined by his passivity, by his indifference to what he does. He merely carries out the bureaucratic tasks he has been set. He is in no sense a subject, and is as far removed as possible from any logic of subjectivation. He is no more than an agent.

Obedience to authority

A few years later, a series of psycho-sociological experiments in a sense gave Hannah Arendt's central idea a new lease of life. Gordon Allport, who was one of the great figures in social psychology, called them 'the Eichmann experiment'. Stanley Milgram asked, in various ways, a number of individuals who had been invited to take part in an academic study to obey the orders of the experimenter (Milgram, 2005 [1974]). They were told to give increasingly powerful electric shocks to someone sitting on the other side of a glass partition whenever that person made a mistake in a learning and memory test. The person who suffered the electric shock was in fact a colleague who was miming pain, and there was in reality no electricity involved. The person administering the electric shocks sometimes stopped quite quickly because he was sickened by the gratuitous violence he was inflicting. Others asked no questions, appeared to have no scruples, and went further in obeying the experimenter's instructions, despite the terrible pain they thought they were inflicting and even though they could see it. The famous experiments were repeated, *ne varietur* or with variations, hundreds of times by different researchers, and were later filmed. They suggested that when agents who are obedient to authority are asked to commit the worst forms of barbarism, they may well fail to see it for what it is and will remain insensitive or indifferent to what they are doing.

Whereas Hannah Arendt put the emphasis on a culture of obedience, Stanley Milgram (2005 (1974): 208) stressed the importance of the situation: 'Often, it is not so much the kind of person a man is as the kind of situation in which he finds himself that determines how he will act'. Judging by these experiments, it is possibly to use violence without being sadistic or cruel, and without feeling any aggressive impulses: 'The act of shocking the victim does not stem from aggressive urges but from the fact that the subjects have become integrated into a social structure and are unable to get out of it' (ibid: 167). Milgram does not, however, necessarily reject the cultural dimensions emphasized by Arendt and does not, in the case of Nazism, underestimate the fact that the Jews had been systematically devalued for years, and that this may have prepared the German people to accept their destruction: 'Systematic devaluation of the victim provides a measure of justification for the brutal treatment of the victims and has been the constant accompaniment of massacres, pogroms, and wars' (ibid: 11).

Milgram found that some of those who took part in his experiments were greatly torn between the moral values that made it unacceptable to inflict electric shocks on their victims, and the obedience that led them to do so. He observed the results, which could be expressed in all sorts of ways, including nervous laughter. One 'subject' told him (ibid: 55): 'I don't know if you were watching me, but my reactions were giggly, and trying to stifle laughter. This isn't the way I usually am. This was a sheer reaction to a totally impossible situation. And my reaction was to the situation of having to hurt somebody. And being totally helpless and caught up in a set of circumstances where I just couldn't deviate and I couldn't try to help'. This important comment raises a major issue: violence can be distressing for the person who inflicts it, even when it seems that he is simply obeying orders and that his conscience or subjectivity should therefore be untroubled. The violence does not always succeed in silencing his conscience, and is therefore accompanied by symptoms that will recall or signal its existence.

The barbarity of 'ordinary men'

After political philosophy in the early 1960s (Hannah Arendt) and then social psychology (Stanley Milgram, ten years later), it was history that took up the debate in the 1990s, thanks mainly to Christopher Browning's important (2001 [1992]) study, which is based on his research into the legal archives on the acts of violence committed by a Nazi battalion on the Eastern front during the Second World War. In Poland, Reserve Police Battalion 101, which was made up of 'ordinary men' and not active members of the Nazi party, found itself in situations where it was ordered to carry out the large-scale massacre of Jews. Operations of this type had begun with an order to select some of the Jews in the village of Jozefow for transport to a labour camp, and to shoot the rest.

How, Browning asks himself, did these ordinary men turn into 'professional killers' after their commanding officer Wilhelm Trapp asked some of them, including the oldest members of the battalion, to say, if they wished, that they did not feel up to taking part in the mission? Can we speak of mere obedience to authority in their case? It is a tempting idea. But the further we go into the events and the analysis, the weaker that idea becomes. Browning's book allows us to demonstrate the limitations of Hannah Arendt's thesis, even when it is backed up by Stanley Milgram's contribution to the debate.

The limitations of a thesis

Stanley Milgram has sometimes been criticized on the grounds that his demonstration was of limited importance because of the very way the work was carried out. The experiments took place in a laboratory and very small numbers were involved. Those who took part were mobilized for only a very short time – scarcely one hour in most cases – and there were no further consequences. If we look at Nazi violence, however, everything changes: the timescale and the density of the mediations between the most minor actors and the rest of the Nazi system. There is no reason to think that we can simply move directly from the laboratory to historical reality and, as Neil J. Kressel notes (2002 [1996]: 168): 'Insofar as Milgram's experimental situation differs in so many essential aspects from the circumstances surrounding mass atrocities in the real world, the study *proves* little about how such crimes could occur'. Milgram's approach tells us nothing as such about the specific historical, social, political, and cultural conditions that lead to such atrocities. It dehistoricizes and depoliticizes their explanation in favour of the general principle of obedience; if the situation is conducive to such behaviour, individuals will obey orders (see also Orne and Holland, 1968). Even so, the fact that Milgram's psycho-social experiments are far removed from any concrete historical action does not provide grounds for dismissing his contribution. On the contrary, his main inspiration played an important role in recent debates about mass atrocities from the late 1980s onwards (Kelman and Hamilton, 1989).

From the perspective that Arendt applies to Eichmann, the criminal is an agent. His mental or psychological passivity towards his own acts, which for him are simply a matter of carrying out bureaucratic orders, and his indifference to their specificity – involvement in mass murder – mean that he is an individual who has been desubjectivated or has never been subjectivated. From that point of view, we are dealing with a non-subject, and definitely not with an anti-subject who has inverted the categories of subjectivation in order to assert himself through the practice of violence itself. The protagonist of the violence is a cog in a machine that makes one think of a system without actors. He obeys laws and orders, and does his duty, as Eichmann said over and over again during his trial: 'Eichmann claimed more than once that his organizational gifts, the coordination of evacuations and deportations achieved by his office, had in fact helped his victims; it had made their fate easier' (Arendt, 1977 [1962]: 190).

THE NON-MEANING HYPOTHESIS

Can we accept the idea that a figure like Eichmann was neither concerned about nor personally involved in his own actions? When it is on such a scale that it becomes possible to speak of the banality of evil, is the system of organized violence a system without actors? If that is the case, anyone involved in the system is ultimately absolved of all responsibility, with the possible exception of a few leaders. Many other senior Nazis – such as Rudolph Hoess, Hermann Göring, Wilhelm Keitel, and Albert Speer – used 'obedience' to explain their actions and even claimed, when their sentence was being passed, that they felt no particular hatred for Jews. Yet investigations and a careful study of the available documents, both written reports and interviews, invalidate that line of defence which simply does not stand up to empirical investigation. When, for instance, Gitta Sereny (1995) was interviewing Albert Speer, she forced him into a corner and made him admit that he did indeed know something about the Final Solution, despite the denials that had allowed him to escape the death penalty at Nuremberg. Speer had only one thing left to say: he thanked God that Sereny had not been one of the Nuremberg prosecutors. There may have been an element of obedience to authority in these Nazi leaders' experience, but there was also a lot of initiative, and an active and an willing involvement in evil.

When applied to those who did no more than stand by and watch as the barbarism took place, the theme of their supposed indifference does not hold up as well as one might think, as we can clearly understand if we read Czeslaw Milosz (1981 [1959]). He suggests that the terrible indifference of the Poles who saw Jews being taken away to a sinister destination with their own eyes in fact masked much more ambiguous feelings.[2] And when it comes to those who were actively involved the thesis obviously has to be called into question, not only in the case of the officers in charge but also for those who merely followed orders. Claude Lanzmann, for example, questions it when he describes himself as 'resolutely opposed to Hannah Arendt's banality of evil thesis. All the men and all these consciences knew what they were doing and what they were involved in: the guard at Treblinka, the railway bureaucrat and the administrator of the Warsaw Ghetto knew' (Lanzmann, 1986: 36). But perhaps we do have to admit that at least some of those who 'knew' were primarily motivated by their need to obey because the culture of obedience had permeated their very being.

The idea of the banality of evil, 'the fearsome, word-and-thought defying *banality of evil*' (Arendt, 1977 [1962]: 252) or the related but less profound idea of bureaucratic violence, or simply carrying out orders or following instructions, is intolerable because it dissociates the actor from the meaning and import of his acts. Hannah Arendt knows full well that the Nazis were inspired by an historical project and were convinced that they were on an exceptional mission. From her perspective, some were responsible for defining the meaning of that mission, whilst others carried it out, as difficult or psychologically painful as it may have been. The actor who corresponds to the banality of evil hypothesis is dissociated from those who were, in one way or another, motivated by their emotions, hatred, or project, and from those who took a sadistic pleasure in inflicting violence. Thus, Arendt (1977 [1962]: 105) cites Himmler addressing the leaders of the *Einstazgruppen*, the high SS and police leaders: 'We realize that what we are expecting from you is '"superhuman", to be "superhumanly inhuman"'. She also specifically states (ibid: 105) that the Nazis 'were not sadists or killers by nature; on the contrary, a systematic attempt was made to weed out all those who derived physical pleasure from what they did ... So that instead of saying: What horrible things I did to people! the murderer would be able to say: What horrible things I had to watch in the pursuance of my duties, how heavily the task weighed upon my shoulders' (ibid: 105, 106) .

The banality of evil thesis leads to the admission that human beings can behave in extremely barbaric ways without knowing or feeling what they are doing, as though they were not motivated by hatred or any other passion. 'This type of criminal', writes Arendt (ibid: 176), 'commits his crimes under circumstances that make it well-nigh impossible for him to know or to feel that he is going wrong'. Eichmann was 'terrifyingly normal' (ibid: 276). This raises a serious legal problem: can we conclude that a crime has been committed when the author does not have the ability to tell the difference between good and evil? Eichmann, Arendt tells us (ibid: 287–8), *'never realized what he was doing ...* He was not stupid. It was sheer thoughtlessness ... that predisposed him to become one of the greatest criminals of that period'. From this point of view, the failure to distinguish between good and evil stems from the absence of any capacity for reflexivity, of the ability to stand back and give a meaning to the violence perpetrated against other human beings.

When the banality of evil explanation does seem to be valid, it refers to agents who are not actors because they exist outside any moral framework and recognize only the principle of obedience to a political authority or the State. Any individual refusal to obey orders and the law is, in these circumstances, a refusal to conform to the rules and laws embodied in the State, whereas for the individuals concerned the only rule that applies is the rule of obeying orders rather than relying on their own moral judgement. This leads Zigmunt Bauman (1993: 13) to say that, from this point of view, 'the stubborn and resilient autonomy of the moral self ... is viewed as the germ of chaos and anarchy'. If he is right, the modern age is one in which reason replaces ethics, in which the State and the market have the effect of 'putting the moral conscience to sleep'. Then there is the impact of technology, which fragments the moral subject' (Christensen, 1998: 64). The life of the moral subject is no more than a sequence of multiple, disparate, processes. Each of them is partial, and therefore ready and able to argue that it is morally not guilty.

It is possible that, when certain people are in the right situation, their violent behaviour does reflect the banality of evil. They obey orders, and their only passion is obedience to some legitimate authority, usually the power of a state. No questions are asked about how that state came into being, or about what popular effects it may have crystallized. But what is the actual arena of this aspect of obedience? How does it relate to the loss of meaning or a plethoric meaning, or to cruelty, and violence for the sake of violence or for the sake of the pleasure it affords, which we will look at in greater depth in the next chapter? At this point it is helpful to look more closely at Christopher Browning's fine historical study, which is both sensitive and detailed.

Police Battalion 101 was initially characterized by behaviours that were sadistic and cruel, but had little to do with obedience (Browning, 2001 [1992]: 11–12).

> The action (in Bialystok on 27 June 1941) began as a pogrom: beating, beard burning and shooting at will as the policeman drove Jews to the marketplace or synagogue. When several Jewish leaders appeared at the headquarters of the 221st Security Division of General Pflugbeil and knelt at his feet, begging for army protection, one member of Police Battalion 309 unzipped his fly and urinated on them while the General turned his back. What started as a pogrom quickly escalated into more systematic mass murder.

On 27 October, another act of mass murder was the subject of a report from the Regional Commander in Slutsk (Lithuania): 'What else concerns this action, I must to my greatest regret emphasize, is last of all that it bordered on sadism', wrote the official (Browning, 2001 [1992]: 21), who went on to describe scenes of unheard-of violence. He was all the more outraged in that he was thinking in economic terms about the far from negligible role the Jews played in this region, and argued that there was no political rationale for exterminating them. Browning (ibid: 41) also describes how the men amused themselves. While the battalion was guarding the Warsaw ghetto, 'the company recreation room was decorated with racist slogans, and a Star of David hung above the bar. A mark was made on the bar door for each Jew shot, and "victory celebrations" were reportedly held on days when high scores were recorded'. In Lodz, 'the guards on the thoroughfare that cut between the two halves of the Lodz ghetto occasionally amused themselves by setting their watches ahead as a pretext for seizing and beating up Poles who were allegedly violating the curfew' (ibid: 41). Later in his book, Browning provides a description of the particularly repugnant figure of Lieutenant Gnade, who was a 'brutal, sadistic drunkard' (ibid: 151) and evokes Sergeant Heinrich Bekemeier, who 'forced a group of Jews to crawl through a mud puddle while singing. When an exhausted old man collapsed and raised his hands to Bekermeier, begging for mercy, the sergeant shot him in the mouth' (ibid: 152).

The many precise and well-documented details take us a long way from the banality of evil and obedience to authority theses. Browning's analyses do, however, touch, albeit less often, on the bureaucratic handling of the Jewish question, and he does so in terms that do support those theses. Everything to do with the rail transports of Jews becomes caricatural – and Raoul Hillberg also draws attention to similar points in his standard (1961 [1955]) account. Browning (2001 [1992]: 33) cites a report complaining that 'the excessively great overloading of most of the cars with 180 to 200 Jews was catastrophic in a way that had tremendously adverse effects on the transport'.

What Browning in fact shows is the interplay between the bureaucrats who organized the destruction and those who carried it out. The latter 'were not desk murderers who could take refuge in distance, routine, and bureaucratic euphemisms that veiled the reality of mass murder ... What happened to the men as the killing stretched on week after week, month after month?' he asks (ibid: 36) How did 'a group of normal middle-aged German men [become] mass murderers'?

There was nothing automatic about their metamorphosis, and in fact it met with some moral resistance, which was itself mingled with a more elementary feeling of disgust. Some members of the battalion refused to take part in the massacres. Trapp, its commanding officer, was unhappy about having to organize this terrible mission. He said he was in 'distress', and complained 'Man ... such jobs don't suit me' (ibid: 58). He wept in private and complained about the orders he was carrying out. Many claimed to find the work repugnant. Some killed but did so selectively: no infants and no small children. Others reacted to the situation by having themselves assigned to other duties and avoiding direct involvement in the killings. Some approached Kramer 'after shooting for some time ... and said they could not continue' (ibid: 62). Others systematically and deliberately missed their targets, and some hid during the killings. All this is far removed from an obedience to authority, but it is also far removed from jouissance and violence for the sake of violence. When someone '"organized" a supply of alcohol for the shooters' at 'some point in the afternoon' (ibid: 61), he was not giving them a treat but making it easier for them to get on with their work. At the end of the day, 'the men were depressed, angered, embittered and shaken. They ate little but drank heavily' (ibid: 69), and felt a sense of shame and horror. Some were later found to be suffering from what were obviously psycho-somatic illnesses. Moral considerations aside this was pure horror, and it demoralized the troops. At least to begin with.

Three logics were at work in the experiences of these 'ordinary men'. They were contradictory and there was considerable tension between them. Bureaucratic logic, which was itself a servant of the Nazi project, would have liked its orders to be carried out by zealous and obedient agents who were indifferent to the meaning of their acts. It came into conflict with, on the one hand, a logic of excess, cruelty, and sadism that went far beyond bureaucratic logic and perverted it and, on the other hand, with a moral logic that resisted evil, found that murder was a step too far, and was mingled with a powerful feeling of horror and disgust.

The logic of obedience to authority needs to combat the logic of morality, and that of good. It must do so if the mass murders are to go on and if the killers are to become hardened. The role of power, the chain of command, leaders and strategies is to set in motion a process of hardening that takes away the disgust, repugnance, shame and horror, or to outline a sort of division of labour. The good policemen in the battalion take charge of the phase that proceeds mass murder in the strict sense, and will not come directly face to face with the horror, whilst others take responsibility for the killings. The killings were, in this case, left to the *Trawniki*, or auxiliaries recruited from the USSR's border regions because of their anti-Communism or anti-Semitism. They were capable of doing the dirtiest jobs, especially when drunk on spirits. The work was usually done in collaboration: it was done more quickly because alcohol was freely available and because the *Trawniki* did much of the real killing, often in the form of shootings that took away the characteristic feature of the earliest massacres: the face-to-face encounter between killer and victim. Mass murder had reached the phase when killing become depersonalized. Even on the Eastern front, which was very different to the world of the camps and the deportations, a cold, bureaucratic organization was beginning to emerge, and it made the killers' job easier.

Browning's analyses clearly show how cold bureaucracy and obedience on the one hand, and anti-Semitic passions and sadistic pleasure on the other, can coexist without coming into conflict. The combination of the two helped to defeat the logic of revulsion, which has less to do with humanism or morality than with disgust, pure and simple. And there comes a moment when there is no more need for the *Trawniki* and their like, when the battalion's men can kill with fewer scruples: 'They become increasingly efficient and calloused executioners' (Browning, 2001 [1992]: 77).

But the coldness of 'ordinary men' who have become hardened owes nothing to bureaucratic or administrative logic. They are not little Eichmanns, and the banality of the evil they do differs from that of Hannah Arendt's thesis. It is a product of a concrete process in which morality has been destroyed by the organized experience of practical killing. The starting point is certainly characterized by obedience to authority, but this coldness is a construct and it is not inherent in the culture of obedience. It is the result or product of experience, and not a basic given. It owes a great deal to the skills, even if they are at times rudimentary, of those who organize such massacres, either on the spot but usually from afar, and want them to take place. In other cases, in which state power plays a less dominant role, the outcome might be different. The violence might be just as cruel, as Zimbardo's experiments (to which we will return) appear to suggest. They demonstrate that sadism can easily appear in certain situations, and we will come back to them. But in this case, 'ordinary men' became cold killers because that is what the Nazi leadership wanted them to become.

The obedience to authority thesis applies to them, at best, *in fine* and not at the beginning of or even during their trajectory. Even at that stage, it can, moreover, be challenged by a different hypothesis. We find traces of it in Browning's book, and it does in a sense reintroduce the meaning of the killers' behaviour. Did they, or some of them, act as they did because they wanted to conform, did not want to dissociate themselves from their group, or from their comrades' or leaders' perception of them? 'By breaking ranks', remarks Browning (ibid: 184–5), 'nonshooters were leaving the "dirty work" to their comrades. Since the battalion had to shoot even if individuals did not, refusing to shoot constituted refusing one's share of an unpleasant collective obligation'.

The banality of evil thesis and the very closely related obedience-to-authority thesis turn the violence of both the Nazi experience on the Eastern front and Eichmann's wartime behaviour into a cold and instrumental behaviour whose goals elude the conscience and will of those who indulge in it in the field. Ultimately, it is possible for evil to be banal only when evil itself is legitimate. And in a Westphalian world, evil is legitimate when the State itself is criminal and elaborates a criminal project, when legitimacy is supplied by a principle that is at once human and superior. Evil becomes an 'act of state', and an expression of *raison d'Etat*. The question then becomes: what makes the killer a criminal when he is acting within the law?

But as we have seen the banality of evil is not self-evident, even in such circumstances. Some of the killers were willing volunteers who took pleasure in what they were doing. Their superiors clearly wanted nothing to do with them. Others resisted in one way or another, which indicates a certain insight into the non-banality of what they were doing. And whilst obedience to authority may have had something to do with the experience of 'ordinary men', it was not a normal attitude and was not part of their culture. It was inculcated into them by a process in which they themselves were in many respects terrorised, manipulated, or at least conditioned. All this does not completely negate either Hannah Arendt's initial inspiration or the implications of Stanley Milgram's experiments. But it does show that they have serious limitations: it is difficult to accept that violence, and especially extreme violence, can occur in circumstances in which there is no meaning at all, or that it is unrelated, in either positive or negative terms, to certain significations or values, perverted or distorted as they may be. Unless – and this is the question we have to look at now – it is inspired or governed by a pleasure principle.

Notes

1 Pierre Vidal-Naquet, Preface to Christopher Browning, *Des Hommes Ordinaires*, Paris: Les Belles Lettres, 1994: xxiv–xxv.
2 On the theme of indifference as a mechanism for denying one's own actions, see the interesting comments of Stanley Cohen (2001).

7

CRUELTY

Why, in so many experiences, must the violence be so excessive? Why does it descend into madness, gratuitous cruelty, or sadism? In some cases, the violence appears to be completely determined by a quest for the pleasure it affords the person who inflicts it; in such cases, it becomes an end in itself and we have to speak of violence for the sake of violence. In other cases it is, rather, the circumstances that make the excesses possible and that permit a cruelty which is certainly very real but secondary in that it begins only as the action proceeds. If the violence is collective, only some of the actors will behave in this way. The reasons for the violence and the excesses sometimes derive their meaning from the *jouissance* the protagonist expects to get from them, but can go far beyond that, unless it is of a different nature and escapes the analysis to such an extent that it can only be put down to madness. In certain cases, even its most useless or superfluous aspects still seem to have some function or a finality that is not restricted to either the direct effects of the destruction or murder, or the liberation of the author's affects and drives. In all these cases, violence for the sake of violence, cruelty, and sadism present anyone who is trying to conceptualize violence with a paradoxical challenge: these aspects of the phenomenon are extreme and often appear to be marginal. They emerge on the fringes of what we spontaneously call 'violence' rather than at its heart, and yet they do constitute its most central core because it is there that we find its purest, most naked and radical form. Perhaps we should even take the view that they do more than any other dimension to define violence.

Excess, *Jouissance*, and Madness

It is not always easy to strike a balance between the meaning, which may be distorted, partly lost or reduced, for example, to an ideological form as it may be, that is expressed through violence, and the savagery and cruelty of the violence itself, which can appear to have nothing to do with its meaning.

Historians have often raised this issue. Pierre Laborie (1996), for instance, raises it in connection with the violence of the post-war 'purges' in France, and admits that, having noted that some of these acts of violence were politically inspired, he is not convinced that 'the logics of the political explain them all'. He suggests that their origins may also lie 'in the opaque regions of depth psychology'. When, in his inaugural lecture to the Collège de France (11 April 1986), Maurice Agulhon looked at the French Revolution and, more specifically, the 'frenzied madness of the Revolutionary Tribunal' and the 'savagery of the infernal columns in the Vendée', he asked himself: 'Did the bloody mass murderers of those terrible years act as they did for ideological reasons, and was this extreme violence an element of Jacobinism, or was it a phenomenon that had broken free from Jacobinism?'

In certain experiences, the violence is from the outset a phenomenon in itself and for itself, and appears to have no end but violence itself. In others, it is only as events unfold that it comes to look like violence for the sake of violence. The excesses and gratuitousness appear and become autonomous only as events unfold, or only when a certain point has been reached. They are part of a process, and may eventually manifest themselves in a 'pure' way. They become dissociated from the meanings that gave rise to them. As Agulhon has shown, this question is central to historiographical debates, and political debates, about the Revolution of 1789, and about the continuity between 1789 and 1793.

In both these cases, this aspect of violence is what Wolfgang Sofsky (1996) describes as 'absolute' and it needs no justification. It obeys its own laws, and no others.

Violence for the sake of violence can occur in many different situations. It may be a matter of mere delinquency or classic criminality, as is often the case in sex crimes, paedophilia, and rape.

The famous case of Gilles de Rais, who committed some abominable child murders in the fifteenth century, and who was evoked by Georges Bataille in his day, and then by Wolfgang Sofsky, can serve as an illustration. His cruelty, which in some respects prefigures the writings of the Marquis de Sade, seems to have a meaning that transcends it. We find in it the *jouissance* of excess, and a sneering contempt for his victims' suffering that goes beyond the emotional level. We see an indifference born of habit and the repetitive ritual of a *mise en scène*. The slaughter is carefully regulated. Sofsky calls this 'the creativity of excess'.

Violence for the sake of violence can also be related to so-called urban violence. In a superbly written book, Bill Buford (1992), for instance, describes the most extreme forms of British hooliganism and shows how some supporters are in fact not interested in football as a spectacle or even in the outcome of the match. For them, the match is no more than something that gives them the opportunity to run wild. Their violence is brutal, bestial, and tribal, and purely hedonistic. They attack not only the other team's supporters but anyone who gets in their way outside the ground, starting with the police. Their violence goes far beyond that of the 'wreckers' who tag along on demonstrations and use them as a pretext for troublemaking, fights and vandalism. Such violence has no social or political meaning and is totally ludic. It has nothing to do with the sporting event that provides the excuse. Meaning disappears completely and gives way to non-meaning and the complete desocialization of subjects who have been reduced to an animal level.

Most descriptions of violence for the sake of violence associated it, as we have said previously, with various forms of criminality and especially with wartime situations. A study of American veterans who fought in Vietnam by Richard Strayer and Lewis Ellenhorn (1975; cited in Bourke, 1999) shows that all the men who had been heavily involved in combat, and one third of those who had had some involvement, had witnessed atrocities or had themselves helped to kill non-combatants. One episode from this war hit the headlines. The My Lai massacre, which was certainly not exceptional, horrified America and the rest of the world because it made the abuses committed by the American army in the field obscenely obvious.

Let us recall the facts. On 16 March 1968, the 11th American Brigade's Charlie Company entered the village of My Lai. By midday its men had murdered 500 unarmed civilians, many of them with bayonets. They laughed as they sodomised and raped the women, using knives to cut open their vaginas in some cases. They scalped the corpses. Lieutenant Calley, who commanded the company, was the only one to be brought to trial. He was found guilty and admitted responsibility for the butchery. He had no doubts: even babies could be enemies, he explained.

The enjoyment of inflicting violence is a constant in the eye-witness accounts given by veterans of recent wars. William Broyles, a former US Marine and editor of the *Texas Monthly* and *Newsweek*, cited by Joanna Bourke, states that when veterans are asked about their experience they say they hated it, that they do not want to talk about it, and that they would prefer it to be 'buried'. But there is also something else: 'somewhere inside themselves they loved it too' (Bourke, 1999: 13). Broyles also described what his men had done to a North Vietnamese soldier they had recently killed: 'They had propped the corpse up against some C-rations, placed sunglasses across his eyes and a cigarette in his mouth, and balanced a "large and perfectly formed" piece of shit on his head'. As an officer, Broyles was outraged, but 'inside ... I was laughing' (1999: 15).

Similarly, John Dower gives terrible descriptions of the atrocities committed by both the Japanese and the Americans during the war in the Pacific. Some American troops cut off the hands of Japanese soldiers for trophies, whilst other collected gold teeth, scalps, or even skulls, toes, and penises. Dower (1986: 66) comments that 'It would have been inconceivable, however, that teeth, ears and skulls could have been collected from German or Italian war dead'.

In wartime, cruelty can involve mocking the victim or fooling around with his body, dead or alive. But it usually involves treating him as an animal. In 1944, Charles Lindbergh lived as a civilian observer with US forces based in New Guinea. He was horrified by the barbarity he witnessed, and noted in his journal that: 'Our men … treat the Japs with less respect than they would give to an animal' (cited Dower, 1986: 70). Violence of this kind can also take the form of a competition in which everyone tries to outdo everyone else – killing more enemies than anyone else then becomes a game. It may involve collecting souvenirs and trophies: the killer has himself photographed with one foot on the corpse, cuts off a scalp or the ears, tears out teeth and fingers … Charles Lindbergh also recounts how, on his way back from Asia, American customs officers in Hawaii asked him if he was bringing back any Japanese bones in his luggage. It was, they told him, just a routine question. One could go on with the more recent example of the war in Iraq and the acts of cruelty that go with it, on the part of both American troops and the private companies on which they rely. The excessive cruelties inflicted in Abu Ghraib prison, for example, were reported all over the world.

In some experiences, finally, it seems that we are faced with something that goes beyond excess and defies all understanding. In his study of violence in the Maya country of Guatemala in the early 1980s, Yvon le Bot (1992) looks at monstrous, incomprehensible outbursts, and strange, 'mad', or irrational behaviour (the soldiers separated the women from the men even though they were going to kill them all). It was as though some delirium had taken hold of them. This was neither pleasure, *jouissance*, nor rationality: this was madness. As Le Bot demonstrates, the madness is not necessarily absolute or complete. It may be combined with rational elements, so much so that it seems that Jacques Semelin's notion of 'delirious rationality' might be applicable to some massacres. Delirious rationality is a combination of cold calculation and madness and corresponds, in Semelin's view, to 'two psychiatric realities. The first is a "psychotic"-type attitude towards an other who has to be destroyed … The psychotic element of the relationship between the killer and his future victim lies in the denial of the "barbarian" other's humanity. "Delirious" can also mean a paranoiac representation of the other, who is perceived as a threat or even as the incarnation of evil' (Semelin, 2001).

The acts of violence we have evoked range from Gilles de Rais to what happened in the Maya country, but they all belong to the same family. There is an excessive, gratuitous side to this violence. We might say that it has its 'accursed share', had not Georges Bataille already given that strong expression a different meaning. But even within this family, there are considerable differences.

Jouissance

Cruelty, as evoked and analysed by Wolfgang Sofsky, is pure libibo or what, referring to torturers, he calls the pleasure of expanding the ego. It is particularly common in acts of mass murder, when violence for the sake of violence has no purpose beyond itself. Violence enjoys total freedom. It has no meaning outside itself. The only meaning of the destruction is destruction. The violence is in control of events. The collective excesses are divorced from any political or social ends. If, according to Sofsky, we wish to understand the practice of mass murder, and how it unfolds, we therefore have to look at how it is perpetrated and not at its goals.

In this perspective, the use of cruelty in mass murder means a liberation of the drives. If we accept Sofsky's argument, it involves the killer's sensuality, a complete loss of inhibitions, and physical pleasure: the killer wants to wade through blood, and to feel what he is doing with his hands and fingers. The good thing about this image is that it brings us closer to the word's etymology because, as Clément Rosset points out (1988: 18), '*cruor*, which is the etymological root of *crudelis* (raw, difficult to digest), refers to scorched, bloody flesh, or in other words naked flesh that has been skinned. It has been therefore reduced to its stark reality and is as bloody as it is difficult to digest'. In some cases, it seems that the physical pleasure is indifferent to the suffering of the victim, or is not informed by it. In others, the victim has to be aware of the pain he suffers if the killer's satisfaction is to be complete. Alphonse, who was one of the Tutsi killers Jean Hatzfeld met, explained to him that the babies were killed more rapidly than the children and the adults: 'The babies could not understand the why of the suffering, it was not worth lingering over them' (Hatzfeld, 2008b: 123). Here, the cruelty includes a message to the victim, who had to understand why he is being hurt. Which suggests that, at least in this experience, the *jouissance* is not just a matter of physical pleasure, and that something else is involved, as the pleasure is possible only if the victim is capable of understanding what is happening to him.

No matter whether they are the primary source of the violence or whether it is the violence that provokes them, sadism and cruelty seem therefore to call for explanations that lead to the idea or image of the irresistible unleashing of a psychic force, or the quasi-sexual pleasure of destroying the other with one's own hands in a murderously bloody fashion. It is close to delirium. Such phenomena appear to result from the activation of hitherto forbidden and hidden archaic or primal drives which are set free when circumstances allow them to emerge. Understanding them may therefore require us to use psychoanalytic categories that can explain intrapsychic tensions and the mechanisms that shape or permit their expression. When 'pure', 'absolute' violence, or violence in and for itself, has to be discussed, psychoanalysis is constantly evoked, no matter whether we are talking about experiences where it appears to result in an instinctual satisfaction, or whether we are talking about a barbarism that stems from pure madness. Jacques Derrida (2000a), for example, takes the view that what we call 'psychoanalysis' is that which, without any theological or other alibis, looks at what is *cleanest* about psychic cruelty. He cites Einstein's letter to Freud, and the argument that, if the power drive and cruel impulses are older and more archaic that the pleasure principle and the reality, which are basically the same, no policies can eradicate them. From this point of view, cruelty is associated with power and the question of the State.

Is cruelty always a clear indication that there is no meaning involved, irrespective of whether it inspires the violence or is triggered by and, so to speak, complements it? Is it devoid of any meaning, and does the pleasure it affords relate to a dimension of the personal subject that apparently exists outside the social and outside culture to a purely biological human nature, and can it be reduced to a psychic economy? Or can we find some meaning in it, even when there appears to be none?

The Functionality of Cruelty

Although still superficial, my first comment is in fact a warning: whilst it may look purely gratuitous and may seem to be violence for the sake of violence, the most extreme cruelty may well be meaningful, at least from the author's point of view. Criminologists are very familiar with this: a crime may well be accompanied by what appears to be pointless acts of cruelty, but they may in fact result from a certain logic and often have a symbolic import. We saw this earlier, when we evoked the psychiatrist James Gilligan's discussion of the case of Ross L. Although the mutilations he inflicted on his victim may look absurd or laughable, it is possible to find more than gratuitousness and non-meaning in them.

This example suggests that we should never make the over-hasty diagnosis that postulates that extreme violence is purely instinctual, an expression of drives, *jouissance*, or dementia. The case of Ross L. is relatively easy to understand in classic anthropological terms. All mutilations of the eyes, mouth, and genitals are highly symbolic and laden with meaning, even though they do not function at the level of reason or rational thought. They may even have a certain functionality. In the case of Ross L their function was magical, as they took away his shame. They also had the more instrumental function of delivering a message. The games that are played with the corpses of those who have been killed in a massacre represent a combination of symbolic dimensions and a sadism that its future victims and the population that is under attack will understand only too well. Germàn Guzman gives some striking examples in his (1962) book on the *Violencia*, or the years of great violence in Colombia.[1] Both the troops of the armed forces and the guerrilla groups adopted their own style of 'cutting' (*corte*). The 'vest cut' (*corte de franela*) consisted of tying the victim to a tree and inflicting a long, deep cut at the base of the neck; the 'tie cut' (*corte de corbata*) was made under the lower jaw – the incision made it possible to extract the tongue, which hung down like a tie; the 'French cut' (*corte francès*) consisted in removing the scalp while the victim was still alive, and so on.[2] Once more, it is possible to read the message that is sent by the barbarity. It is intended to terrorize the victims, and therefore their side or village, and its effects are not restricted to the present. It is a way of telling them what will happen to them when they are dead: they will have no descendents. Hence the importance of anything to do with sex, and with anything to do with normal access to the next life: 'the mutilation of corpses was also used as a *post mortem* punishment' (1962: 85).

We should also generalize on the basis of this lesson: before we talk about violence in terms of madness, irrationality, or non-meaning, we would do well to follow the example of Yvon Le Bot in his (1992) study of the war in the Maya country, and try to look as seriously as we can at other hypotheses, and attempt not to mistake our ignorance, inability to understand, or prejudices for a deep analysis of the meaning of such acts and behaviours, no matter how barbaric they may seem.

The interplay between the human and the inhuman

Some would argue that the extreme violence we refer to as cruelty can be attributed to calculations on the part of the actors: its function may be, for example, to bring the population back into line and to terrorize it still further. This may be true in certain cases. As we have seen, the mass rapes committed by Serbs in Bosnia, especially in the summer of 1992, have been explained as 'psychosexual destruction' (Kressel, 2002 [1996]), and as part of a policy of using terror to convince Croats and Muslims to leave their homes and to allow the creation of ethnically homogeneous Serbian territories. The same policy also gave the groups involved considerable gratification – 'We were ordered to rape so that our morale would be higher', claimed one Serb leader in a Bosnian military prison (Kressel, 2002 [1996]: 3). It should be noted that this policy of terror is a message which, if it is to be effective, must be delivered brutally and rapidly. International opinion must not be given the time to mobilise and to stop it in either military or political terms.

One common feature, which may be consubstantial with cruelty, is not, however, indispensable to the destruction of people, or even the use or establishment of a reign of terror. It is a 'plus' or 'extra', and it is artificial to think of it in terms of calculated utility, or to reduce everything to an instrumental logic. To refer once more to Bosnia, the mass rapes also reflected a desire to inflict pain, with the pleasure of doing so, and to humiliate individuals, and were not just a desire to terrorize a population or to indulge in sadism. One Muslim victim of gang rape is reported as saying (Kressel, 2002 [1996]: 37), 'If they couldn't rape me, they would urinate on me'.

The suggestion that cruelty or barbarity may be functional is not reducible to the idea of an elementary rationality, and therefore to the idea that excess has an instrumental role. At this point in the discussion, the question is whether it is possible to adopt approaches other than those that either see cruelty in terms of the *jouissance* and pleasure it can afford, that see it as delirium or madness, and those that, in contrast, try to detect in it a possible practical utility (forcing the victims to remain silent, terrorizing a population) or a symbolic import (depriving the victim of the means to enter the next world by mutilating him or her).

Primo Levi provides us with an important starting point in a luminous chapter of what was to be his last book. Perhaps because he is describing a very different situation to that written about by Wolfgang Sofsky and is speaking of Nazi camps where the role of the guards was, in theory, to guard prisoners and not to exterminate them, what he says suggests a very different interpretation of cruelty. Primo Levi raises the issue of useless violence and, more generally, of the cruelty of the Nazi guards in the death camps. He sees in it 'one of the fundamental features of Hitlerism', which was based on the principle that 'Before dying, the victim must be degraded, so that the murderer will be less burdened by guilt' (Levi, 1988 [1986]: 100, 101). From this point of view, cruelty is an indication that the actor's subjectivity is uncomfortable with the violence he commits as he goes about his normal tasks, and that the violence is not determined by the cruelty itself. This is a paradoxical mechanism: if the actor is to be able to live with himself when he is behaving violently towards other human beings, they must be treated as though they are non-human. They must be treated in an inhuman way that turns them into things or animals, or at least excludes them from humanity. Levi's text suggests that in order to treat the person he is assaulting as someone who is susceptible to being assaulted, the actor must keep an absolute distance between his victim and himself, and must see him as belonging to a different species. Cruelty makes it psychologically possible to see oneself as a member of humanity. It allows the killer to see himself as a human being, or even a subject, as he turns the other into a non-man, a non-subject, or a being who has been dehumanized because he can be degraded and treated as an object or an animal – even though he is much closer to being a negation of the subject, or an anti-subject who comes into being by denying the humanity of the victim, and by acting in such a way as to negate his or her subjectivity. The negation of the subjectivity of the other becomes a form of self-assertion.

This kind of approach can be illustrated by the collecting of trophies and war souvenirs that was mentioned above. According to Joanna Bourke (1999: 39), 'Souvenirs were regarded as proof that a man had seen active combat and thus had proved himself on the field of battle'. Souvenir-hunting allowed men to associate the death of the 'other', the enemy, with self-esteem.

Contemporary anthropology is coming increasingly closer to history. In addition to the historical studies of Bourke, Dower, and Annette Becker and Stéphane Audoin-Rouzeau (2000), who are all sensitive to this type of analysis, we might mention anthropological studies by two women researchers who are also activists (Grappe and Vidal, in Héritier, 1996). They explain the cruelty that characterized both ethnic cleansing in the Former Yugoslavia and the genocide and mass murders in the Great Lakes region of Africa. Véronique Nahoum Grappe demonstrates (in Héritier, 1996: 289) that, in the Former Yugoslavia, 'the baroque excesses of cruelty and the enigmatic, gratuitous and irrational escalation of violence were not part of a rhetoric that legitimized a policy', and Claudine Vidal reaches similar conclusions about the Tutsi genocide. Like history, contemporary anthropology is becoming increasingly sensitive to suffering, including the suffering inflicted by individuals and groups who have known and lived with their victims for a long time. Historians and anthropologists now speak of 'neighbourhood cruelty', and that notion does, in some cases, seem to be applicable to ethnic cleansing in the Former Yugoslavia and to the Tutsi genocide of 1994, and may also apply to the destruction of the Jews of Jedwabne, who were, as Jan Gross's (2000) study reveals, massacred by their Polish neighbours.

It might be added that it is possible to put forward an interpretation of culture that resembles Primo Levi's but inverts it. In an incisive and well-documented essay, the anthropologist Michael Taussig looked once again at the brutality of the employees of a Peruvian-British consortium that owned rubber plantations in the Putumayo region during the nineteenth century (the Putumayo is a tributary of the Amazon). The Indians were not only forced to work in unjust and difficult conditions, they were terrorised, tortured, and massacred, not so much because they were a somewhat recalcitrant labour force, suggests Taussig, as because the torturers themselves were living in a culture of fear and terror. They were convinced that it was only by using extreme and excessive violence that they could hope to escape the worst horrors, including acts of cannibalism, that might be inflicted on them by the Indians: 'It was only because the Indians were human that they were able to serve as labour – and as subjects of torture. For it is not the victim as animal that gratifies the torturer, but the fact that the victim is human, thus enabling the torturer to become the savage' (Taussig, 2002: 176). Like Primo Levi's, his proposed explanation looks at the interplay between the human and the inhuman but inverts the analysis by demonstrating that the torturer makes no attempt to stay on the human side of the boundary, and succumbs to the opposite temptation of going over to the inhuman side.

Three types of cruelty

Now that we have identified them, is it possible to reconcile the main approaches to cruelty that have been evoked? Wolfgang Sofsky emphasizes the element of pure *jouissance*. Yvon Le Bot and Jacques Semelin emphasize the madness or delirium of the actors, whilst Primo Levi outlines the idea of a relationship with the self in which the protagonist of violence must negate the other in order to become a human being. The positive answer is that these approaches can be seen as three possible, singular, and different expressions of a subject who is, in many respects, what might be called an anti-subject. We will come back to this point in the next chapter.

The first modality we have identified is that of a subject defined solely in terms of libido and *jouissance*. The second is that of a delirious, psychotic, or paranoid subject. The third inscribes the subject in a relationship that is perverse but still meaningful; in extreme cases, the executioner uses even greater violence and introduces a gratuitous element of sadism in order to take responsibility for, or at least to justify, what he himself sees as inhuman behaviour. These dimensions are so different that, when it comes to analysing a concrete situation, it seems that we have to choose between them. Wolfgang Sofsky insists that it is a mistake to believe that human atrocities require the dehumanization of the other, or that human beings can torture and slaughter only those who are not fellow human beings. The way massacres take place proves that the opposite is true; insofar as it is possible to do so, the killer does his own killing, and does it at close quarters. He wants to see death at work, to see the bleeding body and the fear in the victim's eyes. Indeed. But how many torturers say or feel, after the event, that what they have done has destroyed them? They recall with horror the look in the eyes of their victims. As Victor Hugo wrote in *La Légende Des Siècles*, 'The eye was in the tomb, watching Cain'. One of the Hutu killers interviewed by Jean Hatzfeld (2008b: 18–19) admitted:

> I do remember the first person who looked at me at the moment of the deadly blow. Now that was something. The eyes of someone you kill are immortal, if they face you at the fatal instant. They have a terrible black colour. They shake you more than the streams of blood and the death rattles, even in a great turmoil of dying. The eyes of the killed, for the killer, are his calamity if he looks into them.

To what extent does each of these three dimensions of the anti-subject – one consisting of pure *jouissance*, the second which is a form of delirium, and the third which has a certain functionality – derive from a particular psychic economy and particular conditions? One hypothesis has to be ruled out, as it tries to see them as three possible stages in a continuum: madness gives way to *jouissance*, for instance, to produce the third and extreme phase of cruelty, whilst functionality is characteristic of only the intermediary phase in which constraints inevitably restrict it. Madness may, for instance, appear in atrocious murders that no one could have predicted, but it may also appear at the end of a kind of trajectory when the actor resorts to even greater violence. After the war in Vietnam, American cinema produced several films (*Coming Home, Taxi Driver, Rambo* ...) showing how home-coming veterans who had witnessed cruelty, and their own cruelty, in Vietnam descended into the most murderous madness or self-destruction. Similarly, *jouissance* can give rise to extreme behaviours, but it can also get in the way of a colder and more efficient extreme violence. Nazism and some well-structured terrorist organizations resisted the temptations of a hot violence that might have become cruel or even sadistic, and the pleasure it might afford, and tried to force a return to a cold, controlled violence that was rationally oriented towards highly destructive ends.

No matter whether it takes the form of delirium, madness, *jouissance*, or the search for pleasure, 'absolute' violence that is dissociated from any other meaning is not the same as the cruelty or excess of meaning we find in situations where the actor has to come to terms with what is already extreme or shameful violence, and in which further atrocities appear to correspond to what he sees as a vital necessity; in order to live with what he is doing – and with himself – he invents mechanisms which, in a sense, use evil to exorcise evil; faced with an extreme and unbearable situation, the actor survives by venturing still further into the extreme and the unbearable. That is why it is preferable to make, like Françoise Héritier (1996: 273–4), a distinction between extreme violence and extreme cruelty, and to accept that cruelty can have different meanings and can correspond to different logics.

The Importance of the Situation

Excessive violence, gratuitousness, and especially cruelty do not occur in just any context, and it can be assumed that it is all the easier for them to occur when a number of conditions are present.

The prison experiment

From that point of view, Philip Zimbardo's experiments are especially revelatory (see Kressel, 2002 [1996]; Haney et al., 1995). The psychologist had a mock prison built at Stanford University and had 12 students locked up in it. They had volunteered to take part in an experiment about prison life, and the pretence was that they had committed armed robbery. Eleven student volunteers played the role of the guards. All the students were paid, and were chosen from a total of 75 volunteers for their mental stability and maturity. It seemed unlikely that any of them would behave in an 'anti-social' way. Those playing the prisoners' roles were given a guarantee that they would not suffer any physical abuse.

The participants very quickly internalized the conditions of life in prison, and it emerged that the 'guards' were treating the 'inmates' in unpleasant ways, forcing them to carry out degrading tasks and abusing their authority. Some even behaved sadistically towards them. For their part, the prisoners found lots of ways of putting up resistance, but on the whole they became so demoralized that the experiment, which was meant to go on for 15 days, was halted after six.

From our point of view, the main lesson is that in the confined, controlled, and dehumanising space of the prison, brutality and cruelty began to occur very quickly, with some variations from one individual to the next. Zimbardo demonstrates that these aspects of violence (and not just the obedience to authority observed in Milgram's experiments) are always likely to emerge under certain conditions.

Prison is obviously not the only place that encourages cruelty and brutality. In more general terms, situations characterized by impunity, fear and, certain political and cultural training can also encourage excessive cruelty.

Impunity

As many research papers mention, and as Primo Levi also notes, the conviction that one can act with impunity is a decisive factor in the transition to barbarity. A feeling of impunity is almost indispensable to cruelty. It may be provided by the circumstances (the absence of witnesses and especially of journalists) or by the authorities, who turn a blind eye, or encourage or even legitimize transgression in the name of a higher principle, usually a state.

From the point of view of modern democracies, cruelty is transgressive in two senses. It transgresses the law and the state on the one hand, and on the other, a moral value that was established long ago by the sixth commandment. The conviction of impunity does not in itself make cruelty possible. There must also be some encouragement and an ability to break the moral injunction not to kill. That is why the theme of remorse has to be present in any consideration of cruelty; the feeling of having offended morality by being cruel in, for example, time of war, often haunts those who have indulged in that cruel behaviour. They often find it difficult to live a normal life and are permeated by a feeling of unspeakable guilt after the event.

They committed acts of a cruel and murderous violence that involved a direct relationship and actual contact with the victims; one of the reasons that makes modern warfare acceptable to democracies is that it avoids physical confrontation or violence in the true sense of an intimate murderous act. It involves the use of technology that kills from a distance, and ensures that the combatants do not have to bear the psychological and human burden of a murderous face-to-face encounter.

Remorse does not, however, affect everyone who has been involved in cruel games or in violence for the sake of violence. In, for example, the most horrific criminal cases, the murderer who indulged in cannibalism or played appalling games with his victim's body – dead or alive – may very well feel no remorse at all. He is living in a different psychological world and therefore feels no guilt. When they go back to civilian life after taking part in a war in which they behaved with great cruelty and tortured and killed civilians, some veterans feel an intense guilt, whilst others feel none. That is why we have to introduce a distinction: impunity is indeed a necessary precondition for the use of cruelty in all cases, but its meanings can vary, especially when the actor has to break a moral or political law or a taboo that he has internalized, or, at the opposite extreme, when he has internalized the highest moral law of all – 'Thou shalt not kill' – and is then forced by circumstances to break it.

Fear

In certain mass experiences, and especially war, there is all the more room for cruelty in that the killers are not soldiers who are under the control and command of their officers, but individuals and groups who have been left to their own devices. The sociologist Morris Janowitz, and the historian George Mosse, explain this phenomenon by speaking of 'brutalization' (see Shils and Janowtz, 1948). In such cases, the violence can be unbridled, but that does not necessarily mean that it is completely meaningless, or that those involved enjoy violence for the sake of violence. It has, for instance, often been noted that the most excessive behaviours on the battlefield are informed not so much by, or not only by, sadistic impulses as by a wide range of feelings that may emerge from a learning process that is grounded in experience. Omar Bartov demonstrates the point with respect to Hitler's soldiers.[3]

The most powerful of these feelings appears to be fear, especially if an enemy has already been described as capable of committing the worst atrocities: fear is what George L. Mosse (1990) calls a 'disempathy' that makes it possible, or even necessary, to treat the other as someone who is inhuman. Fear can then lead to terrible atrocities which are, at least in part, the products of panic, as Georges Lefebvre (1973 [1932]) clearly demonstrates was the case with the Great Fear of 1789. Fear feeds on stories and rumours that circulate and which are in some cases fed on myths that are more deeply inscribed in a culture or historical memory, and create a climate that may encourage excessive violence. In their study of 'German atrocities' during the First World War, John Horne and Alan Kramer (2001) demonstrate that the German troops who invaded Belgium and then north-eastern France in August 1914 were living in a climate of fear and great tension fuelled by the fear of being attacked by *franc-tireurs* who effectively existed only in their imagination. The 'atrocities' (killing civilians, including men of the Church, and raping women) resulted from a panic exacerbated by alcohol, combined with a living memory of the war of 1870, the myth of the *franc-tireur*, an individual who attacked alone, from ambush, and treacherously. It was also generated by the strategy of the German military authorities, who had a vested interest in spreading terror.

For fear can be used by the authorities, or at least taken into account in their calculations; it can be prepared and orchestrated, or at least inculcated into the imagination of troops who are about to face an enemy. John Dower demonstrates, for example, that propaganda convinced the American troops who fought in the Second World War that the Japanese were nothing more than pure barbarians. Having been told about Japanese war atrocities, real or fictional, they were convinced that they had no alternative and that it was a question of kill or be killed: 'men in battle became obsessed with annihilating the foe' (Dower, 1986: 53). Propaganda, the media, and films had created a cultural image of an enemy who had both a sub-human side, and a superhuman side. The enemy was both an animal that had to be exterminated in the same way that rats and other vermin are exterminated, and a creature endowed with exceptional qualities (fanaticism, a talent for violence, a particular capacity for evil, sexual appetite). The social sciences had their part to play in the radicalization that instilled fear on the battlefield. Dower (1986: 135–6) cites the work of the anthropologist Weston La Barre. In 1945, La Barre observed Japanese-Americans (who were Japanese in his eyes) who were being held in a relocation camp in Utah. He believed that he could demonstrate the existence of 'cultural-psychological differences' between them and Americans. The dominant American characteristics were freedom and democracy, a sense of humour, confidence, a sense of law of equal applicability to all men, whilst the Japanese displayed the very different characteristics of secretiveness, hiding of emotions and attitudes, fanaticism, arrogance, hypochondriasis, sadomasochistic behaviour, and so on. On the battlefield fear heightened, rather than replaced, a desire to avenge comrades who had recently been killed by the enemy, sometimes in cruel ways.

A culture of hatred ...

Leaving aside the specific circumstances that encourage it, does the violence that is unleashed on such a scale in times of war have something to do with the liberation of instincts or drives? Is it the result of a long period of in-depth indoctrination that is non-specific and that takes place in the family and at school, and that accustoms the future actors to reifying or animalizing the enemy, to dehumanizing and debasing them? In some cases the enemy may be identified in advance, and the media can play a decisive role here, as with the calls for hatred and murder than were broadcast on Rwanda's Radio Mille Collines from August 1993 onwards. They paved the way for the genocide of Tutsis and moderate Hutus that began in April 1994, and designated some of the first targets.

Such questions suggest that we have to go back to the thematic of culture. Are cruelty and sadism more present in some cultures than in others, and do those cultures provide a breeding ground that is all the more conducive to violence in that the enemy or the incarnation of evil is clearly delineated? This idea is advanced by Daniel Goldhagen, amongst others. Goldhagen argues that pre-war German political culture included a hatred of Jews and promoted the idea that they 'ought to die' (1997 [1996]: 14) because they were 'pernicious' (ibid: 36). 'The camps ... became institutions in which Germans could indulge and give expression to any ideologically suggested practice, any psychological impetus, by using the minds and bodies of the inmates as instruments of work and objects for every gratification' (ibid: 174).[4] According to Goldhagen, a culture of cruelty and sadism is not a culture of obedience, but a culture of hatred that facilitates and almost legitimizes gratuitous violence.

It is possible to reconcile the registers of fear and culture by noting that, in certain circumstance, actors can be encouraged to take part in forms of extreme violence by reactivating historical fears that are anchored in the collective memory and have become an integral part of a national imaginary. In mass murder and other crimes against humanity, national or ethnic feelings are often stirred up by reminders of the crimes the enemy committed in the past. This allows the organizers to both stir up the fear that the brutalities of the past are about to be repeated and to encourage a desire for revenge or vengeance.

... or inculcation

The available documents suggest, however, that extreme cruelty and violence for the sake of violence do not come naturally, at least in war, and that the reality is in fact very different: men do not want to go to war, do not want to be involved in physical combat, and do not want to kill. In many cases, they have no choice. In such cases, the excesses do not occur because the fighters are left to their own devices and governed by their drives or instincts; they are the result of more or less deliberate preparations on the part of the military authorities. During the Second World War, notes Joanna Bourke, the commanders of American training camps found that their men did not want to kill, and that they had to be motivated, trained, and given a taste for killing. Hence the curious use that was made of social psychology: 'The frustration-aggression formula of the psychologist John Dollard and others – which implied that by increasing frustration, aggressive behaviour could be fostered – was used to legitimate many of the more sadistic aspects of basic training' (Bourke, 1999: 83). 'Transforming fear into anger was a chief preoccupation of military instructors' (ibid: 84). When cruelty and violence for the sake of violence did occur on the battlefield, they were not expressions of primal instincts that had suddenly been unleashed. They were the result of training and conditioning. Which makes it difficult to see them as 'pure' violence. We have already mentioned the My Lai massacre. One of the men who trained Charlie Company for combat said that he was 'pleased' with their performance on 16 March 1968: 'They turned out to be very good soldiers. The fact that they were able to go into My Lai and carry out the orders they had been given, I think this is the direct result of the good training they had' (Bourke, 1999: 187).

It is not just their training that prepares men to use atrocious cruelty on the battlefield. Their conditioning may be the result of a much wider mobilization involving not only political and military actors but also the media, artists, and scientists. In his book on the war in the Pacific that followed the attack on Pearl Harbour, John Dower clearly demonstrates that the atrocities committed on both sides were stimulated by intense propaganda based upon 'stereotyped and even blatant racist thinking' (Dower, 1986: x). In 1937, the US Department of State was still denouncing the slaughter of civilian populations as barbarous and 'in violation of the most elementary principles of those standards of humane conduct which have been developed as an essential part of modern civilization' (Dower 1986: 38). A few years later, the same Department of State considered the allied air raids on Germany and Japan to be necessary, and claimed that any criticism of them was a matter of hopeless idealism, madness, and above all treason: the Japanese deserved to have those 'elementary principles' violated.

Remorse, mental disorders, and defence mechanisms.

One explanation sees cruelty as a form of violence for the sake of violence that, at least in the case of some people, merely waits for the favourable circumstances that will unleash it, whilst a second stresses, in contrast, that it is culturally determined or the product of specific lessons taught in training camps or by deliberate propaganda. According to the first explanation, the author of cruel acts of violence finds an opportunity to unleash drives, or a madness, that his psychic economy previously held back and repressed. There are no grounds for believing that they involve any transgression from his point of view. There is no room for moral considerations in these excesses and this violence for the sake of violence. Violence functions on a different level and is not concerned about morality.

The second explanation is a much better way of understanding the remorse, guilt, and mental disorders (headaches, systematic nightmares, insomnia, digestive problems, or nervous tics) that are observed in, for instance, veterans who have been involved in serious acts of violence. Once again, a note of caution is required. It is not only that, as we have seen, not everyone who has taken part in acts of extreme and cruel acts of violence feels remorse or guilt, or presents psychosomatic problems. The same symptoms are also often presented by individuals, such as soldiers, who were not the authors of barbaric acts, or did not even witness them directly but were associated with them. In their case, the remorse and guilt may well have nothing to do with violence that was inflicted in the past, and may result from a heavy load of determinations, such as the fear they felt at the time, disgust at having been involved in barbaric tasks, or the feeling of having been involved, marginally but collectively, in an inhuman experience. Guilt, and all the other emotions felt by those who have had actually experienced extreme violence, must be seen not only in the light of that past, but also in the light of the present in which they are now living: the society in which they are living may be willing to listen to them or may refuse to do so, and may forgive their excesses or refuse to forgive them.

It has to be added that other mechanisms may come into play in the course of the experience, and especially of a prolonged experience of extreme violence. In his study of the Nazi doctors, Robert Jay Lifton (1986), for example, suggests that we should uses the notions of dissociation and 'doubling' to explain how criminal Nazi doctors were able to protect themselves from their own acts in psychological terms. According to Lifton, they created a second 'self' that was autonomous from their primary self. That self allowed them to come and go between a peaceful and affectionate family life and inhuman experiments without any difficulty. The idea of such a defence mechanism has been strongly criticized: the future Nazi doctors were educated and supported its socio-biological doctrines and racial purity projects long before Auschwitz came into existence, and they had no difficulty in reconciling them with normal family life. Such criticisms by no means invalidate, however, the idea that defence mechanisms allow the worst criminals to distance themselves from their acts, to attenuate their seriousness and to exonerate them of all responsibility. [5]

The most singular aspects of violence, excessive violence for the sake of violence, and cruelty must always be analysed on several different levels. The analysis must look at the actual moment of the violence, but also at what happened to its author before and after that moment. The cruelty may, in some cases, be a product of a psychic economy that was simply waiting for an opportunity to express itself. In other cases, it may have to do with a preparation or even an orchestration that influences individuals so greatly that it becomes psychologically possible to transgress the laws that make atrocities or barbaric acts taboo. The guilt and remorse affect only some individuals – and they are not necessarily the ones who are most guilty. This does not mean that the others are, in psychological terms, passive. On the battlefield itself, circumstances, constraints, and the very process of using violence can encourage atrocities in many different ways. Cruelty and violence as an end in themselves are not a unitary or homogeneous phenomenon, and can be products of different logics.

A brief comment on the State

But can the State itself not act with great cruelty, and not only when it is in the hands of a dictatorial, totalitarian, or simply blood-thirsty power? Does the same cruel act cease to be cruel when it is committed by a state insofar as it has the monopoly on legitimate physical violence that we mentioned in Chapter 2? Does it become more meaningful or more moral because it is legitimate?

The best way to address this question is to look at punishments administered by the State, and especially the death penalty when, as is the case in some American states, it has not been abolished. Is this extreme violence so far removed from barbarism and cruelty, even if everything is done to make it look completely different because the public is not allowed to witness the administration of the punishment or because supposedly clean technologies of death are used? There is in fact no reason why the arguments we have applied to non-state actors should not be applied to the death penalty. Aspects of the capital punishment penalty do indicate that social, political, and cultural answers have been rejected in favour of a brutal solution influenced by the spirit of revenge and resentment. As Austin Sarat demonstrates, capital punishment is the source of some of the greatest dangers American society faces. More specifically, America refuses to look into the social problems that give rise to violence and has adopted a policy of vengeance. Sarat also speaks of its use of crime to turn social groups against each other, the temptations of 'government by crime', and the erosion of basic legal protection and legal values to profit short-term political expedients. More important still, he underlines what 'state killing' implies in terms of the responsibilities of citizens. An almost invisible gesture exonerates citizens from any feeling of responsibility for the death that the State administers in their name. The cruelty of the State – and the above remarks could also be applied to all its punitive apparatuses – is masked by its legitimacy and its truly bureaucratic nature. This does not mean that it does not deserve to be examined for what it is. State violence is not the subject of this book, but it inevitably has to be mentioned, as does state terrorism and government through terror.

Notes

1 Daniel Pécaut's (1987) study remains the standard work on the *Violencia*.

2 Cf. Quintero, who also mentions the monkey cut (*corte de mica*), the ear cut (*corte de oreja*), the goose cut (*corte de ganzo*), and the flower-vase cut (*corte de florero*), in which the head of the victim is cut off. So are his limbs, which are then 'inserted into the trunk as though they were flowers' (p. 54).

3 See Bartov (1991). Bartov also uses the concept of 'brutalization' and notes that, the more time they spent at the front, the more violent German soldiers became.

4 En echo, one of the killers who took part in the genocide in Rwanda, told Hatzfeld (2008b [2003]: 34) 'Some hunted like grazing goats, others like wild beasts. Some hunted slowly because they were afraid, some because they were lazy. Some struck slowly from wickedness, some struck quickly so as to finish up early and go home early to do something else'.

5 Stanley Cohen (2001) is highly critical of Lifton, but has himself made a number of suggestions to explain how the authors of atrocities can attempt to deny any involvement not only to others (the courts, the media ...) but also to themselves.

8

THE MARK OF THE SUBJECT

Perhaps we have to accept that the various perspectives and approaches we have discussed and which we have sharply criticized – but never dismissed – throughout this book are in many respects contradictory and fragmentary. The social sciences depart from ordinary usage, which uses the word 'violence' to refer to a vast range of experiences, but it is true that, different as they may be, even their most serious explanations for violence never question the use of the adjective 'violent'. At best, they extend, or fail to extend, the spectrum of its application by questioning, for example, the pertinence of notions such as that of symbolic violence. In both spontaneous and more reflective usages, the term 'violence' refers to all sorts of phenomena and is defined in many different ways, some resolutely subjectivist and others with objective and universalist ambitions. Should this book, in contrast, therefore be seen as an attempt to deconstruct the term, or as a critique that is intended to put an end to the confusion that results from the use of a single word?

Perhaps the most useful feature of this book is that it describes the available explanations and shows how they differ from one another. Each of these explanations can be used to approach this or that concrete experience, and there is nothing to prevent us from attempting to use several different explanations or to look at violence in different ways, provided that we raise the issue of the overall coherence of the set of tools we are using.

It is helpful, even indispensable, to separate out the registers and to have a clear idea of which instruments are likely to be required to do so. It would, however, be a mistake to restrict the ambitions of this book to providing a *catalogue raisonné* of analytic tools. The central issue it raises is very different, namely the idea that violence is best understood when we introduce the subject of its author or authors, and their experience as a subject in both the lived and imaginary dimensions.

This idea must, above all, not be reduced to an over-simplistic or naïve formulation such as: violence is the direct expression of a subjectivity in conditions that encourage its expression. Violence does not bear the mark of the subject in just one way, and in some cases it may do so in a negative sense. That is the issue we are about to examine. Before we do that, and given that our goal is to make the subject central to the analysis, it is certainly helpful to outline what we mean by 'subject'.

The Notion of the Subject

In intellectual terms, and especially philosophical terms, the notion of the subject derives from many very different traditions and orientations. At times, it has been given a warm welcome, and at others it has been rejected. Since the end of the 1980s, the social sciences have placed more and more emphasis on perspectives that centre on the personal subject, and this is the case all over the world;[1] in the 1960s and 1970s, the most radical versions of structuralism not only divorced structure from subject, but explained everything in structural terms, declared war on the subject, and even went so far as to proclaim the death of the subject.

The impetus given to it by the American and French revolutions meant that the modern idea of the subject was primarily political and juridical. The subject was primarily a citizen. Then came the Industrial Revolution, which no longer saw the subject as, or only as, an essentially political and juridical actor, but primarily as a social being. To be more specific, the central actor in industrial societies – the workers' movement – inspired conceptions of a subject with three main characteristics; the working proletariat was, first, a *social* subject, second, an eminently *collective* subject and, third, a subject with *an historical mission* to fulfil because, when it cast off its chains, it would, as Marx used to say, free the whole of humanity. Intellectual debates, especially in the 1960s and early 1970s, did not so much contrast this type of conception with other conceptions, as reject the very idea of the subject in favour of the idea of structures, agencies, apparatuses, or systems.

From the 1980s onwards, the historical decline of the workers' movement and the rise of collective identities led to a renewed interest in the notion of the subject, which was increasingly associated with identity politics and its actors. The subject then became cultural rather than social and took a religious, ethnic, national, or gendered form. And whilst it remained collective, the definition of the subject now made much more allowance for a personal, singular subject. Both the social sciences and political philosophy increasingly tend to reject 'primordialist' approaches that see cultural identities as naturally-determined phenomena, and even to move away from ideas about reproduction that reduce identities to a legacy or heritage that is passed on more or less automatically. Increasingly, we recognize that, on the contrary, cultural particularisms are invented, transformed, and produced in the course of processes in which individuals make choices and take personal decisions to take on, assume, or bring to life one or another collective identity. This suggests that it a mistake to contrast collective identities with the individualism of the subject; they complement it and are sustained by it. Advocates of the notion of the subject find themselves involved in intellectual debate, not with those who reject it, but with those who see new or revived collective identities, and not least Islam, as a negation of the subject, as inhibitory forces that make the existence or constitution of the subject impossible. They denounce communitarianism on the grounds that it is a threat to the subject, and above all to women-as-subjects.

Political, social, or cultural conceptions of the subject in a sense ground the subject in society. They turn the subject into an actor defined in relation to other actors, by roles or even by a substance. The conception used here differs from them in that it does not derive from any such political, social, or cultural principle. In my view, the subject is neither the product of political rights, or a challenge to a social relationship of domination. The workers' movement, for example, did not come into existence simply because it challenged the masters of labour. And nor is the subject the product of a community. The subject exists before any relationship is established and before there is any action; the subject is a demand, or the possibility of producing one's own existence. It is a relationship with the self, a goal, or a potential that may or may not become a reality thanks to what we can call subjectivation. The subject is, to cite the German sociologist Hans Joas (1996 [1992]: 4), 'the *creative* character of human action'. The notion of the subject refers to the possibility of constructing oneself as an individual, as a singular being capable of formulating choices, and therefore of resisting dominant logics, be they economic, communitarian, technological, or political. The subject is, in other words, a potential meaning that can posit its own existence and produce its own trajectory. This conception overlaps, broadly speaking, with the sociological conception outlined by Alain Touraine in his most recent work, and especially in his long and demanding dialogue with Farhad Khosrokhavar (Touraine and Khosrokhavar, 2000), and it is not far removed from Alan Renaut's more philosophical conception (Renaut et Mesure, 1999).[2] It implies that all human beings must have the same right to be a subject, and to become involved in processes of subjectivation. This implies the notion of democracy, but also that of collective responsibility: how can one be a subject if one does not make the effort to ask about the conditions that allow others to be subjects too? In that sense, Michael Dillon (1997: 162) is right to say that 'modern politics is the politics of subjectivity', just as Robert Fraisse (1997) is right to call for 'policies for the subject', or in other words policies that concentrate on the creation of personal subjects, such as the child at school or the patient in hospital.

This conception would be partial if it ignored everything about subjectivity that comes to terms with the other's failure to become a subject, with the impossibility of becoming a subject. It would, that is, be partial if it was indifferent to or overlooked attempts to prevent the other (and perhaps the self) from becoming a subject or at the production of the antithesis of a subject. It must look at the negation of the subject, the threats to its very existence, its destruction or assaults on its physical or intellectual integrity. The notion of the subject includes, or at the very least implies, its opposite or what we can call the anti-subject: the dark side of being that upsets the categories of the subject. It will be noted that the notion of the subject we are adopting departs considerably from that proposed by psychoanalysis, and especially Lacanian psychoanalysis. For the latter, the 'pure' subject is, as Marcos Zafiropoulos says 'a subject without an ego ... a mere function of the symbolic structure' (2003: 89). For Lacan 'The subject proceeds from his systematic subjection in the field of the other' (1994 [1973]: 188). The subject is assigned its role by various influential determinisms: traumas, lack, family complexes, the death drive, and so on.

Violence and the Subject

If we make the subject the central category of our analysis of violence, as we are about to do, we distance ourselves both from psychological or sociopsychological approaches that try to reveal the links between a personality-type and acting out, and 'situational' approaches that explain violence in terms of a context, the conditions that are conducive to violence, and a situation. What is at stake in the hypothesis of a link between violence and the subject is of a different nature: violence refers either to the impaired ability of a group or individual to become a subject or to function as such, to mechanisms of desubjectivation, or to the expansion or expression of the anti-subject. Personalities and situations may contribute to all this, and can prohibit and prevent the emergence of a subject, but they are primarily products of dynamics and processes in which all kinds of logics – some personal, and others general, social, historical, or political – intermingle. Violence is bound up with the way in which the subject is constructed, or is not constructed, in the inverted form of an anti-subject. It is neither a mere psychological attribute nor just a reflection of a situation.

The suggestion that we should relate violence to the subject is therefore a natural continuation of Part I, where the central idea was to emphasize the main social, political, and cultural changes which, at both the global and the individual level, from the 'planetary' to the most personal level, reinforce the suggestion that the study of violence requires a change of paradigm. The continuity is clearly apparent if we look at the theme of the emergence of victims. In a world in which victims are listened to and are recognized for what they are, and in which they demand justice, reparations, and recognition, violence is no longer defined primarily as something that disturbs the social order and defies the state. Violence is an attack on the physical and moral integrity of individuals and groups. And when contemporary developments urge us to look at violence in terms of the broken or negated subjectivity of those it affects, rather than the failings or excesses of the system in which it arises, how can we not go one step further and look at the subjectivity of those who use it?

The continuity is also apparent when we look at the transformations brought about by globalization or what the word means: the undermining of certain states, greater migratory flows, a cultural fragmentation, new forms of social inequality, and so on. Paradoxically, these major transformations, which operate at a global level, also affect the most individual and personal aspects of people's lives. They affect the body. They help to bring about outbreaks of violence that are not necessarily major collective phenomena, and that can occur at the individual and local level. It becomes easier to understand them if we introduce the hypothesis of phenomena of subjectivation. Arjun Appadurai (2002) provides a remarkable example of the phenomenon in his analysis of the extreme ethnic and genocidal violence committed against Tutsis and moderate Hutus in the late twentieth century in the Great Lakes region of Africa, in outbreaks of violence between Hindus and Sikhs in India, in the Former Yugoslavia, and in China at the end of the Cultural Revolution when there were major outbreaks of cannibalism in Guangxi province. The starting point for Appadurai's argument is globalization, which in some cases gives rise to uncertainties about identity. The ethnic identities concerned become uncertain when frontiers cease to be clearly defined, when migratory flows bring in new populations, when civil wars create displaced persons, when political regimes are transformed, and when new and broader identities are imposed upon those to which the groups in question were accustomed. Identities become uncertain when, to use the expression he borrows from Robert Hayden, communities become unimaginable (as opposed to Anderson's (1983) 'imagined community'). Appadurai is particularly interested in the debauchery of extreme violence, including mutilations, cannibalism, rape, and so on. This kind of violence affects the body, and can suddenly break out amongst ordinary people who have previously lived together on relatively friendly terms. Such ethnic violence, he explains, has to do with uncertainty, the loss of points of reference, and with the fact that people no longer know who they are. It is a response: 'When one or more of these forms of social uncertainty come into play, violence can create a macabre form of certainty and can become a brutal technique ... about "them" and, therefore, "us". This conjuncture takes on a particular significance in the era of globalization' (Appadurai, 2002: 288–9). We kill in order to know who the other is, and to deduce who we are: 'Ethnocidal violence evidently mobilizes some sort of ambient rage about the body as a theatre of deception, of betrayal and of false solidarity' (2002: 295). Whilst it may have something to do with history or politics, it is also 'a horrible effort to expose, penetrate and occupy the material form – the body – of the ethnic other' (2002: 295). Violence is, in other words, used when there is no longer any collective identity, or when that identity has been undermined. It is the terrifying expression of a subject who has lost, or is losing, all identity, of a subject who is fighting for survival. It is 'a logic for the production of "real persons", which links uncertainty, purity, treachery and vivisection' (2002: 298).

If we are to move from the suggestions, which are still relatively descriptive, that structured Part I, and make the subject central to the analysis, we have to take into account the heterogeneity of the modalities and meanings of violence and therefore identify the different modalities of the relationship between the subject and violence. In order to identify them we have to take as our starting point not violence but what produces it, namely a subjectivity that is in one way or another coming to grips with the real. From that point of view, it is possible to identify at least five figures of the subject, each corresponding, in analytic terms, to a different logic of violence. The first is that of the *floating subject* who cannot find the meanings that might allow him to become an actor; the second is that of the *hypersubject* who overloads his behaviour with new meanings; the third is that of the *non-subject*, or an actor whose behaviour is completely determined by orientations that are more or less forced upon him by the power he obeys; the fourth is the *anti-subject* we have already mentioned; and the fifth is that of the *survivor-subject*.

These five figures outline a typology that is therefore based upon differences inscribed in the logics revealed by empirical analysis, and not upon an arbitrary division of the real. It is possible that other typologies will give us a better understanding of the various modalities of the relationship between violence and the subject by moving away from the more concrete examples that were the object of earlier chapters. We might, for example, attempt to identify everything relating to the destruction of the subject, the subject's absence or pathology, or the preconditions for the subject's formation. The great virtue of the typology we are outlining is that it makes simple forms of violence correspond to dimensions of the notion of the subject that are relatively easy to isolate and clear. They are also so distinctive that there is little danger of confusing them.

Five Figures of the Subject

These five categories will be discussed here with the help of a novel vocabulary that may appear somewhat problematic: we do not have the specialist terminology that would pertinently define the figures we have to identify and name. It is to be hoped that further research will suggest a more complete and sophisticated set of terms and notions that are more jargon-free than those outlined here. But as we shall see, this first outline typology does give us a starting point for an examination of the relationship between the subject and violence.

The floating subject

In some experiences, violence corresponds primarily to a loss of meaning. It fills a void which has either just been created or which has to be filled, but not only until much later. As we saw in the discussion of the relationship between violence and conflict in Chapter 1, when a conflicted relationship is established between actors, and even more so when that relationship becomes institutionalized, there is no room for violence because the emergent conflict scarcely impinges upon the consciousness of actors who are themselves having difficulty in emerging. Something similar happens when the conflict is over or a thing of the past. Those who would like it to continue have no longer have any points of reference or relational framework. Violence can therefore appear more easily. This idea was clarified in the section of Chapter 5 devoted to the processes of the loss of meaning. A meaning that once existed may disappear, and no meaning can emerge when some expectation or need cannot yet be clearly formulated because it has no actors and because there is no clear definition of what is at stake. In such situations subjectivity is a very powerful force that urges the individual or group to act, even though the concrete preconditions for action are absent or underdeveloped. Here, the violence corresponds to a subjectivity that cannot find an outlet in a real concrete project or a capacity for action that could prolong it. It defines a subject who cannot, or can no longer, be an actor, or in other words be inserted into a relationship, be it social, political, inter-cultural, or even interpersonal. Such violence is the mark of a subject who is well aware that it is possible that the relations he wishes to be involved in will be established one day, or who refuses to acknowledge the decline or end of the relations within which he still operates. It can be associated with the image of a subject who is neither social, political, nor cultural, and who seems doomed to float; this subject can either foreshadow a future actor, or be embodied in, for example, the artificial or ideological form of an exhausted actor.

In the vocabulary we are outlining, the subject is not 'floating' because he is defined by some social, cultural, political, or other principle – that is, of course, our definition of the subject – but because he is being prevented from emerging, or finds it impossible to transform himself into action, even though he feels the desire or need to do so. The conditions are not yet, or no longer, conducive to action; the only thing that exists is a subjectivity that will be able to, or which was once able to, act as its support. But for the moment that subjectivity is drifting and has no point of anchorage.

The floating subject may be informed by a sharp sense of injustice or non-recognition that exacerbates his distress or anger, or that turns to violence when some minor event demonstrates how the subject is being negated or silenced. A minor event reveals and emphasizes the social or racial discrimination he is experiencing, the brutality of the police, or the iniquitous inadequacies of the legal system ... Explosions of urban violence are common when individuals experience their negation as something intolerable, or when it results from a police 'blunder' or a particularly unacceptable ruling by the courts. The major riots that broke out in Los Angeles in 1992 were, it will be recalled, triggered by the acquittal, despite the video evidence, of the white police officers who had given a savage beating to Rodney King, a black man who had not threatened them in any way. The denial of subjectivity is all the more intolerable in that there is no political way of handling the expectations of the individuals concerned, and in that there can be co recognition of their social or cultural demands.

The floating subject is under the constant threat of desubjectivation, and this can force him to behave angrily, destructively, or self-destructively; he may also resist the loss of meaning, desocialization, and the danger of desocialization by going off in search of a new meaning or new forms of socialization in a different political or cultural environment.

The hyper-subject

In many cases, a subject corresponding to a deficit of meaning does not just turn to violence to express his desire or need to be an actor even though he cannot, or can no longer, become an actor. He may also try to give his life a meaning by giving violence a new or revived meaning. Those meanings may not be the ones he has lost or which he expects, without realizing it, to emerge. As we saw in our discussion of 'excess meaning' in Chapter 5, subjectivity now becomes weighed down with a discourse that can, in extreme cases, come to look like a plethora of meaning. The plethora of meaning allows the subject to move into a different space, and therefore to get beyond the earlier situation of emptiness, loss, and lack. Meaning is now omnipresent, superabundant, and can even seem to spill out from the frame of reference that previously defined the social, political, or cultural dimensions of the subject's previous day-to-day life.

In some cases, a subject in search of a meaning may, so to speak, be content with a shift of meaning. He drifts away from the meaning he has lost, or has yet to find, and looks elsewhere for a new legitimacy that will allow him to act in relations other than those in which he was forged. They may be social, political, or inter-cultural, but they are always real. A peasant in what has become an industrial society commits himself to work-class action. The student or populist intellectual goes to the countryside or the factory to live with the people. The terrorist who once operated in a Western society such as Germany becomes a quasi-mercenary in the service of an Arab state. The most spectacular examples occur when the plethora of meaning has more to do with overspill than with a shift of meaning, and when the subject becomes an actor by internalizing metasocial, metapolitical, or metacultural meaning – which takes us back to the analyses of Chapter 2 above.

Religion often serves this purpose and, more importantly, allows the logic of the plethora of meaning to be taken to extremes. More specifically it justifies acting out, which can in some cases take the extreme form of the sacrifice of the author, who destroys himself through his own action because he is convinced that he will find in the next world something that he cannot find in this world . At the same time his gesture helps, if needs be, to change the balance of power here on earth. When Islamists remove themselves from their society of origin and its problems and tensions, and declare war on a modernity in which they are steeped, but which they believe to be completely destructive, in order a carry out an attack on the United States that will, they hope, bring them recognition and happiness – including sexual happiness – in the next world, their violence is pregnant with a meaning which installs them in a religious metasocial space that is partly oneiric. In such cases, the protagonist of the violence is committed to a logic of hypersubjectivation in which the personal subject asserts himself not so much, or not only, in the here and now, but also, and above all, elsewhere and in a different temporality. Compared with the earlier case of a mere deficit of meaning, that self-assertion adds meaning. We have here an excess of meaning rather than a lack of meaning. It is that excess of meaning that allows us to speak of a hyper-subject. A hyper-subject can be committed to forms of violence that are increasingly artificial and unreal because they are divorced from the experience of those whose lives he claims to be changing. But the hyper-subject can also open up new political and social spaces, and can usher in a new era in which other forms of all kinds of relations can be constructed.

The moment of hyper-subjectivation, of a violence that is bound up with an excess of meaning, may well prefigure or even pave the way for the establishment of new social, political, and intercultural relations and, on a different register, new interpersonal relations. This moment is an essential characteristic of totalitarian phenomena and emergent cults, as it is an indication of both the intense subjectivity of those who are about to be part of that experience and their great heteronomy, which leads them to agree or even want to subordinate their lives to a project or a charismatic leader whose personality is a concentration of a movement's highest aspirations. The protagonists of such phenomena are often convinced that they are in control of their lives, that they are living as they choose to live, and that they are subjects who give a real meaning to their commitment; they are hyper-subjects. At the same time, their obedience to the law of the group or leader, and to the norms that derive from it, is not, in their view, open to discussion. They experience both an excess and a lack of meaning. They are, at least to begin with, at once in control of the lives they have chosen and alienated. Given the object of our discussion, it is only natural to emphasize the links between the hyper-subject and violence. But to reduce this figure of the subject to its self-destructive and destructive aspects would be to do it a great injustice. It would also be a big mistake: the hypersubject can also go off in very different directions and follow paths that do not lead to evil and extreme violence. If we forget that, we reduce religious belief to its murderous implications.

The non-subject

In our discussion of Nazi barbarism in Chapter 6, we came across the banality of evil thesis, which is sometimes associated with the idea of a culture of obedience to authority. Whilst we may have expressed serious reservations, we have to accept that the thesis can be validated, if only very partially. That is what Milgram's experiments and some historical research would suggest.

From this perspective, the executioner, murderer, or killer is not a subject; he is merely obeying orders. He is defined by his passive attitude towards the crime he commits. In his view it is meaningful only in the sense that it shows his respect for law and order. Such subjects have been reduced to the roles they play, and have therefore been desubjectivated or not subjectivated, or at least act without any reference to their personal subjectivity. That is why Hannah Arendt (1977 [1962]: 287–8) could say of Eichmann that: 'It was sheer thoughtlessness ... that predisposed him to become one of the greatest criminals of that period'.

The actor who commits the act of violence is then not a subject. He is merely carrying out orders which can be described as bureaucratic. He is a minor cog in what seems to be a pure system, a machine in which no one has to take responsibility for their actions. The non-meaning of the action leads to the behaviour of a non-subject.

Such behaviour must not be confused with a loss of meaning associated with a floating subjectivity that cannot attach itself to any meaning. The explanation for the violence lies, not in some deficit or lack of meaning that makes the subject express himself through violence, but in a more radical subjectivity-deficit, an inability or refusal to be a subject, whatever the nature of the acts that are committed. The violence therefore cannot be blamed on those who commit it; they have been reduced to the image of the non-subject, and have already been exonerated from any moral responsibility for their actions.

If we reject the non-subject thesis that follows on from Hannah Arendt's analysis of Eichmann, or which can be deduced from Milgram's experiments, we also have to reject the idea that the figure of the non-subject corresponds, empirically, to the historical experience of Nazism. In more general terms, we have to minimize the reality of cultures of obedience. But to the extent that the figure of the non-subject is pertinent and does have a heuristic value, it provides a novel instance of the relationship between violence and the subject: violence is possible precisely because subjectivity is not involved, or is systematically ignored.

The anti-subject

As we saw in Chapter 7, violence can be partly or completely gratuitous and cruel. It may look like a phenomenon that exists in its own right, that has no end other than the satisfaction it affords, that is not bound up with any meaning other than the meaning it constitutes in itself.

In the most extreme cases, such violence appears to relate only to the personality or psychic economy of the individual who inflicts it. It is not socially determined because it is not referred to by any social relations, or even by social relations that no longer exist, and nor is it culturally determined, as it cannot be explained in terms of determinations associated with the culture of some group or sub-group. It appears to be a personal attribute of the individual in question or, rather, to derive from a self-to-self relationship. It has to do with pleasure. It is a source of *jouissance* for its protagonist, who treats his victim or victims as beings who are from the outset dehumanized, sub-human, or supra-human. He reduces them to animality, or even the materiality of objects. If he needs to see them suffer, which is not necessarily the case, and derives pleasure from that specific moment, that is not because his victims are expressing their subjectivity in a positive sense, but solely because he can watch them being negated and mistreated. Sadism is not, in other words, the only component in this type of violence, but it does have its role to play. So too does the masochism that may be associated with it.

It is difficult to describe someone who indulges in violence for the sake of violence as a subject if we define the subject as a potentiality, or as the possibility of being in control of one's experience whilst recognizing that other people have the right to do the same. At the same time, there is no denying that inflicting physical and moral violence on others is intensely subjective. This subjectivity has to do with *jouissance*, with a pleasure that is neither social nor cultural but almost animal, and perhaps anthropological. It appears to be the least socialized, least educated, and most spontaneous aspect of the human personality. It is the very opposite of what one might expect of that dimension of the subject that means that it exists for itself only to the extent that it requires all human beings to exist in that same sense, and marks a definite departure from all humanism and any democratic spirit. Here, we are dealing with a very different aspect of the subject. The anti-subject is characterized by an absolute refusal to regard his victim as a subject; he can then reduce him or her to the level of a thing or an animal over which he can exercise absolute power for the sole purpose of deriving pleasure or satisfaction from violence.

The anti-subject is a strange aspect of individuality. The anti-subject appears to have the attributes of a subject-for-itself but cannot, in situation, enter into any relationship with other individuals, except in the form of sadistic or sadomasochistic acts. The anti-subject therefore has two essential characteristics. First, he is destructive and never constructive and, unlike the subject, does not seek to go on existing through action – or even protest action – or to inscribe the individual concerned in social, political, and intercultural relations. Second, the anti-subject denies his victims the most elementary rights and desubjectivizes them, except in cases where he expects them to derive pleasure from their own negation as in masochism, though that is usually more applicable to sexuality than to even serious or murderous physical violence.

The survivor-subject

The anti-subject is not to be confused with another dimension of the subject that must also be defined without reference to any possibility of action, and therefore without reference to social, political, cultural, or interpersonal relations. This is not a matter of purely destructive drives, of the pleasure of causing others pain, or of violence as an end in itself, but of the self-preservation of someone who feels threatened in their very being. The violence that corresponds to this figure of the subject is what the psychoanalyst Jean Bergeret calls 'fundamental'. This is an 'archaic, dominating violence' that derives from 'a primitive fantasy that simply raises the essential question of the survival of the individual: "The other or me?", "Him or me?", "Survival or death?" or "Survival, even if it means killing the other", without any primary or specific intention of destroying that other …' (Bergeret, 1995: 46).

Having reviewed the work of various authors and various currents within psychoanalysis, Jean Bergeret applies the notion of fundamental violence to a contemporary phenomenon that was particularly obvious in France in the 1980s and 1990s, namely the hate-fuelled violence of young people. The urban riots in the outlying working-class *banlieues*, which received a great deal of media coverage, helped to fuel a feeling of insecurity that was at the heart of national public debates throughout this period, particularly during the presidential and legislative elections of the spring of 2002. Bergeret explains:

> Today's young people are accused of being *violent* and 'aggressive'. We think we can take away the guilt and protect ourselves by advocating (either naively or perfidiously) a *fight against* **violence**. We are in fact talking about symptoms that simply express the precariousness of the interactional epigenesis that is available to so many of our contemporaries. The imaginary family models available to the latent structural elements that are innate in children are no longer capable of playing their dual role of warding off the excitement of over-violent fantasies on the one hand and, on the other, developing attractive libidinal elaborations. (1995: 62)

From this point of view, the violence that was seen at the time as a working-class urban – and male – phenomenon and which was often associated with immigration, is a product of failings on the part of adults who cannot offer the young people concerned adequate models with which they can identify. The young people themselves are well aware of this, see that no one is taking any interest in them, and find it impossible, according to Bergeret, to 'integrate fundamental violence correctly'.

This violence pre-exists the actor, and is something that everyone should be able to 'integrate', manage, and transform into something else. It is not surprising that the behaviour of young people in France's *banlieues* should be 'both extremely destructive and self-destructive, and very violent. Anger, madness and despair are tragic blind alleys, and reflect their inability to creatively negotiate one of the things that the human psyche has always used quite naturally: violence' (1995: 62).

This concept of fundamental violence suggests the idea of a universal anthropological characteristic, a natural quality, an almost animal instinct, a primitive potential, or a drive which a well-organized personality must channel into non-violent behaviour, rather than concealing it. This thesis is not far removed from some of Freud's analyses, and is even closer to René Girard's analysis: human beings are basically afraid of fundamental violence and use myths to conceal it.

Bergeret is not the only psychoanalyst to take an interest in what he calls fundamental violence. But he is, and this is the important point, clearer about the distinction between this form of violence and aggression than most. The goal of aggression is, according to Bergeret, to damage or destroy its object, whereas fundamental violence is a form of self-preservation for the subject. Aggression can be emotionally ambivalent or a mixture of hate and love, but fundamental violence is 'pre-ambivalent', bound up with the life drives and does not come from the death drive.

Bergeret's approach thus allows us to correlate certain expressions or aspects of violence with the pre-condition for the subject's existence: survival. 'Primitive life-narcissism' or fundamental violence is that which guarantees that the self will survive. It allows the individual concerned to save his own skin.

This violence, and the corresponding dimension of the subject, therefore has nothing to do with aggression or sadism. It breaks out when an individual feels, rightly or wrongly (not that it matters) that he is in a situation of existential danger or great peril. It does not deny the other's existence as a subject, even though it may result in the destruction of the other or an attack on the other's physical integrity. It breaks out because, even before the subject can emerge, claim to exist in his creative capacity, and to be in control of his experience, the individual concerned must first protect his physical being and body, and ensure that he will subsequently become the actor of his own existence. Fundamental violence is an expression of the refusal to let the emergent self be crushed or negated.

This violence corresponds to a subject who is not yet capable of becoming an actor, and not to a subject defined by a meaning that has been lost or has yet to emerge. This is a subject who must, in some elementary sense, simply preserve his capacity for being. Fundamental violence is a primal expression of a subject who needs no apprenticeship, no socialization, and no inscription in some culture before he can emerge. It precedes all subjectivation.

Neither the anti-subject nor the survivor-subject is in any position to become a social, political, or cultural actor. For his part, the anti-subject can only create the pre-conditions for destruction, whilst the survivor-subject is striving to ensure that he will become an actor.

Configurations and ambivalence

The typology that has just been outlined describes five figures of the subject, and relates each of them to a particular logic of violence. But it does more than just establish a link between the subject and violence. It constantly introduces a third term: the actor. There would in fact be no violence, or at least much less violence, if the subject did not try in some way to become an actor, or if the creative capacity that defines the actor did not also imply commitment and action – and withdrawal from commitment

We must, however, be very specific about the analytic status of the five figures of the subject that we have identified. In practice, there is no reason why they should systematically appear in their sociological purity or in isolation, or why they should be clearly defined. The idea of individuals or groups that could be reduced, in terms of the sources of their violent behaviours, to a single principle, and therefore to an elementary figure of the subject, is indeed applicable to certain experiences, and especially to the end of trajectories in which all that remains is, it would seem, a logic that corresponds to one or another of our figures of the subject.

But on the whole, an examination of concrete phenomena suggests that these figures are always likely to coexist or to become confused. When it is a matter of collective violence, the individuals involved may well represent one or another of these figures. This gives rise to complex and diversified overall configurations in which, in the case of a collective actor, the relative influence of each component figure is a given that varies greatly from one experience to another. And when it is a matter of individuals, there is no reason why we should not find a very complex combination of various figures of the subject or a co-presence whose modalities of expression are greatly influenced by the situation or environment.

The complexity becomes even greater because violent episodes are often unstable, especially if they last for a long time. Violence often breaks out in contexts that change, or in contexts that it transforms. And the ways in which groups or individuals shape the subject's various configurations at any given moment are therefore distorted. They change over time, in ways that can be both progressive and chaotic. They may change direction, but they can also break down.

The image of a combination or mixture of logics, and therefore of figures of the subject, is itself somewhat inadequate in that it tells us nothing about the relations that exist, or that are established, between the logics of the subject in the course of the experience of violence. From the actor's point of view, violence often marks the end of a trajectory or process, and suddenly resolves what seemed to be a mass of contradictions. The resolution is not normally recognized as such by those who bring it about, but there are exceptions to the rule. To take an example of collective action; research carried out under the supervision of Alain Touraine and François Dubet (1981) has shown that the only way the Occitan movement of the 1970s could reconcile the irreconcilable – a national-identitarian demand and a social protest supported mainly by wine growers – was to use violence. Their lucid refusal to go down that road after debating it condemned the militants' movement to failure, and that was in fact how it ended. Once the analysis has identified the main figures of the subject that may emerge, the question that arises is that of the overall economy within which they are likely to emerge and operate before the moment of fusion, or before one figure becomes dominant and puts its mark on the violence which is beginning or spreading. This raises a huge theoretical issue, and a theory of ambivalence might help to resolve it. Simonetta Tabboni outlines such a theory, which is in the tradition of Georges Sorel, when she explains that: 'Ambivalence is inherent in the *a prioris* that make social life possible, in the processes of cognitive activity, in the normative structures that prescribe incompatible behaviours and attitudes, in the habitus that demand the incessant control and repression of spontaneity and in the institutions of power' (1996: 244). From that point of view, the anti-subject becomes the other side of the coin when the subject is already in place; the plethora of meaning cannot be explained unless we relate it to the meaning deficit, and so on. The ambivalence hypothesis allows us to explore the complex interplay between the various figures of the subject and to look at episodes and figures that the classical social sciences, unlike great literature, could not really come to terms with. That is why anyone who wishes to understand the subjectivity of the protagonists of violence should certainly read great authors such as Shakespeare or Dostoyevsky.

Foundational Violence

In my view, the idea of the subject cannot be dissociated from the idea of self-foundation and autonomy, especially if we differentiate between it and the idea of the hyper-subject and the anti-subject. The idea of the subject places the emphasis on the creative capacity of human beings. Human beings are not just created; they create themselves – by using their brains according to Hegel, and through their labour according to Marx. From that point of view, violence means that the subject has failed, is impotent, or has been perverted. It results from the subject's failures, from the prohibition or impossibility of action, or from its dark side or what is known as the anti-subject. As Hannah Arendt might have said of Eichmann, there is a great difference between the peaceful activities of thought and labour, and acts of violence.

But is it quite impossible to argue that violence can also be a source of subjectivity, and therefore of the ability to create? Can we not invert the argument that has just been outlined, and which takes the subject as its starting point and violence as its point of arrival?

Sacrificial violence

The literature on anthropology has often seen violence as a necessary and foundational precondition for the social bond, which takes us a long way from the ideas we have discussed thus far. From this point of view, violence is not referred to the subject, but to the quasi-functional requirements of the system, of the community it binds together, and of the collective life it makes possible. Human sacrifice and the phenomena of the scapegoat are examples. This type of thesis, which is strikingly illustrated by Yvon Le Bot's study (1994: 208–9) of expiatory sacrifice in Guatemala, has also been theorized by Freud and, more recently, by Walter Burkert and René Girard. The usual suggestion is that by inflicting sacrificial violence on an individual or group, the tribe or primitive society closes ranks and drives out, together with the victim, problems that can, it believes, be blamed on the gods, who are, if we agree with Emile Durkheim, never anything more than a society's self-representation. Sacrifice is, explains René Girard (1999: 16), a regulatory mechanism that allows social violence to be driven out. The expulsion of the bleeding victim, or the lynching that once calmed down a community that was experiencing a rivalrous crisis that was in itself murderous, is then re-enacted in the form of a simulacrum or ritual that masks the foundational process, which may not be recognized for what it is:

> A lynching is the central moment in a sequence comprising at least three moments: 1) a violent crisis or disaster destroys the community, or prevents it from being founded; 2) the lynching restores peace; 3) the community begins to function or to function once more. This way of understanding sacrifice and the scapegoat uncovers a paradox: if they are to function, the mimetic phenomena that are central to this type of argument require 'the persecutors not to realize that they are responsible for either their mimetic rivalry or for the collective phenomenon that releases them They make their victim responsible for their deliverance as well as their misfortunes. Having demonized their victim, they deify him (1999: 18).

As Girard successfully demonstrates, the mechanism must, in other words, be inexplicable.

It was pointed out in Chapter 3 that we reached an anthropological turning point some years ago. Victims are increasingly recognized for what they are in their misfortune and pain, in the violence they have suffered and which has damaged, sometimes beyond repair, their moral and physical integrity. Once victims have a voice, or when it is simply acknowledged that the negation of their physical or moral integrity is implicit in the violence they have suffered, the thesis that violence is functional loses its validity, no matter what so many authors may have to say about, for example, pre-Columbian societies. The power of the rulers becomes an analytic category, as do the screams of their victims. The power relations become apparent and have to be theorized. The interesting thing about Bernard Lempert's (2000) study is that it reveals the relationships that are at work in human sacrifices: those who organize and perform them can never quite prevent their victims from protesting, or at least groaning.

We can discuss the idea of the functionality of so-called foundational violence in more historical terms if we recall that, in most cases, states and nations are born of violence and war – a civil war, or a war with external enemies – and then forget, in accordance with mechanisms that are quite similar to those described by Girard, the initial phases of their construction, if only to allow those who slew one another in the past to forget the violence they inflicted and to learn to live together. In his lecture 'What Is a Nation?' Ernest Renan (1990), for example, clearly states that a nation must forget the violence that surrounded its birth.

Violence founds the subject

Given that our perspective centres on the subject rather than the system, we have to look at a very different idea. From this point of view, violence is a moment or element in the formation and personal construction of the subject. The actual experience of violence cannot be discussed here; let us simply say that trying to recover from the trauma sometimes allows the victims to become subjects. The most impressive examples are, as it happens, provided by women rather than men. One thinks, for instance, of the mobilization of the mothers of the disappeared in Argentina, or of the way women who were abused and then turned into refugees living in the camps of the Former Yugoslavia subsequently transformed their own lives.[3]

The question that arises here is whether or not the subject can be founded on the basis of the experience of violence of which he is the author. From that point of view, can the violence inflicted by an individual be, in certain cases, a cathartic element and can it trigger a process of subjectivation? By using violence, that individual triggers or accelerates a logic that enables him to emerge as a subject. One example, which was often mentioned in France in the 1980s and 1990s, will serve as an illustration. The young people who became involved in riots for the first time had no real understanding of what they were doing, but felt sympathetic to or concerned by the protests that followed a police 'blunder'. For some, their first involvement in violence went no further than that, but it in others it marked the beginning of a career that led to delinquency and then prison, which is itself a breeding ground for crime. For others, it was the starting point for a very different trajectory that could lead to involvement with neighbourhood associations or cultural or sporting activities. It facilitated, in other words, a mobilization of the self, in either creative or political terms, or a subjectivation that was possible only because the moment of violence wrenched the individual away from a day-to-day existence consisting of passivity or alienation. A similar idea can be found in Jean-Paul Sartre's theorization of individual praxis.[4]

In general terms, it has to be recognized that the personal experience of violence is, at least in some cases, a process in which some moments are more decisive than others. Each moment can correspond to a subjectivation that is facilitated or accentuated, or, at the opposite extreme, to a loss of meaning and desubjectivation. But the overall trend is never towards an assertion of the subject in the long term. The assertion never lasts for very long, or at least not if the violence itself continues. And it should be added that careful observation gives the lie to hasty or superficial *judgements* such as those we have just mentioned in connection with young people in France's *banlieues*. Is the subjectivation of an adolescent who takes part in, for example, a riot simply a product of the violence itself, or of a community involvement that could be revealed only by that action? Does it result from the fact that he threw stones or helped to burn down a youth club, or from his impression that he had been able to denounce injustice and to draw the attention of the media and politicians to his neighbourhood, its situation, and its difficulties? My own work on terrorism (Wieviorka, 1995; 2002) suggests that we should be wary of over-facile ideas about acting out. More than one terrorist told me that the decisive moment that led him to join in the armed struggle was not an involvement in some violent foundational moment, but a banal episode that, as such, had nothing to do with violent action.

Violence can be a liberating experience for the subject in certain experiences and for a certain length of time. In such cases, it is the precondition for the emergence and blossoming of the subject's emancipation or self-preservation. That must not, however, conceal or minimize the essential fact that the opposite is true: the force and speed quickly prove to be anything but meaningful, and are an obstacle to the subjectivation of the individual concerned. To continue with the same example, the young revolutionary who turns to terrorism may well feel that he is, perhaps for the first time, in full control of his life when he joins an organization involved in the armed struggle. But he soon has to commit acts whose meaning he cannot really control and becomes trapped into a life that is not conducive to the subject because it is dominated by the constraints of clandestinity and has to obey a hierarchy. The strength of non-violent movements is precisely in the fact that they go far beyond a moralistic pacifism or humanism and take the view that basing political action on violence involves the almost inevitable risk that it will make subjectivation difficult or impossible for those involved.

Violence as transformation

Violence is often an exceptional event; the crime is not repeated and the outbreak of rioting quickly dies down. In other cases, it has to be thought of as a process that can last for a certain length of time, and that has its high points and its low points.

In such cases, it is never stable for any length of time. It cannot be stabilized or controlled by its protagonist, who will be unable to establish a level or threshold at which its intensity can be regulated. Violence is itself a process of change, so much so that some of its manifestations have been described as a spiral or an infernal machine. It moves from 'hot' to 'cold', from untrammelled expressivity to what seems to be highly organized instrumentality, but its stability is no more than provisional. It moves from one level to another, from the infrapolitics of delinquency to the metapolitics of religion. The same actor can be a terrorist one day, and a classic criminal the next. He may be caught up in an increasingly murderous spiral of violence, or may revert to low-level delinquency. In the countless processes that make violence such a many-sided phenomenon, it can easily acquire and lose meanings that constantly transform it. Its protagonist can move from being autonomous (or in other words capable of establishing the orientations and modalities of his own action) to being heteronomous, which means that he becomes the vector for a meaning that does not belong to him. He may even become a hired killer or hit man, or a mercenary in the service of a cause that is not his, or at least not the cause that made him turn to violence.

Violence is always likely to drift away from its original meanings, and its protagonist is always likely to turn to behaviours in which those meanings become lost. By the same criteria, other meanings may emerge. To illustrate the point, we can look at the trajectory of young Khaled Kelkal, who was one of the main protagonists of the wave of Islamist terrorism that hit France in the summer of 1995.[5] The trajectory began with a young man of North African immigrant origin living in the suburbs of Lyon, where his intense feeling of social and racial discrimination blocked his personal development. It ended in extreme violence. Islamism gave that feeling a plethora of meanings, but they had very little to do with any desire, or even a lost desire, to become a subject within French society. A reconstruction of Kelkal's trajectory reveals some episodes of fairly classic delinquency, but also the discovery or rediscovery of an Islamism that encouraged him to become an example and to preach by example, especially to those close to him. Understanding his point of departure does not really allow us to understand his point of arrival, or the decisive moments in his trajectory, which inevitably include changes of direction and moments of rupture. That is unavoidable in the transition from the meaning of a violence that was, in Kelkal's case, greatly influenced by a subjectivity grounded in the social relations and lived experience of young people of immigrant origin living in the suburbs of Lyon, to the meanings of a terrorism designed to promote what had become a radical Islamism.

These comments suggest that it is a mistake to use stable categories to analyse various experiences of violence. Precisely because it is bound up with the subjectivity of actors, violence can be just as diverse as its actors. One or other of the five figures of the subject may be dominant, and all five may coexist in combinations whose stability varies. The subjectivity of the protagonist of violence is not a quantity that diminishes or increases at various stages in his trajectory. It is something that is transformed and in extreme cases perverted. It is something that the researcher must rediscover in even its most fragmentary, impoverished, lost, distorted, or inverted expressions.

Notes

1 On this question, as applied to sociology, see Wieviorka (2000).
2 See the exchange between Renaut and Touraine published as 'Rencontre au sujet du Sujet' (2000).

3 The coauthored *Violence and Subjectivity* (Das et al., 2000) includes several texts showing how subjects can emerge from the lived experience of violence, despite the violence they have suffered, despite the accumulated shame, the traumas and sometimes the pressure to use violence exerted by, for example, a terrorist movement it is not easy to refuse to join.

4 See in particular the discussion of the transition from individual praxis to the pratico-inert in Sartre (1976 [1960]).

5 See Wieviorka (1995). The sociologist Diemar Loch published a particularly interesting interview with Khaled Kelkal in the issue of *Le Monde* dated 7 October 1992. The interview was given in 1992.

CONCLUSION

A Major Dilemma

It may seem that this book is, ultimately, organized around a paradox. It opens with the idea that transformations such as economic globalization, with its effects on states and its implications for violence, call for a change of paradigm. It ends by arguing that our analysis should be centred on the subject, and even the individual subject. In short, it seems to begin by asking us to look at general or 'macro' phenomena and end by re-centring the analysis on something that could not be more 'micro', namely individuals in their subjectivity and almost their intimacy. That suggestion appears to be far removed from the book's original inspiration.

There is in fact nothing paradoxical about this. When properly understood, the notion of globalization does not in fact mean that we now have to analyse everything on a global scale, or that it is all a matter of transnational financial flows, markets without frontiers, and identities that reflect the image of an intense circulation of people all over the word or of the global expansion of some regions. It suggests, rather, that we have to see a phenomenon such as violence, in all its countless expressions, as something that will always present us with a major intellectual dilemma: we can either talk in very general 'global' terms, or we can talk in very particular terms about intimate subjectivity.

To relate violence to the subject does not, in my view, mean outlining a psychological approach; it is a plea to see violence as an effort that is made by the subject, or anti-subject, in contexts or situations whose overall dimensions have to be taken into account. I would happily describe those dimensions as 'total', had not Marcel Mauss given the idea of a 'total social fact' a rather different meaning. We have to recognize that violence is more likely to occur when action seems difficult, when social, political, cultural, or interpersonal relations disappear and give way to the logics of rupture and the loss of meaning, and when the construction of relations gives way to a plethora of, for example, metapolitical meanings, to lack, and to the hypersubjectivity of some and the despair of others.

Great geopolitical changes and global phenomena such as the reenchantment of the world thanks to religion and the rise of ethnic identities do have an influence on lived experience, but they do not in themselves directly or automatically determine the behaviours of the people they concern. They themselves are shaped by the personal, subjective choices of those who cause them to happen. Such changes do not necessarily take away their ability, desire, or impulse to make their own choices, to give a meaning to their lives, to try to go on doing so in artificial ways, to seek pleasure, or quite simply to survive when life itself seems to be under threat. They are not an obstacle to subjectivation; on the contrary, they encourage and exacerbate it, and subjectivation is not a process that occurs outside the system, even though it may come up against difficulties or prove unable to influence it in their turn. Subjectivation is in many respects informed by the situation, but it is also a product of the way the persons concerned perceive that situation. In certain cases, this may lead to violence. Palestinian martyrs, young rioters in France's *banlieues*, and criminal gang members in Los Angeles do not necessarily have to systematically define themselves with reference to globalization or even, more simply, logics that operate on a grand scale. But it is all the easier to understand their behaviour if we see in it the mark of an impossible subject, a floating subject, or an anti-subject who finds within his general conditions of existence, which might be described as 'global', spaces that have been destructured, that are dominated by disruptive forces, and that can be filled by violence rather than any other action, logic, or social, cultural, political, or interpersonal construct.

Good and Evil

In moving from the classical approaches to the hypothesis of the subject, which is central to this book, we are making such a leap that we seem to be calling into question the basic rules of sociology. We are arguing that the subject in fact functions at a pre-social level. Violence is not a product of the social, but of the lack, inadequacies and decline of the social, and, in the most extreme cases, has nothing to do with the social. Ever since the time of Emile Durkheim (see especially Durkheim, 1982 [1895]), sociologists have habitually explained the social in terms of the social, and have refused to make any analytic recourse to what Alain Touraine (1973) calls a metasocial guarantor. Perhaps it is time to admit that my proposals are non-sociological because they come down to centring the analysis on a non-social principle.

If violence is, to adopt Durkheim's terminology, a social fact, and if we are introducing the non-social element of the subject in order to explain it, are we not introducing a new – and hidden – God in order to analyse a phenomenon whose considerable importance in our collective life, preoccupations, debates, and worries calls for a sociological analysis?

Barbarism, cruelty, mass murder, and the extreme phenomena that should, I think, be central to any discussion of violence, defy the classical explanations supplied by the social sciences, even though the latter may help us to understand some aspects of them. The traditional explanations do not tell us why evil can lead to such excesses or why cruelty is not functional. That does not, however, mean that the social sciences do not need to go on studying the subjectivity of the protagonists of violence and the preconditions for the transformation of violence into action. We have to learn to accept the idea that there is a non-social or even an anti-social basis to what is undermining and dehumanizing our collective life, and that it has little to do with its dysfunctionalities and crises. And we have to complement that idea with another idea that in fact allows us to get back to sociology's most classical approaches and categories: the violence of the subject, in the different forms we have identified, emerges in some contexts rather than others, and is more likely to do so when societal ensembles are incoherent, fragmented, or decadent at every level from the most local to the most global.

Until the 1970s and 1980s we lived in a world in which violence was not the central figure of evil, which is what it has become. We discussed social relations and social conflicts, and tensions and collective life, within the framework of nation-states, and possibly in terms of relations between nation-states, and we were, following Max Weber, sensitive to images of religious disenchantment. Indeed, violence had a certain legitimacy, even at the heart of Western societies. We are now preoccupied with major worries rather than hopes for radiant futures or utopias. Violence has replaced conflict, cultural identities are creating tensions and fear, and God is back all over the world, and not only thanks to Islam. Wars have replaced negotiations and the political deficit grows day by day all over the planet as it translates the ideology of the 'clash of civilizations' into a self-fulfilling prophecy. All these phenomena encourage violence, and it is embodied in the various figures of the subject which use the clash of civilizations as a training ground. Violence constitutes evil, and the big question is whether or not we can use good to fight it. And if so, how?

There are three main sets of answers. The first puts the emphasis on the social conditions that are conducive to the expression of violence ('social' is to be understood in the broad sense, and as including the political, cultural, institutional, and juridical dimensions). This suggests the idea that evil lies beyond or beneath the social, whilst good is inscribed within the social. There are two main variants on this idea. One insists, as we have insisted from the very beginning of this book, that all human groups are divided, and that a principle of conflict is enough to ensure that their division can be handled in non-violent ways, that it can be experienced in the form of relations and not ruptures. The other variant is more interested in the unity of the system under consideration, and in its ability to ensure its own integration. It sets great store by the notion of the social bond, or the national-community bond, for example, and has great faith in the mechanisms and institutions that can integrate and socialise, as well as the notion of order. One suggests that problems should be transformed into conflicts, debates, reforms, and negotiations, whilst the other argues that problems should be socialized, prevented, or repressed. Both contrast a social concept of good with violence, or in other words, the most subjective aspects of evil.

A second set of answers points to the limitations of the classic social and political ways of handling violence and of the naivety of believing, for example, that it is possible to negotiate with fanatical terrorists who are prepared to kill themselves. From this point of view, good must also correspond to some metasocial principle if it is to be able to fight evil. Where is that principle to be found? Some would argue that we should look to humanist or ethical values, turn non-violence into a principle that is not open to discussion, and tolerate no exceptions on the part of actors involved in non-violent struggles, whatever their nature. Others say that we should turn to a faith or belief – which is a reminder that whilst religion can produce the hyper-subject of violence, it can also produce the hyper-subject of respect for life and love of others, and indeed that of a non-violence that becomes a guide to action.

Both sets of answers have to admit that what is embodied in the floating subject, the anti-subject, and other figures of evil manifests itself in concrete behaviours, and in social and institutional geopolitical spaces. Violence represents a challenge to the social sciences in that it derives from a principle that operates at a pre-social level whereby there is no 'subject', but it also lies at the heart of social life. That is why the approach outlined here breaks with sociology's classical approaches, and still remains profoundly sociological. It breaks with traditional approaches by making a non-social principle central to the analysis, but remains sociological in that it attempts to analyse the conditions that allow evil to emerge, spread, find expression, or regress. What applies to violence also applies to many other domains: the social sciences' classical age has gone, and we have to invent new analytic tools, paradigms, and modes of approach that correspond to the contemporary world's problems, be it the rise of cultural identities, of racism, of the phenomena of deinstitutionalization, of changes in the workplace, or the return of God.

But perhaps the reader expects this book to end by making more specific suggestions that will allow us to develop policies for action against violence? So let us go back to our typology.

The simplest example is, in theory if not in practice, that of the floating subject. If the floating subject is primarily the product of an absence of conflict, or of difficulties or impossibilities that prevent individuals and groups from transforming their expectations and problems into debates and conflicts, then our first response to violence must be to attempt to compensate for that deficit and those difficulties, either by finding new conflicts that can replace old and exhausted ones, or by recognizing that subjects who cannot, for the moment, promote action are beginning to emerge as actors. If, on the other hand, the floating subject is, rather, the product of a crisis affecting mechanisms of integration or institutions, we have to restore order, authority, and the system's ability to function and to recreate the social bond. If that is the case, the task of the sociologist is to produce the analysis that allows a hierarchical distinction to be established between these types of explanation, which are usually complementary rather than contradictory, and therefore to shed light on the nature of the situation by undertaking concrete research.

Similarly general policies and orientations may be required to deal with the hyper-subject. In this case, the problem is not a deficit of meaning and therefore a lack of conflict or crisis, or the weakness of the social bond. On the contrary, it is the plethora of meaning, which either overloads the conflict and transforms it in rupture, war, or terrorism, whilst potential adversaries are treated as enemies, or which deliberately tries to make the crisis worse. The answer to the floating subject may be to try to get back to a principle of conflict, or to strengthen the social bond. In the case of the hyper-subject, it is more a matter of giving new meaning to the idea of the social bond, or of getting back to conflict, and eliminating the meanings that are perverting it, or blocking its formation, or preventing it from appearing as such. That implies acting in such a way as to ensure that the metasocial or metapolitical dimensions of action, and especially its religious dimensions, cease to overdetermine it by making all negotiations impossible. Otherwise, no reforms, compromises, debates, or discussions are possible, and there can be no individual involvement in the life of the *polis*. This is never easy, especially when the hyper-subject has already come into existence. If the attempt is made too early, the processes of inversion that will lead to violence may, for example, turn the poor or the excluded into a floating subject, and then into desperate individuals who can avoid desubjectivation only by going to extremes. It is likely that our efforts will be in vain, or too late, in which case the only way to put an end to murderous practices is to repress them by using the police, the military, or the legal system.

The set of responses showing that the hyper-subject can also be dealt using other ways also merits examination. These suggest that non-social figures of good should be promoted, even if, and perhaps especially if, those figures belong to the same cultural space of the hyper-subject under consideration. To put it simply, the response to a radical Islamism that is turning into terrorism should be a call to recognize and support a so-called 'moderate' Islam, especially if it can divorce religion from the political and refer only to the former register. In more general terms, this orientation is an argument in favour of human rights, absolute respect for life and the physical and moral integrity of all human beings, and recognition of the Other, and has no qualms about seeking support from concrete groups or communities, even if it means ignoring the sovereignty of states or the abstract universalism that sees nothing but individuals in the public space.

These comments, and this kind of argument, might be extended to other figures of the subject of violence. The problem is that, as we move further away from the floating subject and the hyper-subject, the more difficult it becomes to see how the protagonists can rediscover a meaning, conflict, or the social bond. A case can certainly be made, in fairly general terms, for education policies, both at school and in the home, that prevent the emergence of personalities that are more inclined than others towards violence. One can just as easily call for more effective and more systematic repressive and legal apparatuses that could bring the authors of mass murders and the organizers of genocides to trial at a supranational level. But such policies and apparatuses cannot answer the underlying question: is it possible to conceive of a world without violence, or of a humanity that has rid itself of perverted or inverted figures of the subject?

BIBLIOGRAPHY

ADDI, Lahouri (2002) *Sociologie et anthropologie chez Pierre Bourdieu*. Paris: La Découverte.

ALTHEIDE, David L. (2002) *Creating Fear: News and the Concept of Crisis*. New York: Aldine de Gruyter.

ANDERSON, Benedict (1983) *Imagined Communities: Reflections on the Origin and Spread of Nationalism*. London: Verso.

ANGOUSTURES, Aline and Valérie Pascal (1996) 'Diasporas et financement des conflits', in Rufin and Rufin (1996): 495–542.

APPADURAI, Arjun (2002) 'Dead Certainty: Ethnic Violence in the Era of Globalization', in Hinton (2002): 286–304.

ARENDT, Hannah (1970 [1969]) *On Violence*. New York: Harcourt Brace.

— (1977 [1962]) *Eichmann in Jerusalem: A Report on the Banality of Evil*. Harmondsworth: Penguin.

— (1985 [1951]) *The Origins of Totalitarianism*. New York: Harcourt (new edn. with added preface).

ARON, Raymond (1966 [1962]) *Peace and War: A Theory of International Relations* (trans. Richard Howard and Annette Baker Fox). London: Weidenfeld and Nicolson.

— (1970 [1967]) *Main Currents in Sociological Thought. Vol 2. Durkheim, Pareto, Weber*, (trans. Richard Howard and Helen Weaver). Harmondsworth: Penguin.

AUDET, Jean and Jean-François Katz (1999) *Précis de Victimologie Générale*. Paris: Dunod.

AUDOIN-ROUZEAU, Stéphane and Annette Becker (2000) *14–18. Retrouver la guerre*. Paris: Gallimard.

BADIE, Bertrand and Pierre Birnbaum (1979) *Sociologie de l'Etat*. Paris: Hachette.

BADINTER, Elisabeth (2006 [2003]) *Dead End Feminism*, (tr. Julia Borossa). Cambridge: Polity.

BAKER, Robert K. and Sandra J. Ball (1969) *A Staff Report to the National Commission on the Cause and Prevention of Violence*.

BALANDIER, Georges (1992) *Le Pouvoir sur Scènes*. Paris: Balland.

BARKER, Martin and Julian Petley (1997) *Ill Effects: The Media/Violence Debate*. London: Routledge.

BARTOV, Omar (1991) *Hitler's Army: Soldiers, Nazis and War in the Third Reich*. New York and London: Oxford University Press.

BAUDRILLARD, Jean (1995) 'Le Degré Xerox de la violence', *Libération* , 2 October.

BAUDRY, Patrick (1997) *La pornographie et ses images*. Paris: Armand Colin.

BAUMAN, Zygmunt (1989) *Modernity and the Holocaust.* Cambridge: Polity.
— (1993) *Post-Modern Ethics.* Oxford: Blackwell.
BAYART, Jean-François (1996) 'L'Historicité de l'Etat importé', *Les Cahiers du CERI,* 15.
BAZENGUISSA-GANGA, Rémy (1996) 'Milices politiques et bandes armées. Enquête sur la violence politique et sociale des jeunes déclassés', *Les Etudes du CERI,* 13, April.
BENJAMIN, Walter (1996 [1921]) 'Critique of Violence' (trans. Edmund Jephcot), *Selected Writings Vol I, 1913–1926,* edited by Marcus Bullock and Michael W. Jennings. Harvard: Belknap. pp. 236–52.
BERGERET, Jean (1995) *Freud, la violence et la dépression.* Paris: PUF.
BOIME, Albert (ed.) (1996) *Violence and Utopia: The Work of Jerome Boime.* Lanham, NY and London: University Press of America.
BOURKE, Joanna (1999) *An Intimate History of Killing: Face-to-Face Killing in Twentieth-Century Warfare.* London: Granta.
BOZARSLAN, Hamit (1997) *La Question Kurde: Etats et minorités au Moyen-Orient.* Paris: Presses de Sciences Po.
BRAUD, Philippe (2004) *Violences Politiques.* Paris: Seuil, Collections 'Points'.
BRODEUR, Jean-Paul (1995) 'Violence spéculaire', *Lignes* 25, May.
— (2003) *Les Visages de la Police.* Montréal: Presses Universitaires de Montréal.
— and Dominique Monjardet (eds) (2003) 'Connaître la police: Grands texts de la recherche anglo-saxonne , *Les Cahiers de la Sécurité Intérieure,* Hors série.
BROWNING, Christopher R. (2001 [1992]) *Ordinary Men: Police Battalion 101 and the Final Solution in Poland.* Harmondsworh: Penguin.
BRUCKNER, Pascal (1999) *La Tentation de l'innocence.* Paris: Grasset.
BUFORD, Bill (1992) *Among the Thugs.* London: Mandarin.

CALVI, Fabrizio (1982) *Camarade P. 52.* Paris: Grasset.
CASTEL, Robert (1995) *Les Métamorphoses de la Question Sociale.* Paris: Fayard.
CHAUMONT, Jean-Michel (1997) *La Concurrence des Victimes: Génocide, identité, reconnaissance.* Paris: La Découverte.
CHERKI, Alice (2000) *Frantz Fanon: Portrait.* Paris: Seuil.
CHESNAIS, Jean-Claude (1981) *Histoire de la Violence.* Paris: Robert Laffont.
CHESTERMAN, Simon (ed.) (2001) *Civilians in War.* Boulder, CO: Lynne Rienne.
CHEVALIER, Louis (1973 [1958]) *Labouring Classes and Dangerous Classes in Paris During the First Half of the Nineteenth Century* (trans. Frank Jellineck). London: Routledge and Kegan Paul.
CHRISTENSEN, Birgit (1998) 'Principe et morale. L'ère post-moderne et le droit d'avoir des droits', in Marie-Claire Caluz-Tschopp, *Hannah Arendt: la banalité du mal comme mal politique.* Paris: L'Harmattan.
COHEN, Stanley (2001) *States of Denial: Knowing about Atrocities and Suffering.* Cambridge: Polity.
COMTESSE DE SEGUR (2008 [1865]) *Un Bon Petit Diable.* Paris: Livre de Poche.
COSER, Lewis (1956) *The Function of Social Conflict.* Glencoe, IL: Free.

DAGNAUD, Monique (1999) 'Violence des jeunes, violence des images' , *Enfances et psy,* 6, March.
— (2003) *Médias et Violence: l'état du débat.* Paris: La Documentation française.
DAMIANI, Carole (1997) *Les Victimes: violences publiques et crimes privés.* Paris: Bayard.
DAS, Veena, Arthur Kleinman, Mamphele Ramphele, and Paul Reynolds (eds) (2000) *Violence and Subjectivity.* Berkeley, CA: University of California Press.

DELLA PORTA, Donatella (ed) (1984) *Terrorismi in Italia*. Bologna: Il Mulino.

DELMAS, Philippe (1995) *Le Bel Avenir de la Guerre*. Paris: Gallimard.

DELMAS-MARTY, Mireille (2002) 'Les crimes internationaux peuvent-ils contriber au débat entre universalisme et relativisme des valeurs?', in Antonio Cassese and Mireille Delmas-Marty (eds), *Crimes Internationaux et Jurisdictions Internationales: valeurs, politique et droit*. Paris: PUF.

DERRIDA, Jacques (2000a) *Etats d'âme de la Psychanalyse. Adresse aux Etats Généraux de la Psychanalyse*. Paris: Galilée.

— (2000b), 'Le siècle et le pardon', in *Foi et Savoir*. Paris: Seuil.

DERRIENNIC, Jean-Pierre (2001) *Les Guerres Civiles*. Paris: Presses des Sciences Po.

DESBARATS, Carole (1995) 'La Frontière', *Trafic,* 13.

DILLON, Michael (1997) 'Otherwise than Self-Determination: The Moral Freedom of *Oedipus Asphaleos*', in Vries and Weber (1997).

DOUBNOV, Simon (1988) *Histoire d'un Soldat Juif, 1880–1915*. Paris: Cerf.

DOWER, John (1986) *War without Mercy: Race and Power in the Pacific War*. New York: Pantheon.

DUBET, François (1987) La Galère: jeunes en survie. Paris: Fagard.

DURKHEIM, Emile (1982 [1895]) *The Rules of Sociological Method and Selected Texts on Sociology and its Method* (trans. W. D. Halls). Basingstoke: Macmillan.

— (1915 [1912]) *The Elementary Forms of Religious Life* (trans. J. W. Swain). London: Allen and Unwin.

ECO, Umberto (1976) *Dalla periferia all'imperio*. Milan: Bompiani.

EHRENBERG, Alain (1995) *L'Individu Incertain*. Paris: Calmann-Lévy.

EINSTEIN, Albert and Sigmund Freud (1985 [1932]) 'Why War?' in *The Penguin Freud Library. Vol. 12. Civilization, Society and Religion*. Harmondsworth: Penguin.

EISENSTADT, Schmuel and Wolfgang Schluchter (1998) 'Paths to Early Modernities: A Comparative View', *Daedelus*, vol. 127, no. 3: 4–7.

ELIAS, Norbert (1994 [1939]) *The Civilizing Process: The History of Manners and State Formation and Civilization (*trans. Edmund Jephcott). Oxford: Blackwell.

ENGELS, Frederick (1976 [1878]) *Anti-Dühring (Herr Eugen Dühring's Revolution in Science)*. Peking: Foreign Languages Press.

ENZENSBERGER, Hans Magnus (1992) *Die Grosse Wanderung*. Frankfurt am Main: Suhrkamp.

FANON, Frantz (2004 [1961]) *The Wretched of the Earth* (trans. Richard Philcox). New York: Grove.

FRAISSE, Robert (1997) 'Pour une politique des sujets singuliers', in François Dubet and Michel Wieviorka (eds), *Penser le Sujet: autour d'Alain Touraine*. Paris: Fayard. pp. 551–64.

FRAU-MEIGS, Divina and Sophie Jehel (1997) *Les Ecrans de la Violence: enjeux économiques et responsabilités sociales*. Paris: Economica.

FUKUYAMA, Francis (1992) *The End of History and the Last Men*. London: Hamish Hamilton.

FUREDI, Frank (2005 [1997]) *Culture of Fear: Risk-Taking and the Morality of Low Expectations*. London: Continuum (revised edn.).

GAVI, Philippe, Jean-Paul Sartre and Pierre Victor (1971) *On a Raison de se Révolter*. Paris: Gallimard.

GERBNER, George (1988) *Violence and Terror in the Mass Media, Reports and Papers on Mass Communications No 102*. Paris: UNESCO.

GEREMEK, Bronislaw (1987 [1971]) *The Margins of Society in Late Medieval Paris* (tr. Jean Birrel). Cambridge: Cambridge University Press.

GILLIGAN, James, MD (1996) *Violence: Our Deadly Epidemic and its Causes.* New York. Putnam.

GILROY, Paul (1987) *There Ain't No Black in the Union Jack.* London: Hutchinson.

GIRARD, René (1999) 'Violence et religion', in *Violences d'aujourd'hui, Violence de toujours,* XXXVIIe Rencontres Internationales de Genève. Lausanne: L'Age d'homme.

GITLIN, Todd (2001) *Media Unlimited: How the Torrent of Images and Sounds Overwhelms Our Lives.* New York: Metropolitan.

GLUCKSMANN, André (2002) *Dostoïevsky à Manhattan.* Paris: Robert Laffont.

GOLDHAGEN, Daniel Jonah (1997 [1996]) *Hitler's Willing Executioners: Ordinary Germans and the Holocaust.* London: Abacus.

GÖLE, Nilófer (2000),' Snapshots of Islamic Modernities', *Daedelus,* 129 (1): 91–116.

GOURGOURIS, Stathis (1997) 'Enlightenment and *Paratonia*', in Vries and Weber (1997).

GROSS, Jan Tomasz (2002 [2000]) *Les Voisins: 10 juillet 1941: un massacre de Juifs en Pologne.* Paris: Fayard.

GUILANE, Jean and Jean Zammit (2001) *Le Sentier de la Guerre: visages de la violence préhistorique.* Paris: Seuil.

GUZMAN, Germàn (1962) *La Violencia en Colombia. Bogotà* (Ed. Tercer Mundo, second edn.).

HACKER, Friedrich (1976) *Terreur et Terrorisme.* Paris: Flammarion.

HAMILTON, James Towler (1998) *Channelling Violence: The Economic Market for Violent Television Programming.* Princeton: Princeton University Press.

HANEY, Craig, Curtis Banks, and Philip Zimbardo (1995) 'A Study of Prisoners and Guards in a Simulated Prison', in Elliott Aranson (ed.), *Readings About the Social Animal.* New York: Freeman. pp. 52–67.

HANSSEN, Beatrice (1997) 'On the Politics of Pure Means: Benjamin, Arendt, Foucault', in Vries and Weber, 1997.

HASSNER, Pierre (1995) *La Violence et La Paix: de la bombe atomique au nettoyage éthnique.* Paris: Ed. Esprit.

— (1998) 'From War and Peace to Violence and Intervention. Permanent Moral Dilemmas under Changing Political and Technological Conditions', in Moore (1998): 9–27.

— and Roland Marchal (eds) (2003) *Guerres et Sociétés: Etat et violence après la Guerre Froide.* Paris: Khartala.

HATZFELD, Jean (2008a [2000]) *Into the Quick of Life: The Rwandan Genocide: The Survivors Speak* (trans. Gerry Feehilly). London: Serpent's Tail.

— (2008b [2003]) *A Time for Machetes: The Rwandan Genocide: The Killers Speak* (trans. Linda Coverdale). London: Serpent's Tail.

HERITIER, Françoise (ed) (1996) *De La Violence.* Paris: Odile Jacob.

HILLBERG, Raoul (1961 [1955]) *The Destruction of the European Jews.* Chicago: Quadrangle.

HINTON, Alexander Laban (2002) *Genocide: An Anthropological History.* Oxford: Blackwell.

HOBSBAWM, Eric (1992 [1990]) *Nations and Nationalism since 1780: Programme, Myth, Reality.* Cambridge: Cambridge University Press (second edn).

HORNE, John and Alan Kramer (2001) *German Atrocities: A History of Denial.* New Haven and London: Yale University Press.

HUGHES, Robert (1993) *The Culture of Complaint: The Fraying of America*. New York: Oxford University Press.

HUGO, Victor (1982 [1862]) *Les Misérables* (trans. Norman Denny). Harmondsworth: Penguin.

HUNTINGTON, Samuel P. (1997) *The Clash of Civilizations and the Remaking of World Order*. London: Simon and Schuster.

JOAS, Hans (1996 [1992]) *The Creativity of Action* (trans. Jeremy Gaines and Paul Keast). Cambridge: Polity.

JOHNSON, Jeremy G. (2000) 'Television Viewing and Aggressive Behaviour During Adolescence and Adulthood', *Science*, 295, 29 March.

JULLIARD, Jacques (1965) *Clemenceau, briseur de grèves*. Paris: Julliard.

KATZ, Elihu (1988) 'On Conceptualising Media Effects: Another Look' in S. Oskamp (ed.), *Television as a Social Issue*. Thousand Oaks, CA, and London: Sage.

KELMAN, Herbert C. and V. Lee Hamilton (1989) *Crimes of Obedience: Towards A Social Psychology of Authority and Responsibility*. New Haven: Yale University Press.

KHOSROKHAVAR, Farhad (1992) *Rupture de L'unanimisme dans la Revolution Iranienne*. Thèse pour le doctorat d'Etat. Paris: EHESS.

— (1995) *L'Islamisme et la Mort, le Martyre Révolutionnaire en Iran*. Paris: L'Harmattan.

— (2001) 'Le Modèle bassidji', *Cultures et Conflits*, nos. 29–30, Winter.

— (2005 [2002]) *Suicide Bombers: Allah's New Martyrs* (trans. David Macey). London and Ann Arbor: Pluto.

KRESSEL, Neil J. (2002 [1996]) *Mass Hate: The Global Rise of Genocide and Terror*. Cambridge, MA: Westview. (revised and updated ed.).

KRIEGEL, Blandine (2002) *La Violence a la Television, Rapport de Mmme Blandine Kriegel a M. Jean-Jacques Aillagon, Ministre de la Culture et de la Communication*. Paris: Ministre de la Culture et de la Communication.

LABAT, Séverine (1995) *Les Islamistes Algériens*. Paris: Seuil.

LABORIE, Pierre (1996) 'Violence politique et imaginaire collectif. L'Example de l'épuration' in *Violances et Pouvoirs Politiques (texts réunis par Michel Bertran, Natacha Laurent et Michel Taillefer)*. Toulouse: Presses Universitaires du Mirail.

LACAN, Jacques (1994 [1973]) *The Four Fundamental Concepts of Psychoanalysis* (trans. Alan Sheridan, with a new introduction by David Macey). Harmondsworth: Penguin.

LAGRANGES, Hugues (1995) *La Civilité à l'épreuve: Crime et sentiment d'insécurité*. Paris: PUF.

— (2001) *De l'affrontement à l'épreuve: Violences, délinquance et usage de drogues*. Paris: Syros.

LANZMANN, Claude (1986) 'Les Non-lieux de la mémoire' in Jean-Bertrand Pontalis (ed), *L'Amour de la Haine*. Paris: Gallimard, Collection 'Folio'.

LAQUEUR, Walter (1982) *The Terrible Secret: The Suppression of the Truth about Hitler's 'Final Solution'*. Harmondsworth: Penguin (new edn.).

LARSEN, Otto N. (1968) *Violence and the Mass Media*. Evanston and New York: Harper and Row.

LAZARSFELD, Paul, et al. (1972 [1932]) *Marienthal: The Sociology of an Unemployed Community* (trans. the author, with John Reginall and Thomas Elsansser). London: Tavistock.

LE BOT, Yvon (1992) *La Guerre en Terre Maya: communauté, violence et modernité au Guatemala (1970–1992)*. Paris: Karthala.

— (1994) *Violence de la modernité en Amérique latine: indianite, société et pouvoir*. Paris: Karthala.

LE BRETON, David (1991) *Passions du Risque*. Paris: Métailé.

LEFEBVRE, Georges (1973 [1932]) *The Great Fear of 1789: Rural Panic in Revolutionary France* (trans. Joan White). London: New Left.

LEMPERT, Bernard (2000) *Critique de la raison sacrificielle*. Paris: Seuil.

— (2002) *Le Retour de l'intolérance: Sectairisme et chasses aux sorcières*. Paris: Fayard.

LEPOUTRE, Daniel (1997) *Coeur de Banlieue: Codes, rites et langages*. Paris: Odile Jacob.

LEVI, Primo (1988 [1986]) *The Drowned and the Saved* (trans. Raymond Rosenthal). London: Abacus.

LIEBES, Tamar and Elihu Katz (1990) *The Export of Meaning. Cross-Cultural Readings of Dallas*. New York and Oxford: Oxford University Press.

LIFTON, Robert Jay (1986) *The Nazi Doctors: Medical Killing and the Psychology of Genocide*. New York: Basic.

MAITRON, Jean (1983) *Histoire du Movement Anarchiste*. Paris: La Découverte.

MAMOU, Jacky (2001) L' Humanitaire expliqué *à mes enfants*. Paris: Seuil.

MANNHEIM, Karl (1936 [1929]) *Ideology and Utopia: An Introduction to the Sociology of Knowledge* (trans. Louis Wirth and Edwards Shils). London: Routledge and Kegan Paul.

MARCHAL, Roland (1993) 'Les mooryan de Mogadiscio. Formes de la violence dans un espace urbain et de guerre', *Cahiers d'Etudes africaines*, 33 (2): 295–320.

MARTINEZ, Andrea (1990) *La Violence à la Television: état des conaissances scientifiques*, Direction de la programmation télévisée du CRTS, Canada.

MARTINEZ, Luis (1995) 'Les Groupes islamistes entre guérrilla et négoce. Vers une consolidation du regime algérien', *Les Etudes du CERI 3.*

MARTUCCELLI, Danilo (2001) *Dominations Ordinaires*. Paris: Balland.

MERTON, Robert (1957) *Social Theory and Social Structure*. Glencoe, IL: Free.

MICHAUD, Yves (1978) *Violence et politique*. Paris: Gallimard.

— (2002) *Changements dans la violence: essai sur la bienveillance universelle et la peur*. Paris: Odile Jacob.

MILGRAM, Stanley (2005 [1974]) *Obedience to Authority: An Experimental View*. London: Pinter & Martin.

MILLET, Catherine (2002 [2001]) *The Sexual Life of Catherine M.* (trans. Adriana Hunter). New York: Grove.

MILOSZ, Czeslaw (1981 [1959]) *Native Realm: A Search for Self-Definition* (trans. Catherine S. Leach). London: Sidgwick and Jackson.

MIRONESCO, Christine (1982) *La Logique du conflit: théorie et mythes de la sociologie contemporaine*. Lausanne: Pierre-Marcel Faure.

MONGIN, Olivier (1997) *La Violence des images, ou comment s'en débarrasser*. Paris: Seuil.

MOORE, Jonathan (ed.) (1998) *Hard Choices: Moral Dilemmas in Humanitarian Intervention*. New York: Rowmer and Littlefield.

MOSSE, George L. (1990) *Fallen Soldiers: Reshaping the Memory of World Wars*. New York and London: Oxford University Press.

MYRDAL, Günner (1944) *An American Dilemma: The Negro Problem and Modern Democracy.* New York: Harper and Row.

NABULSI, Karma (2001) 'Evolving Conceptions of Civilians and Belligerents: One Hundred Years after the Hague Peace Conferences', in Chesterman (2001): 9–24.
NATIONAL TELEVISION VIOLENCE STUDY (1996) *National Television Study: Executive Summary 1994–1995 and Scientific Papers 1994–1995,* Studio City, CA.: Mediascope.
NGOUPOANDÉ, Jean-Paul (2002) 'L'Afrique suicidaire', *Le Monde.* 18 May.

OCQUETEAU, Frédéric (2002) *Déclin de l'état webérien et recomposition des fonctions policières dans les sociétés de la modernité tardive,* Habilitation à diriger les recherches, Paris.
ORNE, Martin T. J. and Charles H. Holland (1968) 'On the Ecological Validity of Laboratory Deception', *International Journal of Psychiatry* 6: 282–93.
OSKAMP, Stuart (ed.) (1988) *Television as a Social Issue.* Newbury Park, CA and London: Sage.

PADIS, Marc-Olivier (2000) 'De l'art du conflit à l'art de l'esquive', *Esprit* 268, October.
PÉCAUT, Daniel (1987) *L'Ordre et la Violence: evolution sociopolitique de la Colombie entre 1930 et 1953.* Paris: Editions de l'EHESS.
PERALVA, Angelina (2001) *Violence et Démocratie: le paradoxe brésilien.* Paris: Balland.
— and Eric Macé (2003) *Médias et violences urbaines: débats politiques et construction journalistique.* Paris: La Documentation française.
PEREZ-AGOTÉ, Alfonso (2002) *Profecia autocumplida y duel non resueleto. La violencias vacca en el siglo XXI,* Center for Basque Studies, University of Nevada-Reno.
PERROT, Michelle (2001) *Les Ombres de l'histoire: crime et chatiment aux XIXe siècle.* Paris: Flammarion.
PIERRET, Régis (1996) *Les Apaches à Paris au Début du Siècle.* Paris: Diplôme de l'EHESS.
PINHEIRO, Paol Sergio (1996) 'Institutions and Impunity: Violence, Crime and Police System in New Democratic Countries (The Brazilian Experience in the Context of Latin American Countries'. Paper read at the international seminar *Strategies of Police Intervention in the Modern State,* São Paolo, September.
POTTER, James (1999) *On Media Violence.* London and Thousand Oaks, CA: Sage.

QUINTERO, William Roberto Pabob, *La Mort et les morts: Rites mortuaries et violence politique en Colombia au XXe siècle,* Mémoire de DEA, Paris: EPHE

RABINOVITCH, Itamar (1984) *The War for Lebanon.* New York: Cornell University Press.
RENAN, Ernest (1990 [1882]) 'What Is A Nation?' (trans. Martin Thom), in Homi K. Bhabha, (ed.), *Nation and Narration.* London: Routledge. pp. 8–22.
RENAUT, Alain and Sylvie Mesure (1999) *Alter Ego: les paradoxes de l'identité démocratique.* Paris: Aubier.
— and Alain Touraine (2000) 'Rencontre au sujet du Sujet', *Le Mondes des débats,* November: 26–8.
ROBERTS, Donald F., Ulla G. Foehr, Victoria J. Rideout, and Mollyan Brodie, (1999) *Kids' Media: A Comprehensive National Analysis of Children's Media.* Menlo Park, CA: Kaiser Family Foundation.

ROCHÉ, Sebastian (1994) *Insécurités et Liberté*. Paris: Seuil.

ROSSET , Clément (1988) *Le principe de Cruauté*. Paris: Minuit.

ROY, Olivier (1996) 'Groupes de solidarité au Moyen-Orient et en Asie Centrale', *Les Cahiers du CERI*, 16.

RUFIN, Jean-Christophe (1996) 'Les economies de guerre dans les conflits internes', in Rufin and Rufin (1996).

RUFIN, Jean-François and Jean-Christophe Rufin (1996) *Economie des Guerres Civiles*, Paris: Hachette, Collection 'Pluriel'.

SALAMÉ, Ghassan (1996) *Appels d'Empire: ingérences et resistances à l'âge de la mondialisation*. Paris: Fayard.

SALAS, Denis (2001) *La Justice, une revolution démocratique*. Paris: Desclée de Brouwer.

SARTRE, Jean-Paul (1976 [1960]) *Critique of Dialectical Reason* (trans. Alan Sheridan-Smith) edited by Jonathan Ree. London: New Left.

— (2004 [1961]) 'Preface' in Fanon (2004): xliii–lxii.

SCARMAN, Lord (1982 [1981]) *The Scarman Report: The Brixton Disorders, 10–12 April 1981*. Harmondsworth: Penguin.

SEMELIN, Jacques (2002) 'Du massacre au processus génocidaire' (Communication au colloque sur la violence extreme, Paris 29–30 novembre 2001), *Revue Internationale de Sciences Sociales*, 174, December.

SERENY, Gitta (1995) *Albert Speer: His Battle with Truth*. New York: Knopf.

SHILS, Edward and Morris Janowitz (1948) 'Cohesion and Distintegration in the Wehrmacht in World War II', *Public Opinion Quarterly* 12: 280–315.

SILBERMAN, Charles (1978) *Criminal Violence: Criminal Justice*. New York: Random House.

SIMMEL, Georg (1955 [1925]) *Conflict and The Web of Group Affiliations* (trans. Kurt H. Wolff, with a foreword by Everett C. Hughes). Glencoe, IL: Free.

SMITH, Philip (1997) 'Civil Society and Violence: Narrative Forms and the Regulation of Social Conflict', in Jennifer Turpin and Lester, R. Kurtz (eds), *The Web of Violence: From Interpersonal to Global*. Urbana and Chicago: University of Illinois Press. pp. 99–115.

SOFSKY, Wolfgang (1996) *Traktat über die Gewalt*. Frankfurt am Main: Fischer.

SOREL, Georges (1961 [1908]) *Reflections on Violence* (trans. T. E. Hulme, introduction by Edward A. Shils). London: Collier-MacMillan.

STOETZEL, Jean (1963) *La Psychologie Sociale*. Paris: Flammarion.

STORA, Benjamin (1997) *Imaginaire de la Guerre: Algérie-Viêtnam, en France et aux Etats-Unis*. Paris: La Découverte.

STRAYER, Richard and Lewis Ellenhorn (1975) 'Vietnam Veterans: A Study Exploring Adjustment Patterns and Attitudes', *Journal of Social Issues*, 31–4.

TABBONI, Simonetta (1996) 'Le Multiculturalisme et l'ambivalence de l'étranger', in Michel Wieviorka (ed.), *Une Société Fragmentée?* Paris: La Découverte.

TAUSSIG, Michael (2002) 'Culture of Terror – Space of Death: Roger Casement's Putomayo Report and the Explanation of Torture', in Hinton (2002): 164–91.

THOMPSON, Irene Taviss (2000) *In Conflict No Longer: Self and Society in Contemporary America*. Lanham, MD: Roman and Littlefield.

TILLY, Charles (1986) *La France Conteste de 1600 à nos jours*. Paris: Fayard.

TISSERON, Serge (2003) *Les Bienfaits des Images*. Paris: Odile Jacob.

TOURAINE, Alain (1966) *La Conscience Ouvrière*. Paris: Seuil.

— (1973) *Production de la société*. Paris: Seuil.

— (1995 [1992]) *Critique of Modernity* (trans. David Macey). Oxford: Blackwell.

— (1997 [1994]) *What Is Democracy?* (trans. David Macey). Boulder, CO: Westview.

— and François Dubet, et al. (1981) *Le Pays contre l'état*. Paris: Seuil.

— and Michel Wieviorka and François Dubet (1987 [1984]) *The Workers' Movement* (trans. Ian Patterson). Cambridge: Cambridge University Press.

— and Farhad Khosrokhavar (2000) *La Recherche de Soi: dialogue sur le sujet*. Paris: Fayard.

TRINH, Sylvaine (2001) 'Aum Shinrikyo: secte et violence', *Cultures et conflits* 29–30: 229–90.

VIGNARELLO, Georges (1998) 'L'Invention de la violence morale', *Sociétés et représentations* 6, June.

Violence à la television. Rapport de Mme. Blandine Kriegel à M. Jean-Jacques Allagon, Ministre de la Culture at de la Communication, Paris 2002.

Violences aujourd'hui, violences de toujours: XXXIIe Rencontre Internationale de Genève, Lausanne: L'Age d'homme.

VRIES, Hent de and Samuel Weber (eds). (1997) *Violence, Identity and Self-Determination*. Stanford: Stanford University Press.

WEBER, Max (1968 [1956]) *Economy and Society: An Outline of Interpretive Sociology, Vol 1*. (trans. Guenter Roth and Claus Wittish). New York: Bedminster.

— (2004 [1919]) 'Politics as a Vocation in *The Vocation Lecture*' (trans. Rodney Livingston, edited with an introduction by David Owen and Tracy B. Story). Indinopolis and Cambridge: Hackett.

WIESEL, Elie (1985 [1967]) 'On Jewish Values in the Post-Holocaust Future', in *Against Silence. The Voice and Vision of Elie Wiesel*, selected and edited by Irving Abrahams. New York: Holocaust Library (vol I: 203–7).

WIEVIORKA, Annette (1992) *Déportation et Génocide: entre la mémoire et l'oubli*. Paris: Plon.

WIEVIORKA, Michel (1989). *Sociétés et Terrorisme*. Paris: Fayard.

— (1995) *Face au Terrorisme*. Paris: Liana Levi.

— (1997) 'Quatre figures du nationalisme: la question de la violence', in Pierre Birnbaum, ed., *Sociologie des nationalismes*. Paris: PUF. pp. 369–86.

— (1998) *L'Ere du Témoin*. Paris: Plon.

— (ed.) (1999) *Violence en France*.

— (2000) 'Sociologies post-classique ou decline de la sociologis?', *Cahiers internationaux de sociologie*, CVIII, July: 5–35.

— (2001) *La Différence*. Paris: Balland.

— (2002) 'Terrorismes: une Rupture historique', *Ramses*: 29–41.

— (2003) 'An Old Theme Revisited: Sociology and Ideology', in Elizer Ben-Rafael (ed.), *Sociology and Ideology*. Leiden: Brill. pp. 79–100.

— and Jocelyne Ohana (ed.) (2001) *La Différence Culturelle: Vers une reformulation des débats*. Paris: Balland.

— and Dominique Wolton (1987) *Terrorism à la une: media, terrorisme et démocratie*. Paris: Gallimard.

WILSON, William Julius (1979) *The Declining Significance of Race*. Chicago: University of Chicago Press.

— (1987) *The Truly Disadvantaged: The Inner City, the Underclass and Public Policy*. Chicago: University of Chicago Press.

YOUNG, Marlene A. (1988) 'The Crime Victim's Movement', in Frank O. Ochberg MD (ed.), *Post-Traumatic Therapy and Victims of Violence*. New York: Brunner/Mazel. pp. 319–29.

ZAFIROPOULOS, Marcos (2003) *Lacan et Lévi-Strauss ou le Retour à Freud*. Paris: PUF.
ZAUBERMAN, Renée and Philippe Robert (1995) *Du Côté des Victims: un autre regard sur la violence*. Paris: L'Harmattan.
ZECCHINI, Laurent (1996) 'Les "Freemen" – comme très souvent les membres de milices d'extrême droite sont des "paumés" de la société américaine', *Le Monde*, 30 July.

INDEX

Supporting researchers for more than forty years

Research methods have always been at the core of SAGE's publishing. Sara Miller McCune founded SAGE in 1965 and soon after, she published SAGE's first methods book, Public Policy Evaluation. A few years later, she launched the Quantitative Applications in the Social Sciences series – affectionately known as the "little green books".

Always at the forefront of developing and supporting new approaches in methods, SAGE published early groundbreaking texts and journals in the fields of qualitative methods and evaluation.

Today, more than forty years and two million little green books later, SAGE continues to push the boundaries with a growing list of more than 1,200 research methods books, journals, and reference works across the social, behavioral, and health sciences.

From qualitative, quantitative, mixed methods to evaluation, SAGE is the essential resource for academics and practitioners looking for the latest methods by leading scholars.

www.sagepublications.com

The Qualitative Research Kit

Edited by Uwe Flick

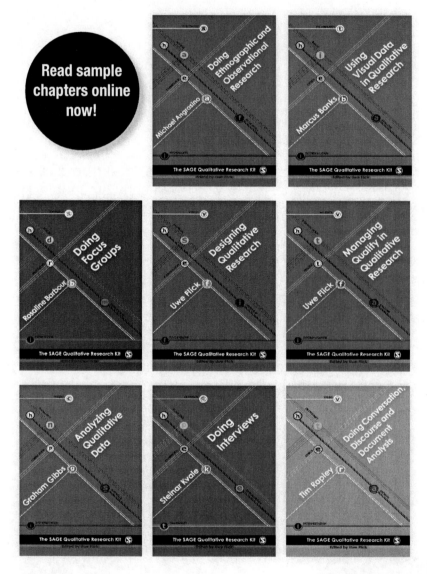

Doing Ethnographic and Observational Research — Michael Angrosino

Using Visual Data in Qualitative Research — Marcus Banks

Doing Focus Groups — Rosaline Barbour

Designing Qualitative Research — Uwe Flick

Managing Quality in Qualitative Research — Uwe Flick

Analyzing Qualitative Data — Graham Gibbs

Doing Interviews — Steinar Kvale

Doing Conversation, Discourse and Document Analysis — Tim Rapley

The SAGE Qualitative Research Kit
Edited by Uwe Flick

www.sagepub.co.uk

SAGE